EL INFIERNO

WITHDRAWN
FROM
STOCK

PIETER TRITTON

EL INFIERNO

DRUGS, GANGS, RIOTS AND MURDER
My time inside Ecuador's toughest prisons

EBURY
PRESS

3 5 7 9 10 8 6 4 2

Ebury Press, an imprint of Ebury Publishing
20 Vauxhall Bridge Road
London SW1V 2SA

Ebury Press is part of the Penguin Random House group
of companies whose addresses can be found
at global.penguinrandomhouse.com

Penguin
Random House
UK

First published by Ebury Press in 2017

*This book is a work of non-fiction based on the life,
experiences and recollections of the author. In some
cases names of people / places / dates / sequences of
the detail of events have been changed.*

www.penguin.co.uk

A CIP catalogue record for this book is available
from the British Library

ISBN 9781785035616

Printed and bound in Great Britain by Clays Ltd, St Ives PLC

This book is dedicated to the memory of my mother Joan Anderson and to all the friends who didn't make it home.

CONTENTS

CHAPTER ONE
LOOKING DOWN THE LINE

I'm sitting in a garden in the blazing heat of a French summer, trying to recall all the events of the last decade or so. Eleven years have passed since I last sat at this table. I'm a very different person to the one who left our house in France all those years ago. I'm sick, for one thing, and I have a very different perspective on life. This is what happened, a story I could never have invented.

I arrived at the same house in the middle of France sometime in June 2005 after being smuggled out of Britain by the Turkish mafia in the boot of an old Mercedes car. Most of the people smuggling is in the opposite direction these days.

I had had to leave Britain in a hurry, as things were getting too hot for me. A few months earlier there had been a huge bust of an apartment in Edinburgh, in which the police had uncovered a 'cocaine laboratory'. They had arrested two Colombians, and seized cocaine, precursor chemicals, mixing agents, a 15-ton floor-standing press and lots of other equipment, along with pieces of a tent groundsheet. This raid had hit the headlines big time. It was mentioned on all channels of the BBC, ITV and Channel 4, and covered by nearly every national newspaper.

Following months and months of heavy surveillance, the Serious Organised Crime Agency, or SOCA, had received various pieces of intelligence from all the informants in the case. The key informant had tipped them off that something was about to take place in Edinburgh. Two Colombians I knew arrived at a flat in Leith, the docks area of the city, in which I had been staying occasionally. I had left the flat having spotted two plain-clothes police officers in an unmarked car watching the building to the rear. I took a taxi to the Balmoral Hotel on Princes Street, leaving the white Transit van I had on hire parked directly across the road from the flat. I had told the Colombians I would call them in the morning, at 10am. I had a restless night, hardly able to sleep for worrying about what might be happening.

I awoke the following morning, ate breakfast, showered and packed my bag. At this point I called the Colombians to see how the job was progressing, but all their phones were off. My mouth began to dry up, a feeling of intense anxiety spreading through my body. They never turned their phones off. My instincts were screaming at me so loudly I thought the people in the next room might hear them.

The police were working hard to try to implicate me in this whole scenario and it had got to the point where I didn't feel like taking a chance. So I decided to disappear to France to sit it out and see what happened. I had to stop using all my phones, bank cards and any other electronics that could leave a trail.

I arrived in a cold, dank Calais where my Turkish couriers said goodbye and promised to sort me out with a car soon, as one of them owed me money. I decided to hire a

French car to get by with until they turned up with a vehicle. After much wrangling, I persuaded the hire company to let me pay cash and leave cash deposits and I was mobile.

I arrived at our house, which my father had bought some 25 years previously, the next day and settled in, relieved to have at least put some distance between me and all the trouble. I called my girlfriend, Nicky, and asked her to collect a car the Turks now had ready for me, and to drive it over to France. I also asked if she could collect my clothes from the flat I had been living in behind my parents' house. Once she had the car packed I told her to drive to Dover, bringing her daughter Emily with her, so they could have a holiday for a few days. I arranged to meet her in Paris and return the hire car to an office there at the same time. We would then all drive back south to the French house and have a week or so there, before she and Emily flew back to England from the local airport.

Nicky made it to Paris and checked into a hotel in a suburb in the north, and I arrived the following day. We chatted on the terrace of a cafe while watching Emily exploring a park next to the hotel. It was nice to be in their company once again.

The following day, we drove the Renault the Turks had provided all the way back to the house. Over the next few days I showed them round. Emily was quickly bored by the countryside and yearned to be back in Paris. After a few days she began to demand to go home or back to Paris or else she would run away. We asked her what she wanted to do, but it was always the same reply: 'Go home or go back to Paris.'

Next morning when Nicky and I came down for breakfast there was no sign of Emily. She had done a runner. We started to panic at the thought of this pretty fifteen-year-old trying to hitch-hike her way to Paris, not speaking any French. We jumped in the car and started to search the area, passing through villages and towns asking anyone we saw if they had noticed a young girl of her description. No one had.

After driving around for several hours and calling her phone repeatedly to no avail, we decided to contact the police. Not exactly the people I most wanted to talk to, but we had no choice. We found a very friendly officer at a local police station who spoke reasonable English and made a full report of what had happened. It was getting dark by now and Nicky was distraught. The gendarmes took the situation very seriously and began searching the area. They told us to go home and wait. We made our way back to the house, hoping and praying she would be there. It was a terrible experience.

We pulled up outside the house to find lights on that hadn't been when we had departed. We raced into the house, calling Emily's name, and found her snuggled up in her bed asleep. We woke her up to make sure she was OK and to find out where she had gone. It turned out that she had just gone up to the village a quarter of a mile away and sat on the steps of the church, chatting to a young English boy who was there on holiday. She told us she had seen us driving past several times on our search for her. I was fairly mad with her. I called the police to let them know she was back. What seemed like minutes later a riot van full of gendarmes arrived at the house.

Great, I thought. Just what I bloody need! I'm in hiding from the British police and now I've got a houseful of French ones.

They insisted on talking to Emily on her own to ensure that everything was OK at home with us. Once they were satisfied, they left. I decided to put Nicky and Emily on the next flight back to England. Emily was upset and really not enjoying herself, and I didn't want a repeat performance happening, thus drawing even more attention from the gendarmes. We said our farewells and off they went. That was the last time I ever saw Emily.

Why have I started my story with this minor incident? To say sorry, Emily. Sorry for all that happened next. Sorry for your mum's arrest. Sorry for the prison sentence she got and never deserved. And sorry for all those years you and she missed together. And you are just one of the many people I want to say sorry to, for all the pain and anguish I caused.

Some days after they left, I spoke to one of my partners. Using a pay phone for anonymity, I dialled the number with trepidation, just imagining all those computers about to click into action at the first syllable of my voice. Voice recognition was a real worry. I generally wouldn't talk on a phone in a car, hotel room or any building – anywhere I thought they might be able to intercept the call. However, at times it was, to some extent, unavoidable, and this was one of those times. I listened to the phone begin to ring, wondering if I shouldn't just hang up now while I still could and call it a day altogether.

Following the raid on the apartment in Scotland the police were already extremely keen to interview me. On one occasion, I had called the police station in Edinburgh to speak to one of the officers heading up the case after they had threatened to cause my sister, Sarah, a lot of problems, even though she had no involvement in or even knowledge of what I had been doing. When I was finally connected the officer to whom I was speaking asked in a friendly manner if I could 'please come in for a wee chat'. To which I replied, 'I'm afraid I'm not in Scotland at the moment and probably won't be coming back up there for quite some time as I am a little busy at the moment.' In a very civil manner, I then asked, 'Please leave my sister out of this whole situation. She is not involved and you know she's not.'

'Right you are then. We will think about it but would very much like you to pop in to answer some questions the next chance you get,' said the officer, barely able to stop himself from exploding.

I really could feel the long arm of the law reaching right down the phone line and taking a firm grip around my throat. After that, I had known it was just a question of time before the forensic test results came back to them, at which point they would most certainly come looking for me. I called the Turks and asked for a one-way lift out of England.

I had only been out of prison a couple of years having been first arrested in England in May 2000, the day after Nicky's birthday. The police had discovered 5,000 ecstasy tablets, along with several kilos of marijuana, 2kg of amphetamines and a couple of ounces of cocaine. The end result, after spending nearly two years on remand at Gloucester prison, was a five-year prison sentence, most of which I spent in category A maximum security conditions. I served nearly three years and was given parole. It was during this time I had decided that if I was going to traffic drugs then it would only be cocaine – small volume, high value – and I was going right to the source, Colombia, in order to buy it. I would then arrange the shipping and sale once it was back in Britain.

After my release in 2003, I set about looking for a good connection. It was not long before I was introduced to Nico, who was a Colombian, had all the necessary contacts and who could make the arrangements in his country. Hence our partnership was formed.

6

'Hello, hello.' Nico's voice hit my eardrum, jolting me out of my thoughts.

'Nico, it's me.'

'Hey man, where you bin?' Nico asked, in his heavy Colombian accent. 'I bin really worried about chu man, where you bin? I thought chu was dead!'

'I had to get out of the country after all the trouble up in Edinburgh.'

'Yeah man, *la policia* is going crazy for you. They got a hard on for you my friend. Better not come back here soon. Where you staying?'

Again with the questions. It had been happening too much of late and a few of us had begun to have some doubts about Nico. He and a couple of other South Americans had been arrested earlier on in 2004 when the police raided a flat they were using as a small laboratory and discovered three kilos of pure cocaine and a hydraulic press, along with various chemicals. All the others had received prison sentences but Nico had somehow managed to get released after six months with no charge. Following his release, Nico became extremely inquisitive and would ask strange questions that generally in the drugs business you just don't ask, such as, 'what car you driving?', 'where you going?', 'where you been?' – just weird questions. Something was wrong.

I avoided the question. 'Is there anything ready over in Colombia with El Comandante?' I asked. This was the nickname of our man over in Colombia – an ex-marine turned paramilitary of the Revolutionary Armed Forces of Colombia.

'Yeah, Comandante has a small one ready with just a couple. You wanna go over, get outta the way for a while and organise that?'

So there was a small job ready and waiting to be collected, if I felt up to organising everything. On this occasion, it was supposed to be two kilos of finest Peruvian flake cocaine impregnated in the groundsheet of a small tent. It had already been transported from Cali in Colombia to Quito in Ecuador. All I had to do was pay for it there and find a 'mule', or passenger, to carry it back to England. I had access to both these – the mule and the money – I just didn't want to go back to prison. They had way too much evidence on me in England. But I decided to give it one last go.

When Nico and the others had been arrested we had an agreement between the three partners – Nico, me and one other – that if anyone got locked up it was the responsibility of whoever was free to look after the families of the others in prison. I kept my word and paid all their bills for the six months Nico was away and presented him with £40,000 in cash when he was freed. A welcome home gesture.

Nico had been the one who had shown me the system of impregnation. At the time this technique was fairly new. People had been soaking clothes in a solution containing the cocaine for a long time. The problem with that was the smell was easily detected by a sniffer dog. It also crystallised on the material and would make it stiffer and therefore quite noticeable.

The method we used was a lot more advanced but also far harder to do. The cocaine was dissolved in a solution of various chemicals and then combined with a type of plastic while it too was in a liquid state. This then had to be dried, ensuring the plastic was as thin as possible. Once dry, you had a piece of plastic very similar to the rubber used for inner tubes of mountain bikes. It had no smell, could not be detected by X-ray or scanner and we put in a chemical to counteract the reactive test the police use. These sheets were then incorporated into the lining of something. In our case, it was the middle layer of the groundsheet for a tent. We could put in as much as five kilograms of cocaine in one go.

Once the tent arrived at its destination we would go through a reverse process, again using various solvents and acids, to extract the cocaine. Only the pure cocaine would come out. We would normally lose 10–15 per cent in volume in the process. This method was extremely good and is still in use, only today cocaine can be put in virtually anything and then extracted – polystyrene, plastics, paper, wood, perfume, wine, vodka, cosmetics and even glass. There are so many ways now. If you picked up the item you would have absolutely no idea that you were holding two or three kilos of pure cocaine, worth nearly £100,000 at today's wholesale prices in London. That's one hell of an expensive tent.

The job seemed straightforward and the risks minimal as only five people knew my approximate whereabouts, four of whom were family. I decided that it would also give me a chance to meet up with El Comandante. I wanted a face-to-face with him in order to plan out our next operation and change the location to somewhere in Europe, but not France. The reason for not working in France was the fact that my family had a house there. Don't shit where you eat.

I arranged for a friend from the UK to fly over with £25,000. We spent an enjoyable weekend drinking wine and catching up on events back home in Britain, including the newspaper reports of the bust in Edinburgh. When my friend left I headed up to Paris to go to the airport and buy tickets to Quito, using cash to avoid leaving any trail. Over the next couple of days, having bought the tickets, I stayed in a boutique hotel at the top of the Champs-Élysées just the other side of the Arc de Triomphe. I used my time to find an amenable bureau de change where I could change £20,000 into euros with no questions asked and no ID required. This, as you can imagine, is a very delicate procedure, even more so post-9/11 when cash is immediately viewed as suspicious. Thanks to the €500 note, the euro was the perfect currency for my purposes. In dollars, of course, the biggest denomination is the hundred dollar bill, meaning the neat little package of cash I needed to carry would have to be five times bigger.

I spent a good few hours wandering up and down the Champs-Élysées reconnoitring the various bureaux, looking for an independent one as shady in appearance as possible. The big chains such as Travelex were out, and it took me a while to find a bureau I liked the look of. It was located halfway down a touristy street, recessed from the road in a gloomy-looking small arcade that did not look very busy. Behind the 2-inch bulletproof glass sat a large Arab-looking man dragging on a Gauloises, sporting a chunky gold Rolex on his fat wrist. He had a slightly nervous look about him. Perfect. I approached the counter and pulled out an already separated bundle of some £600.

'Would it be possible to change these notes to euros? I'm afraid I have forgotten to bring my ID, is that a problem?'

The Arab took a long draw on the Gauloises while his eyes peered through lenses nearly as thick as the glass behind which he sat.

'No problem at all, Monsieur, no problem.'

Yes, perfect.

'Would I be able to change any more?' I asked as he was handing over the first bundle, producing a couple of thousand more.

'Yes, yes, no problem. How much you have to change?' This man liked money and liked easy money even more.

'Well, twenty thousand in total.'

'Bon, no problem, we do it in four or five goes, come back every hour.'

Perhaps not so perfect. The hour delay could be so the system didn't show anything suspicious, or it could be that I would be walking into a trap when I returned. Just long enough to call the gendarmes and have me arrested. I looked closely at his face and decided that this was someone who you could do a deal with.

I spent the next few hours wandering up and down the Champs-Élysées, calling in every hour between coffees to change wads of notes. On one occasion, a group of tourists came in behind me and had to wait while the money counter whirred away checking €6,000 in high-denomination notes. By the end of the afternoon a small bag of English banknotes had been reduced in size to a slim envelope fitting easily in the inside pocket of my jacket. Excellent.

The plan was for Nicky to join me in Quito a couple of days after I had concluded my business, so that we could enjoy a holiday together and I could show her the country. The mule's flight was due to arrive roughly two weeks after I had dealt with the initial exchange with El Comandante, when he would hand over the tent containing the impregnated cocaine. I thought that if there was any heat from the police it would have died down by then. In the meantime, I would hold on to the tent. We had an unblemished track record so far as the mules were concerned. Not a single one had been arrested. This was very important to me as I never wanted to see anyone go to prison; I did as much as I possibly could to minimise the risks they faced, and it had worked so far.

So, in short, I would go to Ecuador, get the tent, spend a couple of weeks with Nicky, pass on the tent to the mule and send him on his way, return to France, grab a change of clothes and head out to my mate's place in Thailand and wait there for the money to be transferred to me after the business was concluded. Nice and simple.

While I was in Paris, my father and stepmother arrived at the house for a visit. When I returned to the house early the next evening they were in the garden having dinner and enjoying the warmth. I had a few days before I flew to Quito and was looking forward to spending some time with them.

Of course, they wanted to know why I was going to South America. I told them I was going to Ecuador to buy a container load of Panama hats, which I planned to sell at cricket matches. They asked loads of questions about how I could charge enough for the hats to make it pay and wondered what I was doing going out to South America again. They knew I had been out to Colombia, Ecuador and Venezuela five or more times that year. They also asked why I was going so soon after the incident in Edinburgh, which I had told them was nothing to do with me.

I hate lying and felt terrible about it. I could see the worry in my father's eyes. He really didn't want me to go out there this time. I was beginning to feel that I didn't really want to go myself. I would much rather relax at the house with my family, drink some wine and eat good food instead. But too many people were involved by this point and wheels had been set in motion.

The day before my flight I packed my large black holdall for the trip. Early the next morning I got up and had breakfast with my father. He once again asked if my trip was really necessary. I was committed, but it was all beginning to feel wrong. We drove into the local town so I could catch an early train up to Paris. The two of us stood on the quiet platform awaiting the train. It was one of those cool, slightly misty mornings you get before a hot day. As the train pulled into the station my father embraced me and said, 'Take care, son. Go careful and look after yourself. Hope to see you soon. Love you.'

He rarely said that he loved me, but I knew that he did. I boarded the train, found my seat and then went back to the window in the carriage door. I watched my father standing on the platform in the mist as the train pulled away.

CHAPTER TWO
THE BUST

'*Queto, no lo mueves, manos arriba!*' Stop, don't move, hands up!

Nicky and I were laughing and joking as we strolled down the corridor. Nicky had flown into Quito that morning and we were returning from a great dinner in an upmarket restaurant close to the hotel where we were staying on Avenida Amazonas, in the new part of the city, high up in the Andes. I slid the card key into the lock and, just as it clicked open, all hell broke loose. A group of heavily armed men in plain clothes charged down the corridor towards us, guns drawn, wearing balaclavas – shit! I knew it was the police. They might as well have been wearing badges.

I looked at Nicky, who was in shock.

'Don't say or sign anything! Let me do the talking—' I whispered urgently.

They were on us by the end of the sentence. We were grabbed and led into the hotel suite: Nicky into the bedroom and me into the living room. That sick feeling was washing over me from the adrenalin coursing through my system but I tried to keep it under control. The Ecuadorian police are renowned for being corrupt. I was hopeful I'd be able to broker some sort of deal.

The police rapidly located the rucksack containing the tent with the cocaine impregnated in its rubber ground-sheet. They had obviously been into the suite while we were out as they went straight to it, making a great show of being surprised by their find. They searched both Nicky and me, emptying our pockets, and opened the safe in the bedroom, revealing about $2,500 in cash, passports and phones, which were all bagged up as evidence.

One of the Ecuadorian police officers, who seemed to be in charge, spoke some English, so I subtly tried to get his attention.

'Is there some other way we can resolve this problem?' I quietly asked. 'I can get $25,000 here within the hour if we could just forget about this misunderstanding – after all there are no drugs in evidence, only an old camping tent.'

'Señor, we are the Ecuadorian police force. We do not receive money. We are not corrupt.' I almost laughed out loud. Yeah, sure thing *tonto*!

It was at this point that I realised that this operation was being overseen by someone else. I imagined that the British police must be in the background, making sure that this way out was closed to me and that I was definitely arrested. Otherwise the Ecuadorians would almost certainly have jumped at the offer.

We were handcuffed, taken to the elevator and down to the underground car park of the hotel where a car was waiting for each of us, along with four police armed with M16 assault rifles and side arms. We were whisked away through the familiar streets of Quito, back towards the airport where poor Nicky had just arrived that very morning and to the headquarters of Interpol, who, it turned out, had made the arrests. The dark streets flashed by in a haze, my mind whirling as I imagined the repercussions.

Upon arriving at the Interpol HQ, the cars were driven into a courtyard through a solid steel gate, bordered by watchtowers with armed guards. Nicky and I were led from the cars into a nondescript three-storey building that from the outside resembled any other small office premises, but within it held dark, dank communal cells. Down badly lit narrow corridors the men's cells lay directly ahead and the women's to the right, both facing on to an enclosed and roofed courtyard.

Racing through my mind were thoughts of my family, how they were going to react once I was able to call them. What was I going to say? My parents were going to be devastated, as was Emily. She was with her grandparents, who had no idea even as to our whereabouts. I also really needed to contact my friends in Britain to tell them to clear everything up and disappear for a couple of weeks. I didn't want anyone else to be arrested.

I immediately asked that the British embassy be informed of our arrests as I knew they were obliged to help out to some extent, although I guessed they probably already knew, if I was right and the British police were involved. I knew they had had us under heavy surveillance for several months in Britain. I was also fairly sure several people were acting as police informants against me as I had been tipped off by family members, corrupt police and just that sixth sense we all have. This was the culmination of their efforts for sure. It was probable that Nico was responsible for my capture as he had arranged this whole deal. No one else knew I was out here. There had been too many coincidences all pointing the finger of doubt towards Nico.

The British police tended to operate out of the embassy or closely with them when investigating cross-border crime. The Ecuadorian police said they would contact the embassy if I provided them with the number. How the hell was I supposed to do that? They assured me they would do their best to contact them, but for the time being we would have to wait. Waiting was something I was to become very accustomed to doing.

CHAPTER THREE
INTO THE DARKNESS

It was approaching midnight when I was reunited with Nicky, first allowing me to give her a hug and kiss.

'Look at me, Nicky,' I said, and she tilted her head and looked into my eyes. 'I promise you I will get you out of here. I'm not sure how long it's going to take but I absolutely assure you I will get you out. I will do whatever it takes.'

She simply replied 'OK' and put her head back against my chest.

She was shocked and bewildered. Knowing the pain I was causing the one I loved was like a knife to the stomach. I held her in one final embrace that I never wanted to end, trying to reassure her, feeling her warm, shaking body against mine. Then the police separated us and I watched as the barred doors closed behind her and the women in the holding cell began greeting her.

Now it was my turn. The police officers led me towards the men's holding area. It looked like a dark hole from which it seemed if I entered I might never return. The officer pulled back the gate and pointed towards the left-hand side of the holding area. Directly in front of the gate was a wall and a corridor leading to the left, along which I could just make out entrances to cells, two on each side. A solitary light bulb hung from a cable, illuminating a shower area and toilet. As I advanced cautiously the gate behind me closed with a resounding clang. This is a sound you will only ever hear in prison, and one you can never forget. It is the sound of defeat, of loss and helplessness, of utter despair. It is followed shortly afterwards by the grinding of metal on metal as the key to your destiny turns. At this point all control over your life is suspended and you are a prisoner.

I advanced warily down the corridor bracing myself for contact or attack from another prisoner, but nobody emerged. Strange. The ringing silence of the darkness intensified a little more as I moved towards the bathroom area at the end of the corridor and the smell of urine and faeces began to tickle my nose. The second cell on my right was also empty. What the fuck was going on? I could hear the women chattering away, their voices drifting down the corridor. I sat down heavily on the bottom bunk, no more than a concrete shelf designed to take a mattress – of course there was none – along with a whole lot more of nothing. At this point the weight of the problem began pressing down not only on my shoulders but over my entire body, as if I was in a diving bell with the pressure being slowly increased. I sat there in the dark and cold trying to collect my thoughts.

At this point I was still optimistic because they hadn't actually charged me yet with any specific quantity. The cocaine impregnated in the rubber groundsheet was not visible to the naked eye. Perhaps the police thought there were only a few grams, as they hadn't mentioned anything about kilos yet. We hadn't lost a single load in over two years of operating. Please, please let it be so.

My thoughts, which were beginning to spiral out of control, were interrupted by a cough and hushed murmuring from the other end of the corridor, but still no one appeared. It began to dawn on me that perhaps the police were trying to hold me separately from the other prisoners for whatever reason. I continued to sit there, listening to the night slowly sliding by, the traffic passing on the road in front and the nearby airport where I'd landed a few days earlier.

I thought back to the day of my arrival and the few peculiarities that now, on reflection, were starting to make sense. The first was at passport control, where a pretty Ecuadorian police officer with a clipboard was standing to the side, examining everybody's face. Seeing me, she did an almost comical double take as if she could barely hide her excitement. She hurried off and out of sight through a door, I now realised to inform her supervisors of my arrival. At immigration, I casually looked behind me and noticed the same police officer with the clipboard had reappeared, now in the company of a male officer. They were having an animated discussion and kept glancing in my direction. I tried to steady my nerves as the €25,000 in my inside jacket pocket burned a hole in my chest. I knew full well that this alone would mean a prolonged stay in the prison in Quito.

I presented my passport to the official in the control booth, who swiped it. There was an immediate change in her face from one of abject boredom to interest and excitement. I had passed through this control on four previous occasions without a blink or second look. 'Please could you wait here one moment, sir, I have to check something,' and off she disappeared with the passport. This hadn't happened before. Was there some kind of marker on my passport, I wondered. After a few minutes, she returned and apologised for the wait, and began joking around and almost flirting with me, saying, 'You could teach me English any time. I would love some lessons from you.'

All this behaviour had set alarm bells ringing, but I had chosen to ignore them. As I sat in the cell I wished that I had walked away then and there. Taken a bus to Colombia or Peru and disappeared as quickly as possible. But I hadn't. I couldn't sleep and just sat there pondering my fate for the rest of the night, wondering how I might get us out of this one, or at least minimise the damage.

The days and nights in Ecuador are of equal length. The sun appears at about 6am and disappears again at around 6pm, seven days a week, 52 weeks of the year. So at 5.30am the walls of the cell started to turn a pallid grey. Around this time the airport kicked into life and the acrid smell of aviation fuel penetrated my dungeon, reminding me of the flight I should have taken and was now going to miss in the coming week. I could hear the roar of the turbines from the jets as they took off and landed. The traffic on the road to the front of the Interpol station had picked up as well and there was a steady hum of cars passing by, people on their way to work and school, going about their normal lives.

I stuck my head out of the cell doorway a couple of times to see who was in the other end of the holding area, but I couldn't see anyone. It was fully light when someone finally emerged and came down to use the toilet. He was a thin-looking guy around 32 years old, clean-shaven and respectable-looking. He introduced himself in broken English. 'Hello good morning. My name is Hassan. I am from Lebanon.' He had a soft gentle tone of voice and pleasant friendly manner. I warmed to him immediately. 'You are English?' he asked me.

'Yes, from the south, 100 miles west of London,' I replied. 'My name is Pieter.'

'Ah, very good, I know London. I have been three or four times, I like it very much. Many pretty girls.' I laughed and we were friends.

'I'm glad to have met someone who speaks English. My girlfriend is in the womens' holding cell.'

'Why are you here?' Hassan asked. 'The guard tell us all, "Move, quick, quick. Big international *traficante* is coming. No one speak to him or you get big trouble."'

Blimey, I thought, as I listened and it dawned on me that I was the big-time trafficker he was talking about. Shit! The police were taking this very seriously indeed.

'Do you want to move back to this end?' I enquired, feeling bad that my arrival had caused all the other people in custody to be cramped together in a small cell the other end.

'I ask guard first. I no want trouble, guards very bad here.' He looked a bit nervous at the mention of the guards. God only knows what sort of torture techniques they used on people here. Hassan went to use the toilet. When he came back he asked, 'What did they catch you with? Drug?'

'Yes. They arrested me in a hotel on Avenida Amazonas called Mercure.'

'I am here for drugs as well. They say we are big organisation. That we are terrorists! Pa. The *policia* say we send cocaine to Hezbollah in my country and they buy guns and bombs and kill many people. I have *grande problema* my friend.' He looked deflated by saying this. 'I go ask guards if we can come back here. We can share cell. My brother is here as well and some other friends. I bring them now.'

'OK, great,' I replied. Off he went into the darkness at the other end of the corridor.

Before long other people started to appear. Some introduced themselves, others not. I think there were about ten of us at this point, four of whom were Hassan's co-defendants. They were all Arab, all educated and well travelled. Most spoke English. Quite a few of the Ecuadorians appeared to be emaciated, skeletal shells ravaged by drug abuse. Only one spoke English. He had been arrested for possession of a gram of weed – one joint.

Hassan had spoken to the guards in fluent Spanish to find out if they were permitted to move back into the cells in my end so they could have more space. I would spend the next six weeks living with Hassan and his friends until we were finally transferred. During this period they helped me a lot with translation, explaining how the prison was, dos and don'ts, food and general support.

It was the second or third day when the vice consul from the British embassy in Quito arrived to speak with me and Nicky. As I had guessed they were already aware owing to the involvement of the British police. They had instigated the arrest having passed intelligence to the Ecuadorians as to my whereabouts, the purpose of my visit and – crucially – the method we were using to smuggle the cocaine out of the country. This the Ecuadorian police had let slip at some point when boasting about having captured me. It was further confirmed when I received some papers from the prosecutor. On the very first page was the sentence 'we were called by a female officer from the British police who informed us of your arrival and intentions to traffic drugs, namely cocaine, from this country to Europe'.

The vice consul, a woman called Rachel, brought both Nicky and me a fleece blanket, toiletries and some food, along with an information pack outlining exactly what they could and couldn't do to help.

I asked Rachel, 'How can the embassy assist Nicky and me legally? Are you obliged to provide a lawyer free of charge to us as in Britain? Does legal aid apply here?'

This barrage of questions was turning into an overwhelming tidal wave. Rachel raised her hands, signalling for me to stop. But I already had an idea as to what the answer was going to be.

'I'm afraid we can't interfere or be seen to be meddling in another country's legal system. I'm very sorry but we can't offer any help on the legal front other than providing a list of lawyers we recommend.'

Nicky's face dropped. I hadn't really expected any help from the British government in trying to regain our freedom, as I was now sure it was they who were doing their utmost to lock me up. But Nicky had been more optimistic, believing the embassy was duty bound to pay for a lawyer and go out of their way to make sure we were freed.

'We have a list of reputable lawyers with whom the embassy has worked in the past,' Rachel went on. 'The problem in this country is that a lot of the supposed lawyers are unqualified and out to con you. We have had several other British inmates robbed of large quantities of cash. You have to be very careful when it comes to lawyers.'

She handed us each a copy of the list, which ran to several pages. The information pack also included a great deal about daily life in the prison, how to receive money transfers, communication with family, and some Spanish translations of common words and phrases. The basic process of how the legal system worked in Ecuador was outlined.

During the first meeting Rachel revealed that she had actually been told by the British authorities to have nothing to do with me, not even to speak to me, which she said was the first time this had ever happened. She asked if this was a reflection of the seriousness of the case back in Britain, which it obviously was. Rachel very kindly offered to contact our families and allowed me to make a call to my father and step-mother, who were still in France. Needless to say, it was one of the hardest phone calls I have ever had to make. They were horrified and ever so upset. My mother, who was in England, was distraught and almost unable to comprehend what had happened. It broke my heart. Nicky also called her parents, who were devastated and beside themselves with worry.

Rachel left behind a pen, writing paper, envelopes and some books so we could write letters and read a bit to pass the time. We had to get food brought in every day because Interpol provided nothing. The embassy took care of this and sent their driver in daily with a good quantity of food.

When Rachel had gone, I looked at the list of lawyers in some depth and chose a firm who seemed reputable and spoke English. I contacted the embassy and asked if they could make the necessary arrangements. A couple of days later they arrived in full regalia. Two lawyers, nice suits, secretaries, assistants, the works, which drew more than a little attention from the other prisoners.

Both Nicky and I were let out to discuss the case with the lawyers and sign a form stating that they were to act on our behalf. They assured me that they would be able to secure the minimum sentence of four years or even get me released. Nicky, they said, should be no problem at all as she had only been in the country for six hours before being arrested and was obviously innocent. They asked that we give them some time to review the evidence and to see what they could work out. They informed me that they had to return a week later in order to take the first statement from me, something demanded by Ecuadorian law. With that they were gone. The question of fees had been left open as they wanted to assess what they were going to be taking on before quoting me a figure.

One of the prisoners had managed to smuggle in a mobile phone. With the help of Hassan interpreting, I could pay the guy who owned it and use the phone. I was able to call a few of my contacts whose numbers I had memorised and from them get other people's numbers. In this way, I warned everybody that I had run into trouble and for them all to clear up whatever they were doing and lie low. I now know that those few phone calls saved a number people from having to spend many years locked up.

Around this time, a young Colombian guy, Juan, and his mother were led in and placed in respective cells. They were charged with possessing a tiny amount of cocaine, less than ten grams. He was absolutely distraught that his mother had been detained because of a crime he had committed. After they had been there a few days his lawyer turned up. They all went off and had a meeting to discuss their case. His mother could go free if he paid the sum of $90, but he was penniless and became extremely upset at the prospect of his mother being imprisoned. I had been watching and listening and I decided to intervene. That amount to me was nothing – especially considering what I was spending on lawyers – but it could buy the freedom of this woman. I tapped him on the shoulder and held out the $90 and gestured that he should take it. He couldn't believe it and broke down in tears, thanking me over and over again. Within a few hours his mother was free and Juan was happy. It felt good to have helped out.

As there were no mattresses provided, I had been sleeping on my clothes. The Arabs explained that I could have a mattress brought in if I paid the police a little money. I thought they were joking, but no. This was Ecuador after all.

I arranged with my family for a fair chunk of money to be sent over via the Foreign Office to the embassy in Quito. This was free of charge and would mean I could start things moving with the case and also be able to buy Nicky and me a mattress each. This was a huge relief for our aching backs, arms and legs. The first night, it felt like the softest, deepest, most luxurious mattress ever made, even though it was only a thin piece of foam.

Nicky collapsed after the fourth or fifth day, having drunk the tap water and contracted a virus. The local ambulance service had had to come in and put her on a drip for a few hours, which seemed to sort her out. I felt like it was me who had poisoned her. In a way, I had.

Nicky and I were able to speak to each other twenty-four hours a day because our holding cells faced one another across the small internal courtyard. We supported each other through these tough days and it made an enormous difference to both of us just being able to communicate and give each other the occasional hug. We would spend our days trying to work out our defence case or just chatting to one another to while away the hours. I could see the strain beginning to show on her face as the days passed slowly.

A week went by without much happening and then the lawyers arrived. We were led to an office area and the interview started. On the charge sheet from the police it appeared that they had listed a quantity of just 7.8 grams of cocaine. I couldn't believe it at first, but then thought that perhaps this was all the surface residue they had managed to accumulate and they had not found the cocaine that was impregnated in the rubber groundsheet. This meant that no drugs were visible to the naked eye, even if you had cut the rubber, as the cocaine was now a piece of rubber itself. Hiding the cocaine this way so it could pass through the X-ray scanner and fool the sniffer dogs was almost foolproof – unless an informant directed the authorities to it. This must have been what had happened in my case. I hadn't disclosed that I knew anything about any drugs at this point, so the police had no idea how much was concealed. I questioned the lawyer on this and he confirmed that yes, they had only charged me over this small amount. I was ecstatic. I knew this sort of quantity was a minor offence so we should be out of there very soon without them ever knowing about the two kilograms in the groundsheet.

I proceeded with the statement that Nicky and I had rehearsed over and over again through the gates of our cells, across the gloomy courtyard. I stuck to the story that I knew nothing of any drugs. I was merely there for a holiday, and a friend had asked me to bring this tent back as a favour having left it behind on a previous trip. This kind of excuse the police must have heard countless times (in fact probably every time). The difference in this case was the fact that they didn't have blocks of cocaine or bags of powder as evidence – a big advantage, or so I thought.

After the statements were concluded, I broached the subject of the lawyers' fees. The one with whom I had been communicating the most, as he spoke English, sat there in his fancy suit looking nervous and began toying with the ring on his pinkie finger.

'How much are you going to charge me?' His beady little eyes darted around the room and the ring-twisting became more furious.

'$250,000 and we guarantee a sentence of no more than four years, out after two and you will be held in the best prison with all the big mafiosi.'

I stood up slowly and focused my gaze on the man squirming in front of me.

'You are joking, aren't you? I can get a better lawyer cheaper in London. You're insane. I'm afraid there is no way I'm paying that amount. It's completely out of the question.'

The lawyers left, promising to consult their partners and try to bring the price down. As I was led back through the narrow corridors of the Interpol station I still couldn't believe what I had heard.

The Arabs all found it highly amusing. Hassan said, 'They are thieves, robbers, they want to steal your money.'

It kept them entertained for at least two days. Hassan then sat me down and explained that here in Ecuador the lawyers were the biggest thieves of all and frequently robbed people of huge sums of money having promised them all manner of fantastic unrealities. Hassan had a very good lawyer who was representing not only him but a few of the others. She was local and well-connected. Being well-connected was everything here: it was who you knew or had access to that kept you out of prison. You didn't even need a proper qualification to call yourself a lawyer. Anyone could get away with this as long as they had contacts in the judicial system. Bribery, Hassan explained, was the norm here – pay the police, pay the judges, pay whoever you needed to in order to get out. Hassan kindly offered to introduce me to the lawyer, whose name was Eva. She was due to visit him in the next couple of days to discuss their case. He promised me she would take a fraction of the money and do the job properly. I asked how much and he said 20, maybe 30, thousand dollars. That sounded more like it. I would be quite prepared to give her extra if she did a good job and got me a short sentence. Still uppermost in my mind was the fact that they thought it was only 7.8 grams. My God, they might even return the tent! That would be hilarious. In the end, though, the joke was to be on me.

CHAPTER FOUR
WE COME TO A FULL STOP

For about another week I sat in the grim Interpol cells trying to convince myself that the police had missed their chance. They were only charging me with 7.8 grams, as confirmed by the high-flying lawyers. Nicky, who would have grasped at any straw, seized this one with eagerness and held on tight. We started to believe we would be released in a week or so, maybe a bit longer in my case as I would take the blame.

Rachel, the vice consul from the embassy, dropped in to see if we were OK and not being waterboarded or tortured as most of the locals were. I brought up the subject of the charges with her and slowly, almost mournfully, she corrected me. 'No, no, I'm very sorry Pieter but you are definitely charged with 7.8 kilograms, not grams.'

It felt as if she had stuck an ice-cold blade in my stomach and then twisted it. I knew full well it was only 2 kilos of cocaine that had gone into the groundsheet, so what the hell? I showed her the paperwork, where it read 7.875 grams of cocaine. I mean it actually said GRAMS not bloody kilos. There was a decimal point, a distinct black dot, separating the 7 from the 8. The vice consul looked at me with a very sorrowful expression and explained that I was charged with 7,875 grams, which equates to 7.8kg. In Britain, we would place a comma when writing 7,875. In Ecuador, it turned out, they use a full stop instead.

I couldn't believe it. The game was up, so I explained to Rachel there was no way it was nearly eight kilos; I knew it was a lot, lot less. Her answer shocked me. In Ecuador if the drugs are impregnated in something they will weigh the entire object in which they are contained. In this case, of course, it was a bloody tent – poles, pegs and all. Well, in that case I would ask them to extract the drugs in order to establish exactly how much was there and hope they messed up in the process. I was told they wouldn't do this, though I could make an application to the judge requesting that the drugs be extracted at my own cost.

I was led back to the cells and asked everyone to give me some space. I explained the mistake of a decimal point to the Arabs, who thought it amusing but also consoled me. What the hell had those lawyers been talking about when they confirmed it was 7.8 grams? Surely they should know? Rather worrying to think the people representing me, who held my destiny in their clammy hands, didn't even know this. What other mistakes might they make? I knew I had to get rid of them, which is exactly what I did. Fuck! What next? Nicky's straw snapped and so did she when I told her that we were going nowhere fast. Deep down I knew it had been an outside chance of getting away with it, but that didn't stop it being crushingly disappointing.

Hassan's lawyer Eva was young – I guessed mid to late twenties – very well presented, friendly and attractive. I imagined all these attributes probably assisted when in negotiations

31

with the judges. Eva spoke not a word of English apart from
to say hello and I at this point spoke very little Spanish, so
Hassan offered to interpret and we got down to discussing
the case. Eva didn't mince her words and one of the first
things she ever said to me, which I'll never forget was, 'It
would be easier to get you freed from a murder charge than
a drugs case.' The problem, she explained, was *los gringos*,
the hated Americans, in particular the Drug Enforcement
Agency, who at this time operated in Ecuador. When the
Americans said jump, the Ecuadorian government jumped,
high and with enthusiasm, in return for cash, arms and
protection.

Apparently, the American government in its war on drugs
paid the Ecuadorians anything from $5,000 for every
capture and prosecution of traffickers and mules, and up to
$10,000 if they were heading stateside to the land of the not
so free. Added to this, in my case there was the extra
problem of pressure from the British police and government,
who wanted my head on a block for the case in Britain; I was
wanted for conspiracy to import over 85 kilograms of cocaine
over a period of two years with three small laboratories
processing it. With so many eyes watching my case it was
going to be hard to carry out any negotiations with the prosecution or judges – in other words to bribe them. I explained
to Eva the British police were all over this and that they may
well ask for my extradition back to Britain. She was unwor-
ried by this. What happened in Ecuador stayed in Ecuador.
Like Las Vegas, I guess. Although in this case it was me who
would be staying.

According to Eva, the sentences had categories, which
began at eight years for mules, went up to 12 years for the
owner of the drugs or the boss, and then 16 years for more
serious cases, and 25 years for the very large cases and

bosses of cartels. It wouldn't make any difference if it was 1kg or 1 ton, they treated you alike. In the end it really just came down to money and how much you were prepared to pay for your freedom. On that note, we discussed how much Eva wanted for her services and we agreed on $25,000 for her fees for both Nicky and me, excluding any extras i.e. bribes, paperwork and costs. We agreed I should pay part up front and the rest in instalments as I saw results.

At this point, Eva wasn't sure just how much I might have to spend in the way of bribes in order to either get us out of this hell completely or negotiate minimal sentences. She asked to be given some time to go away and read the papers so she could work out exactly what was going on and the best way in which to deal with it. She recommended that we stick to our current story that we had no idea there were any drugs present in the bag. Eva was very optimistic that she would be able to secure Nicky's release, but that it would take a few months for the process to play out. We signed the contract giving Eva access to the papers regarding our case.

When Eva went that day, she left both Nicky and me with hope in our hearts and feeling more optimistic about our futures. I thanked Hassan over and over, and promised that I would assist him and his brother if they needed help. He was modest as ever and made no big deal about it all, so we sat down on my new mattress on the concrete bunk and cracked some boiled eggs and ate them with salt, pepper and cucumber to celebrate.

I informed the embassy in Quito that I had changed lawyers from the ones on their recommended list to Eva. I gave them her details and asked them to make contact and instructed them to pay her $8,000 from the money my family had transferred over via the Foreign Office in London. Rachel explained that she had received an invoice from the first law firm. I had asked Eva roughly how much I should pay them and she had made it clear that I should pay no more than $500. I was shocked when Rachel told me they were demanding $8,000 just for sitting in on an interview and two meetings. I immediately told her I was not going to be paying this and they would be lucky if they received anything now.

This worried her, and she told me, 'You have to pay them something or it could cause you problems.'

'Problems? PROBLEMS? Do you think I could have more problems than I do already? What are they going to do? Put me in prison?'

When I next saw Eva she had read through the case papers and also brought me a copy to look through. In British prisons in general you had to have a copy of your depositions so people could check you out and make sure you weren't a sex offender or a snitch (informant). If you didn't produce your papers you could possibly encounter problems from fellow prisoners. It really was a big deal. The other inmates at the Interpol station thought I was being strange to insist on having my papers. In Ecuador, everyone kept their papers to themselves, if they even had them, and didn't really discuss their cases much with each other.

The Interpol headquarters was the centre for anti-narcotics and in the main dealt with drugs offences and associated crimes. I was expecting a great pile of papers like you might get in a prison in Britain or America, with all your depositions, witness statements, surveillance etc., but here I received perhaps just 30 pages. More of a general summary than anything specific.

I asked Eva when I would be going to court. She explained that you have a pre-trial hearing and then a trial with three judges. The first hearing wouldn't be for a good few months yet, four to six months being the usual wait. However, due to the current chaotic state of the Ecuadorian justice system there were people in the prisons who had been waiting on remand without sentence, without even a hearing, for as much as five years. This shocked me. I thought, there's no way in hell I'm waiting for five years without even having had a hearing. Yet again Eva reassured me that everything could be manipulated if you had enough money. Cases could be slowed down, speeded up, evidence lost or changed – anything was possible.

She explained that the first thing we needed to concentrate on was getting moved from Interpol to the main prison but avoid going via the holding area that most prisoners had to wait in until allocated a wing. This was called the *calabozo*, or dungeon, and was notorious. You would be robbed and probably beaten before leaving it. Eva was therefore making arrangements for me to be transferred – along with the Arabs – to the same wing and decent cells without having to endure the *calabozo*.

Eva's boyfriend was a Colombian guy who was also a prisoner and on the same wing we were going to be allocated to. This meant she would be able to speak to me on a regular basis as she went to see him most visit days. Eva seemed to be very genuine and I was immensely grateful to Hassan for having introduced us.

The next important stage was ensuring that Nicky's and my papers ended up in a 'good' courtroom or tribunal – preferably one where Eva had good relations with the secretary of the courtroom and the three judges. They would be open to 'negotiation'. To achieve this, she was going to have to pay off the people in the Ministry of Justice who decided to which tribunal your case would be attributed. This is called the *sorteo*, or draw. It was like fixing the World

Cup draw – you could imagine them picking the balls out. But obviously instead of football matches it was legal cases and instead of stadiums, courtrooms. This meant only one thing: the *sorteo* had to be sorted out.

For $5,000, Eva managed to have my case allotted to a tribunal where she was friendly with the judges. It seems she was as good as her word. It was expensive but at least she got things done. She had negotiated with the judges in this tribunal previously, so knew they were open to offers. This was music to my ears. Eva said she would begin negotiations immediately with a view to having Nicky's case thrown out and me being sentenced to the minimum of eight years.

However, there was one major problem with this. The British police were keeping a close eye on the case as they knew how corrupt the legal system was here. The judges were going to be wary about being too blatant in taking bribes. Furthermore, I now knew that the British police wanted to extradite me if I was sentenced to less than ten years. They also made it very clear that if I served anything less than six years they would re-sentence me on my return to Britain. They were out for blood and said that had I been arrested in Britain I would have faced a minimum 20-year prison sentence, which would have meant serving at least ten years. There was no bloody way I was serving ten years anywhere! I planned to be out after no more than three years at the very most.

CHAPTER FIVE
INTO HELL

Five slow, traumatic weeks had passed, with me and Nicky being held in the dark, dank cells of Interpol without once glimpsing sunlight or being permitted a single breath of fresh air. During this time the whole prison system in Ecuador was in crisis. A protest by the prisoners had closed the main prison, which meant no transfers were taking place because everywhere was in a state of lockdown.

It was then that my very first chance of escape came. The Interpol building was tucked away out of sight of the street behind a row of commercial premises. I had been looking around, assessing possible ways to escape from the building, but couldn't really see any. We were never taken outside for fresh air or sun and the only occasions we were allowed out of the cells were when the embassy or lawyer came to visit. These visits were closely supervised by armed police. There was no obvious means of getting out.

Then, in a moment of frustration, I came across one weakness. I had been sitting on the concrete shelf that acted as my bunk and, feeling angry, had hit the wall behind me. I was surprised when there was a low hollow thud. Instead of a solid wall it appeared to be a fairly flimsy partition wall. I tapped some more, over an area in the middle of the cell.

The whole wall appeared to be very thin indeed. My mind started racing. Imagine. The guards never came in to check the cells, they just came to the gate and did a roll call, often without even verifying it was the right person responding when their name was called.

I had to find out what was on the other side of this wall. I didn't want to dig through just to land in the sergeant's office. And I didn't have any implements with which to dig, nor any idea of where I would go once I got out. I had no money, no ID, no contacts and couldn't speak the language. Another huge consideration was that it would also mean abandoning Nicky to her fate. I thought about this a lot, and found a time to talk it over with her. I explained carefully and as best I could. We knew by now what sort of sentence I was facing and she selflessly told me to go for it if I thought I stood a good chance of making a break.

I needed help but didn't know who to turn to. I knew Hassan wouldn't be interested so I asked another guy who I had been talking to. I pulled him aside and quietly explained my discovery and the need for digging tools. Within minutes he had one of his friends scratching carefully away at the wall with a metal fork, with me and him keeping watch at the gate in case anyone came. He knew the area and told me there were offices the other side of the wall, which were closed at the weekends and had no security personnel watching them. A window of opportunity.

The guy doing the digging had picked a spot under the bottom of the lower concrete sleeping shelf. When viewed from the doorway of the cell it was completely in shadow, so couldn't be seen unless you got on your hands and knees. He was slowly making the wall thinner and thinner, so as not to actually break through. Things were going well when the guy who had been helping me was transferred on to the remand centre, the CDP (Centre for Detention and Prevention), located next to the prison. The very next day both Nicky and I heard we would also, finally, be transferred, thus ending our chances of escaping from Interpol. So close!

I heard shortly afterwards that the police had discovered the hole, beaten everyone, repaired it and swapped the women into these cells and the men into the women's. I often wondered if I would have succeeded and just how far away I would have got.

It may have been a disappointment not to have had a shot at escaping, but it was a relief to be finally leaving the terrible conditions we had been living in. We should have only spent a couple of nights there, but it had now been over five weeks.

However, transfer to the main prison, Penal Garcia Moreno, meant separation from Nicky. She was taking it all hard. She was the first to leave, with a bunch of the other women, who promised to look after her once they reached the women's prison. The group included a woman called María, who spoke good English and looked out for Nicky. Her husband Nizar was also connected to the Arabs, but had been captured at an earlier date and was awaiting the arrival of Hassan and his friends in the main prison.

They reassured me that within three months I should be able to arrange for her to visit me every Thursday – inter-prison – for the whole day for *íntima*, or a conjugal visit. She was tearful and so was I, seeing her disappearing, not knowing where or when I would next see her and what kind of hardships she would endure. I told her I would make contact by phone as soon as possible and instructed her to get a mobile number to our lawyer. I would also make sure she had plenty of money to keep her going.

After Nicky was taken off we had to wait a few hours, during which 'the colonel', a fellow inmate reassured me she would be all right. He was an ex-colonel of police who had been arrested with 300 kilograms of pure Peruvian cocaine. He spoke good English, which he'd learnt while serving a lengthy prison sentence in North America following his extradition some years earlier on drug trafficking charges. When the transport returned, the colonel, the Arabs, myself and a bunch of others were loaded into an armoured box van with no windows, under armed guard. We began a bumpy trip along the choked streets of Quito to the Garcia Moreno prison in the old sector of the city. We first had to go to the CDP, from where we would be allocated to our wings in the prison, a bit like county jail in the USA. This place was notorious for being violent and very basic, so I was feeling fairly apprehensive. We pulled up outside the CDP, which is next to the prison on a dead-end street opposite a market.

Carrying our mattresses and bags, we were led through a high iron gate and through another door in the side of what looked like an office building. This opened up on to a court-yard or small exercise yard, with a three-storey concrete structure on the left that resembled a half-built car park. I could see through the bars of the ground floor a dark, open space in which some gruesome ghouls with filthy-looking faces were milling about like something out of a zombie horror film. I could see a couple of them brandishing knives quite openly and gesturing through the bars in my direction that they intended to cut my throat. Fuck!

'Bloody hell!' I exclaimed. 'We're not being placed in there, are we Adnan?' A note of panic was creeping into my voice. Adnan, Hassan's friend, turned to me, smiling. 'Don't worry my friend, *we* are not going in there, just you!' He was laughing by now, along with a couple of the others who had overheard. 'No, no. I am joking. We all go top floor, penthouse with all the foreigners and traffickers. These people bad people, killers, robbers, drug addicts. No good. Very bad people.'

I looked through the bars at the desperate crazed faces of human beings caged like wild animals. I was frightened.

'Come on, we go,' Adnan said, and I followed him, Hassan and the others. As we passed by, arms came flying out of the windows, trying to grab our bags – or possibly us.

The top floor of the CDP was a long, open area in which people had constructed wooden bunks, some with curtains across them for privacy made from whatever they could get their hands on or bribe the guards to bring in. The Arabs who had taken me under their wing were well-received and invited me to share with them. Within the hour they had a mobile phone and were calling their families and friends. They promised to let me use it the next day to phone England, so that I could speak to my family.

The conditions were a little better here. At least there was fresh air coming through an open window, and everywhere was cleaner. There was a toilet cubicle that offered some privacy and a makeshift cold-water shower at one end. Here people could cook, play cards, talk, smoke. Occasionally fights broke out.

The day after our arrival we were allowed into the exercise yard for a couple of hours to finally get some sun. It was a good feeling to be outside breathing reasonably fresh air after being locked up so long. It was during one of these exercise periods that I first witnessed real brutality by the prison guards.

Juan, the young Colombian I had helped out in the Interpol station by paying for his mother to be released, had decided to climb the chain fence in the yard to call to her – she had come to try to visit him. I was laughing and joking with one of the Arabs as we walked around the yard when a guard spotted Juan, who by this time was almost at the top of the fence. The guard went ballistic, cursing in Spanish, and rushed to fetch a five-foot-long piece of wood from the office. He started towards Juan, who was now descending rapidly. He hit the ground running, just as the guard gave an almighty swing of the bat. It made contact with the kid's legs, grounding him instantly. He then dealt a couple more blows across Juan's legs and back, leaving the guy in a crumpled heap, sobbing. I thought his legs must be broken but luckily it turned out he was just bruised. It shocked me how quick and brutal the punishment had been and without warning or a caution, and this was only for a minor infraction. What would happen if you had a fight or genuinely tried to escape?

On Saturday and Sunday we were permitted a visit and it wasn't long before the colonel's family arrived, bearing food and drinks. He called me over and introduced me to his wife and his daughter, who was very attractive. He half-jokingly said he would like me to stay in Ecuador, marry his daughter and go into business with him exporting prawns. I should probably have taken him up on his offer as we were to meet again many years later. We spent the afternoon eating chicken, drinking cola and chatting as best we could, he interpreting between his daughter and me.

My lawyer Eva came to visit both me and Hassan to bring us documents to sign, allowing her to proceed with her preparation of the defence. She explained that we would not be staying long in the CDP as she was in the process of making arrangements for us to be transferred to the prison more quickly than normal (for a fee) and to be put on the best wing. In Hassan's case she was arranging for him to share a cell with his brother.

We spent about a week in the CDP and from there, for the 'fee' of $200, we managed to bypass the *calabozo*.

In E wing – a kind of holding area where we were to be kept until we moved up to the main prison – we were greeted by a crowd wanting to inspect this new group of inmates. Within minutes I was talking to an English lad called Nick, who came from near Manchester. It felt surreal meeting someone from home in such an alien environment. Although, at the end of the day, prison is prison wherever in the world you are: bars and walls, solid doors.

We dumped our bags and mattresses in the holding area and Nick said he would show me around. I was apprehensive about leaving my kit as I could see all the eager looks of the inmates at the prospect of a new haul of expensive clothes, shoes, electronics, toiletries – all of which could be stolen and sold or swapped for drugs. We decided among ourselves that someone from our group would stay with the bags at all times. Just as well, because when I returned, I could hear one of the Arabs shouting at a guy who had been trying to cut a deal for my stuff to watch his mouth and fuck off.

From my guided tour, I could see that it was a typical three-storey stone prison, open in the middle with cells and landings on either side. There were at least 300 prisoners living on each wing, generally three per cell but sometimes as many as six or seven. The cell doors were metal, but oddly enough they seemed to be locked from the inside, which was new to me. Another peculiarity was that there were shops run by prisoners, offering pretty much anything from bread, cola and sweets to vegetables, rice, meat and chicken. Cash, Nick explained, was allowed in the prison and there was a whole micro-economy within the walls, much akin to a small village, with grocers' shops, laundries, bakers, clothes sellers, ironmongers – but also dealing in drugs, firearms, alcohol, prostitution, gambling and the sale of cells.

One of the first things Nick told me about himself was that he had been stabbed several times. When I asked him why, he became a bit defensive and said he had been in a fight. I soon found out that Nick was actually on this wing for his own protection because of drug debts in the main prison. I knew from time spent in British prisons that you generally only ended up in serious fights if you got into debt, allowed yourself to be victimised or there was something 'not right' about you – maybe you were a sex offender or grass. I knew it was going to be slightly different here, as it had already been forcefully explained to me that being a foreigner meant you were regarded as a cash cow and therefore likely to be a target of extortion or robbery.

I was glad of the tour as the Arabs and I ended up spending about four or five days sleeping fifteen to twenty of us in a space barely big enough for two people as we waited to be moved into the main prison. We spent our time taking it in turns to sleep like sardines and in the day we would sit around in the exercise yard or in other people's cells, chatting.

I quickly discovered that the regime at Garcia Moreno was quite different to any English prison I knew of. The guards would start coming into the prison at around 6am to take the padlocks off the cell doors. At 8am they would carry out a count and everyone had to be at their cells. It didn't matter if you were lying in bed, just so long as you were present. Failure to make the count could result in your being taken to the *calabozo* or punishment block, or otherwise having to bribe the guard ten or twenty dollars. After this count you were then free to roam around the wing until they locked the cell door in the evening at nine o'clock. The exercise yard was usually closed at 5pm when they would take another count and the last count was at 9pm – bang-up. You rarely saw the guards. You could tell this was not a place of rehabilitation, merely of containment: a human warehouse.

However, one thing that really shook me was a cell midway along one of the landings that was permanently locked. There was a plaque on the wall next to it with the name of a former president of Ecuador. He had been imprisoned and subsequently murdered in that very room. This made me think, if an ex-president can be murdered in here, then how easy is it to kill another inmate or, more to the point, to be killed yourself? This I would soon find out once we were moved into the main section of the prison a few days later.

I found out from someone else that Nick had originally been arrested with his father. However, his father had become ill after a couple of years in the poor conditions of the prison and very sadly died here. I felt so sorry for Nick. It is one of the worst things that can happen to you in prison, a parent or sibling dying while you were locked up. It must have been terrible for the both of them. I quietly thought to myself that I hope neither of my parents dies before I am released. My mother was a constant worry, with her poor health and now the added stress of my situation. It weighed heavily on my mind.

CHAPTER SIX
C WING, GARCIA MORENO PRISON

After a few days living like sardines in a can, we were finally moved into the main prison and C wing, where the majority of the foreigners were housed. This I was pleased about. At least we would be in a proper cell and not sleeping on the floor, and also it would be great to meet the other Brits, of whom there were three or four, and some other English speakers.

Dumping our gear down in a pile, we waited to be allocated to cells. This task fell not to the officers but to the *caporal* – an inmate who is an elected representative charged with managing the wing, similar to the Number One on a British prison wing. The *caporal* of C wing was named Youseff, and on first appearance he could easily have been mistaken for the governor of the prison. He was a heavyset Egyptian of six foot two inches, well dressed in a shirt and dark trousers with smart leather shoes and coiffured black hair. Youseff guided us up three flights of stairs to the top floor, passing on the way a small gym, some offices and the telephone kiosks (*cabinas*). Youseff then began sorting out which cells we were going to be staying in. In the case of the Arabs this had been arranged in advance thanks to Eva, and about $2,000.

My first experience of corruption on C wing came within a few minutes of meeting *caporal* Youseff. He explained to me that everyone coming onto the wing had to pay a small fee called the *ingresso*, or entrance fee. This varied between the wings, C wing's being the highest at about $70. This money went into the wing's fund for maintenance and upkeep. There was also a separate tax or charge of one or two dollars a week, collected every Sunday and called the *guardia*. This money was used to pay the guards off daily to ensure they didn't hassle people on the wing too much and that they turned a blind eye to basic infractions, making everyone's life a little more bearable.

Youseff explained that I could buy a cell, which was a new concept to me. The average cell price was $2,000 and you also paid a fee to the *caporal* to witness the transaction between you and the current owner. A contract would be drawn up and you would then pay a fee to the person in admin. This wasn't supposed to happen but the authorities turned a blind eye as they were getting paid. You still had to have at least two people living with you but it meant you had your space, which was particularly important on visit days. These were all day Wednesday, Saturday and Sunday from 9am to 5pm, and once every two weeks your girlfriend, wife or a prostitute could stay the night in your cell on the Saturday. This was music to my ears. Sex in prison!

I thought I would wait a while before I bought a cell, as I was determined to get out of here soon and I viewed buying a cell as settling down and being resigned to being in for the long haul. I should have bought one then and there!

I was allocated to a cell owned by a Frenchman called Jean, who shared it with a German by the name of Johann. Jean spoke only a little English and was a slim, athletic-looking guy with quite a highly strung, nervous manner about him, who rarely sat still. Johann spoke good English and was distinctly Aryan-looking with blonde hair, blue eyes and pale skin. He was quite stocky and a relaxed friendly guy, but with that serious German nature. They were both serving sentences of eight years.

Two of the English-speaking guys had heard that another Brit had just arrived, so came to introduce themselves. The first was perhaps 60, an old boy by the name of Arthur, who had a grandfatherly manner. He was of medium build and about the same height as me – five foot ten – with short grey hair brushed to one side and blue eyes that peered at me over the tops of the spectacles that rested on his nose. He introduced himself in a softly-spoken south London accent, which was nice to hear. Arthur was sentenced to eight years and had been in the prison over two years already, so was well accustomed to the place. The second guy, Victor, was Colombian but had been raised around the Brixton area of London so spoke English perfectly. He was about my age, early thirties, and muscular from working out in the gym. He had short black hair and dark skin. Victor had been in the prison some three years and was reaching the end of his sentence – or at least approaching a possible release date.

Another Brit appeared a little later. Felix was a tall, solid black guy from London, of Nigerian descent, and had been studying medicine. He was two years off finishing when he decided to act as a mule and carry a few kilos of cocaine back to Britain to help finance his studies. He didn't make it out of the airport in Quito and was awaiting sentencing. He was well-spoken and intelligent with a kind face, but had shifty eyes. There was something about him I didn't quite trust.

Each wing in Garcia Moreno prison housed between 300 and 500 men, an overall total of well over 1,500, although the prison was originally designed to hold far fewer. The prison was for men over the age of 18, convicted or charged with crimes ranging from petty theft through to drug trafficking, rape and murder. There were also a number of serial killers held there. Very few of the foreigners were being held for murder – virtually all of them were in for drugs offences. The sentences in the prison ranged from a few months up to 25 years, with exceptionally bad cases receiving a whopping 35 years with no parole.

The inmates of C wing were almost all foreigners, with 40 to 50 nationalities represented. There were a lot of Spanish men, probably since they were the most obvious target of traffickers because of their shared language and ease of obtaining a visa. There were quite a few Russians and Africans, with Nigeria in particular well represented. There were many Colombians in the prison but they tended to live on D wing, which was more or less controlled by them. A number of the Colombians were or had been professional assassins for the drug cartels of Colombia, carrying out contract killings.

B wing was almost entirely Ecuadorian with a few foreigners – just one Englishman and a number of Colombians. Arthur and Victor warned me to be careful over on B wing as the locals could get 'a bit funny' and sometimes took exception to foreigners wandering around in their territory. They explained that it was run in the main by a gang from Quito whose head was a dangerous young guy called Enrique, along with another called Christian, both of whom had committed multiple murders.

Some of the bigger traffickers were being held on A wing, which was a smaller, self-contained maximum-security wing, controlled directly by the police and not the prison guards. These traffickers were usually being held with several other members of a cartel, often up to 15 people on charges of trafficking anything up to ten tons of cocaine. Broken down, that is ten million grams, and after being cut with other substances more like 20 million grams of cocaine for sale. That's a lot of blow!

I soon discovered that the remand and sentenced prisoners weren't separated as in some prisons in the west, nor was there any differentiation between short-, mid- or long-term prisoners, everyone instead being thrown in together. It seemed to me that the authorities didn't really care what happened within the walls of the prison just so long as it was contained there. This job of containment came down to the guards and the police. The guards maintained internal security and in general didn't seem to be armed apart from with pepper spray or tasers and batons. The head guard, or *jefe de guia*, had a pistol of some kind. In comparison, the police, who patrolled the perimeter, were armed to the teeth with M16 assault rifles, various machine guns and Glock 9mm sidearms. They were under orders to shoot to kill anyone trying to escape.

It wasn't just the Brits who warned me how dangerous the place was. It seemed there was an average of one or two murders a week – usually by knife, but sometimes there would be gunfights between gangs for control of one of the wings. The thought of being in the middle of a gunfight in a prison wasn't a happy one for me, particularly without a gun. This was something I had to think about. I would have to be careful here. Any arguments or fights could end in death pretty easily.

I had also heard about the riots – the ones that had prevented my transfer from the Interpol station. The aim of the riots was to draw attention to the plight of the prisoners and their families. It had so far been futile, which could only mean one thing – we were in for more. It looked as though I had arrived at a very volatile time.

On one of my first evenings on the wing there was a guy cutting people's hair with electric clippers near where the communal TV hung on the second floor, very close to my cell. I was standing nearby, chatting, and, as a joke, the guy with the clippers buzzed the side of my head, cutting some of my hair off. I didn't find this funny and before I knew it we had squared up to each other. People intervened and broke it up. Only later did someone tell me that the guy with whom I had been fighting was a *sicario*, or hitman, for a Colombian cartel and the son of a *capo*, or mafia boss, who was in the maximum-security wing charged with trafficking nine tons of cocaine. I had only been there a week and had already made an enemy of one of the most deadly and feared people in the prison. Luckily, Tigre, as he was called, was suddenly transferred for some other problem, thus creating space between us.

Towards the end of my first week Felix, the black guy from London, took me to meet the boss of B wing. An hour after I'd met the guy, there was a lot of commotion and Felix came to find me to tell me that the boss I had just been talking to was dead, having been shot, stabbed and hanged to give the pretence of a suicide. Now, it's fairly obvious that you don't shoot and stab yourself before hanging your own body up. However, the authorities there didn't care and it was chalked up as just another suicide, one less problem for them.

So that was my welcome to C wing: riots, a boss murdered and making an enemy of a Colombian *sicario*, all within a week. And it was starting to seem that I was looking at a sentence of at least 12 years – some people had even suggested it might be 25 years. At this rate, I wouldn't even last six months.

CHAPTER SEVEN
JUST ANOTHER DAY IN PARADISE

The cells at Garcia Moreno prison were small, about six feet by eight with two bunks and one person sleeping on a roll mat or mattress on the floor. This was my current position and it meant I had to get up and out of the way just prior to the first count at 8am so that the cell was clear to move around in. I would fold up my bedding, roll up the mattress and store it under the bottom bunk. It was a pain, but I wasn't yet ready to buy a cell.

The main benefit of having your own cell was that you could relax by yourself whenever you wanted to. Not owning one meant basically wandering around from 8.30am until 9pm or spending time in friends' cells. It was awkward. I tried to set a routine, which I have always found passes the time best in prison. Occupy the hours and the days go a lot more quickly.

First thing in the morning, I would go down to the exercise yard and spend at least an hour doing circuit training with a few others. I would then have a shower outdoors in the exercise yard to freshen up. I had discovered that

Arthur, the old boy, was a keen player of cribbage, a card game I had been taught by my father. When I was a child, helping him on a building site in my school holidays, we would play in the pub at lunchtimes. I didn't get to play games with my father that often so it meant a lot. I remember a police officer telling my dad to get me out of there one lunchtime, thus stopping our game, and me resenting the police after that.

I would find Arthur and together we would sit at one of the restaurants in the small exercise yard of C wing, playing crib for a good couple of hours. I would buy us both breakfast/brunch from Ivan, the gregarious Russian who ran it. He was an ex-KGB officer with huge hands, a real Russian bear. He would cook us large plates of chicken livers and a massive Spanish omelette.

While Arthur and I played crib, Ivan would sit and drink strong coffee – often laced with alcohol – smoking cigarettes and swearing in throaty Russian at anyone who came too close to his restaurant, which was in a red metal Coca-Cola stand-cum-shed. I learned a few words of Russian from him, nearly all of them swear words, mostly because of the frequency with which he used them. This was generally how my mornings were spent, as well as reading a book, calling family and friends, and planning either to defend the case or try to escape.

My first near escape from the prison came not long after arriving there and being allocated to C wing. It involved Martha, an interpreter I had hired on the recommendation of the embassy. We had a meeting arranged at the prison in order to run through exactly what I planned to say in my defence. She had spoken with the director himself, who had kindly offered her the use of his office. This was located at the entrance to the prison, to the right of the main door as you face the building.

It was a Wednesday and visit day as normal. A guard came looking for me mid-morning and told me I was to follow him to the director's office as there was a visitor waiting for me from the embassy. We were allowed our own clothing in the prison, so I was dressed quite smartly in a blue fisherman's jumper and beige trousers with tan shoes. I followed the guard off the wing, through the centre and down the narrow, dimly lit corridor, heading towards the main gate. We were stopped at the end of the corridor by the *jefe de guia*, who wanted to know where the guard was taking me. The guard showed him the pass stamped by the director and this was sufficient to open the main gate. The 'gate' was actually a very solid old wooden door, with dozens of metal rivets holding in place iron reinforcing that had barred the way to freedom for countless lost souls, some of whom never made it out alive.

We passed through it and down a set of old stone steps, turning left into the director's office. There sat Martha, a smartly dressed middle-aged Ecuadorian. The director ushered us into his space and then disappeared to give us privacy. Martha told me the director had allowed us as much time as was necessary to go over the details. She went on to tell me that the embassy had in fact taken care of booking the appointment, which explained why the director was being so amenable. The staff from the British embassy were highly respected in Ecuador and treated most courteously wherever they went.

We spent the next 45 minutes going over my defence, Martha suggesting changes she thought would improve how well it might be received by the three judges. Once we had finished we walked out of the office to where there were visitors being searched before going into the prison for their visit. Martha said goodbye and turned to the left on to a concrete ramp that led down to a police checkpoint and then the road.

I went to turn right to go back through the main entrance door and into the prison. A lone guard stood on the steps aimlessly gazing about, paying no particular attention to anyone and particularly not me. I paused for a minute, watching the visitors filing past me and being searched. Could I make it if I turned left on to the ramp, as Martha had done? Would I be able to get past the police checkpoint without arousing suspicion? I knew they generally held your IDs here if you were going into the prison, but in Martha's case I wasn't sure because she only went to the director's office and not actually into the prison. Perhaps I could tell them the same thing – that I had been to see the director and not speak in Spanish: 'Sorry, must be on my way now old chap. Toodle pip!'

I just wasn't sure what the procedure was. Damn it! I was outside the prison. I was free. No one was paying me any attention. My mind was spinning out of control, uncertain as to what to do next. I gritted my teeth and turned to my right, towards the prison and captivity. I felt sick. The guard stopped me and asked where I thought I was going. I couldn't believe it – he didn't even know I was a prisoner. Shit! I actually had to ask him to 'please open the door so I can go back in because I'm a prisoner'. I was nearly in tears walking back up the long narrow passageway, knowing that I may have just committed one of the worst errors ever in my life – well, second that is to being caught. I should have just had a go then and there and tried to bluff my way through. But I didn't and I very much regretted that decision a few times in the following years. It was *Midnight Express* for real. Who knows, perhaps I would have ended up dead.

At lunchtime, between noon and one o'clock, when the sun was at its most extreme microwave strength, I would avoid being outside. Quito, being on the equator and at nearly 2,500 metres altitude, is a great deal closer to the sun than Brighton beach or Weston-super-Mare. It takes just a couple of hours to achieve what the average sunbather manages in weeks on one of those beaches. If you do expose your skin to the solar radiation of this midday sun you can see red blotches start to appear where your flesh is actively cooking. This is the perfect recipe for skin cancer, especially with the lack of protection we had. I got burnt and ended up with sunstroke several times. Often the newcomers, particularly the Europeans, would rush to get a good suntan and end up making themselves very ill.

Being ill in prison is never a good idea. And here, this prison being a third world one 5,000 miles from my loving family home, comfortable bed and the NHS, it was probably the worst idea ever – apart from, that is, trying to traffic nearly eight kilos of cocaine in Ecuador. From my and Nicky's very first meeting with the embassy staff they had cautioned us to be careful with our health in the prison: wash your hands frequently, stay clean in general, don't smoke, drink alcohol or take drugs, try not to become ill and avoid people with diseases. Of course, this was virtually impossible in a prison full of sick people. The embassy staff had stressed to us the importance of keeping strong both physically and mentally if we wanted to make it through this ordeal alive. Just being in prison takes its toll on you in so many ways: the poor diet, stress, lack of sleep, lack of daylight in some places, lack of exercise, lack of stimulation, little contact with family and friends, the generally all-male environment and poor conditions. One of the big problems in Ecuador, both in prison and on the street, is the fact that very little education is free, and at this time what there was of the national health service was run down and swamped by mismanagement and poor funding. Ignorance really does breed disease.

The prison had a doctor present most days and you could get a diagnosis from him and also prescriptions, but then you had to give them to a visitor to purchase and bring in the medication, which could take time. If you became seriously ill in prison and couldn't pay for the medication, you died. It was as simple as that. If it was a medical emergency then you'd have to be carried to the entrance of the prison where you would have to wait until various people, including the director, had signed documents to allow you to be taken to hospital – as long as you could pay. A lot of people would die in the time it took for the director to sign, guard escort to be organised and the ambulance to arrive.

The dentist was pretty much the same but he only came in twice a week. He would do the basics, such as extractions, but if you wanted your teeth cleaned or filled or anything other than essential work done, then you paid. Once your wallet opened, so did your mouth!

Ideally you should be in perfect health when you started your sentence, with brilliant teeth and 20/20 vision. People who had been in the prison a long time explained to me that they were generally OK for the first three or four years, but after that their health deteriorated. I thought to myself, there's no way I will still be in prison then.

Most people on C wing had a two-ring electric cooker in their cells that they used for cooking food, along with a fridge. Some even had microwaves. Everyone had kettles and toasters and most had a TV, DVD player and hi-fi. Some had satellite TV, via a dish mounted on the side of the wing. I quickly understood that as long as you had money you could have pretty much anything you wanted. I even started to think that maybe it was lucky I had been arrested here rather than in England. At least here there were possibilities ... as long as you had *el dinero*.

On one occasion I was in our cell, congratulating myself with the way I was settling in and figuring out how the prison worked. I had a routine and there seemed to be lots of opportunities to arrange things for my own comfort, and maybe even make some money. Just then my cellmate Jean, who had been in D wing seeing a friend, came hurrying back in. He explained that one of the African guys had just been stabbed to death and all the Africans were up in arms about it – literally. They were being held back at the gate by the heavily armed guards, who wouldn't let them past as they were hell-bent on taking revenge.

Jean explained what had happened. One of the Africans had been using the payphone when another inmate came up to him and asked to use the phone. The African tried to explain his credit was about to run out and he didn't have enough on his phone card. At this point the other guy pulled a large kitchen knife and stabbed him to death. Just for a phone call. That's how dangerous this place was. Everything could change in a split second and with absolutely no warning or provocation your life could be ended quicker than you can blow a candle out. I was shocked and from then on treated virtually everyone with a degree of caution and trepidation.

After the 8am count, the next count was not until 5pm. We would all have to be back on our own wing and in our cells for it, but after that you were left to do whatever you wanted. I would usually go to the gym for a couple of hours with my

Russian friend Sasha, then have a shower and cook dinner. The remainder of the time would be spent chatting, making phone calls and playing games.

The final count of the day was at 9pm when we were locked in our cells for the night. By this point I was usually relieved to finally get the door closed so that I could relax and not have to be constantly on my guard. There would always be a mad rush in the last 15 minutes before lock-up as people dashed about getting whatever they needed for the rest of the night – food, films, cigarettes, alcohol or drugs. You would quite often be able to spot who had drugs for sale on the wing as at this hour there would be a feeding frenzy with a queue of anxious people getting enough coke, crack or weed to see them through the long night – nothing worse than running out of supplies at 1am just as the party's getting started, locked behind a steel door.

I tried not to count the days, weeks and months too much as that is a sure way to send yourself crazy in prison. Time becomes meaningless unless you are nearing the end of your sentence or a parole date. I banned calendars from my cell but it is quite satisfying, to know you are one day nearer to hopefully going home if you can only survive.

CHAPTER EIGHT
WHISKY GALORE

I soon realised that I was living with one of C wing's main alcohol suppliers. One evening I interrupted Jean in the process of cooking up his next batch. I could see he was wondering whether or not I could be trusted to keep my mouth shut. I put his worries to rest by quickly offering to help out.

Jean had developed a technique of distilling medicinal alcohol to make it drinkable and not lethal at the same time. He had someone at the clinic selling it to him as well as permission to bring in a certain amount on visit days. He would cook this up in the cell using his secret method, which involved burning some of it off and adding vinegar and I believe sugar. We would then decant it into half-litre water bottles and there you are – the best spring water you ever drank!

Jean and Johann had dug out a section of the tiled floor below Jean's bed, in the back corner well in the shadow. To cover this, they had cast a concrete top and painted it to match the rest of the black and white tiled floor. Nearly all the cells in the prison were peppered with these little cubby-hole hiding places the locals called *caletas*. Some of them were most ingenious and so well made that they would probably never be found. They were in the walls, floors, ceilings, doors, fixtures and fittings, furniture, electronics, drains, absolutely everywhere. You have to remember of course that these people were professional smugglers well used to concealing ton upon ton of blocks of cocaine in all manner of spaces.

The *caleta* that Jean and Johann had constructed was big enough to be able to hold several bottles of the finest liquor, our mobile phones and chargers, all the cutlery, kitchen knives and any drugs that may have been in the cell. In the event of a search by the police or guards after our doors were locked at 9pm, it would be my job, being closest to the *caleta*, to hide everything quickly. Once I had my mattress down and we were about to watch a film, as we did most evenings, I would make sure the *caleta* was slightly open and all the items to go in it were close to hand so I could act at a moment's notice. If a search did happen, we would usually have advance warning, as other prisoners would start shouting '*onze, onze*' – the number eleven in Spanish. The phone number for the emergency services in Ecuador is 911, hence *onze*.

I had learned this system the hard way. During my first few days at the CDP before we were moved to the main prison, I was sitting on a bunk bed happily chatting away to a friend in Britain using Hassan's phone when there was some shouting – including a word I later found out was '*onze*' – and a guard appeared and promptly seized the phone, still hot from my ear, as I was trying to finish the conversation. Hassan got it back after bribing the guard, which was when he explained the *onze* system to me so that I wouldn't lose any more phones.

As we were the suppliers of the alcohol, obviously we would have a few drinks ourselves and sometimes a few bags of cocaine to go with it. The prison was awash with drugs of almost every kind, but the four main ones were cannabis in weed form, cocaine, base and heroin. The drug the locals called 'base' is what we in Europe and America normally call crack cocaine. However, base in Ecuador, and apparently Colombia too, is actually a by-product of the cocaine purification process. This they called *polvo*, which is Spanish for powder. This powder was a yellowy colour and had a texture rather like breadcrumbs or molasses sugar. It had a horrible smell from all the chemicals it contained and the use of gasoline in the process, which probably caused the yellow colour. When it was smoked it absolutely reeked.

The effect was similar to crack cocaine, just not as strong or intense and not very pleasant. I had never seen this drug in Europe. The reason for this was that all the pure cocaine – the best product – is exported to the countries where it will fetch the most money and only the rubbish by-product is sold locally. We would sometimes get our hands on something good, but not that often. My trafficker's brain immediately kicked in when I saw an opportunity; no one was selling crack cocaine or high-quality coke. A lot of the foreigners were complaining about the quality not being good as they were used to buying good Peruvian and Bolivian flake. This and the fact that I was living on the wing with all the foreigners, who generally consumed the most and had the most income, added up to one thing. An opportunity. I would have to tread extremely carefully as I didn't want to rock the boat and piss off any of the locals, who would probably take umbrage at some foreigner suddenly taking over their patch. I would have to take my time and build up friends and backing, hence protection. I estimated it would take quite a while.

Johann and I would sometimes go over to B wing or D wing looking to score some coke, which Johann was particularly fond of. I remember one occasion, towards the end of Johann's sentence, when he had persuaded a fairly heavy character by the nickname of Commando to give him 50 grams on credit. Johann had convinced the shaven-headed, thuggish Commando that he was going to sell the coke on C wing and become the wing dealer. He had picked the *cadada*, bi-weekly sleepover, as the day to commence operations as everyone had a party then. Commando came over to C wing and met with Johann in the cell I had rented for the night in order to give Johann the coke and explain when he wanted his money. Once he was done explaining everything, he produced a sizeable bag of white powder he had stashed in his boxer shorts. Johann's face lit up at the sight of this extra-large 'party in a bag' and I just knew he was not going to sell a single grain of that coke. As soon as Commando departed the cell Johann turned to me, smiled and said, 'Fancy a line then?' Here we go, I thought and sniffed the first of the evening. I turned to Johann and asked him whether or not he planned to sell the coke, to which he replied in his German accent, 'Pa! Sell zis coke, *nein tu es quazy*. I going to have a big fiesta hahaha!'

I said, 'Are you mad Johann? That guy's a bloody psycho who will cut your balls off for a couple of dollars, let alone a few hundred. He's going to kill you if you don't pay him.'

By now Johann was as high as a kite caught in hurricane winds and couldn't care less.

'Ha. Fuck him. That faggot don't do nothing. Anyway, I go home very soon, ha ha. Another line,' he said, holding out the bag with shaky hands. He lay back on the bottom bunk, made himself comfortable, rested the bag of coke on his chest and from his pocket produced a small teaspoon and began to literally shovel coke up his nose. I became so worried he was going to overdose that I asked him to leave as that was the last thing I needed. Luckily for Johann there were no delays in him going free and he made it out by the skin of his teeth.

A favourite pastime of crooks and villains is planning further escapades or capers. A great deal of this took place within the walls of Garcia Moreno. If you think about it, within the same prison there were people involved in the drug trafficking business from the very bottom to the very top. There were members of mafias from Russia, Bulgaria, Serbia, Italy, Albania, Africa and Britain. We had cartel bosses and *capos*, captains of boats and planes, mules. Nationalities from all corners of the globe were represented, nearly all of whom knew people hidden away in those remotest corners all wanting to buy that crystalline analgesic white powdery substance: cocaine. Let the game commence!

As well as the local internal trafficking, there was a huge potential for making some very good new contacts. Prison, wherever in the world you are, can be turned to your benefit if you view it as an opportunity to meet new people and expand your contacts. In the Quito prison at this time there were members of Colombian and Mexican cartels ranging from workers all the way up to the very *capos* themselves. On top of this you also had people from all over the globe with access to untold numbers of buyers and also means of entry via airports, seaports, container ports and a multitude of other ways in which to get drugs into a country. I immediately saw the huge potential to organise something that could prove to be very financially rewarding. We had the suppliers, the shippers and the buyers all under one roof, literally. It just needed someone to try to organise everyone into action, which would take a good deal of diplomacy. That someone was me.

I already had a fairly well-organised network with far-reaching contacts, who were all still there and keen to work. I decided to start putting the word out that I had buyers in Europe ready and waiting with cash for whatever quantity could be delivered. It wasn't long before people started to approach me asking if this or that were possible. The only thing I was interested in was if the cocaine was on the ground in Europe, preferably Britain. Trying to arrange people in airports and seaports with guarantees was almost impossible and also very dangerous because if anything went wrong they would be coming to me for their money.

I was told three things when I arrived at the prison: don't get into debt, don't do drugs and don't do business unless you want problems. The problem here was there was no getting away from your problems. You had to face up to them and deal with them. If you had become involved in a drug deal with someone else in the prison and it went wrong, leaving you owing them a serious amount of money, there was literally nowhere to run or hide. I didn't intend to undertake any business unless I knew that I had it covered in the event it all went horribly wrong. I decided that, on the whole, it was best to wait for a few months to get the feel of things, wait for my sentence to be confirmed and take it from there. After all, there was no real rush. I was possibly looking at a very long sentence.

CHAPTER NINE
NICKY

One of the first things I had arranged after I arrived at Garcia Moreno was a mobile phone because I was spending a fortune on the *cabinas* – a percentage of which was enriching Youseff, the *caporal*, and his *junta* as they had a monopoly over all the phone cards sold in the prison, as well as a host of other items. The phone allowed Nicky and me to maintain daily contact, which really kept us going. She was totally unaccustomed to a prison environment, let alone in a foreign country with everyone speaking another language. The worst part of the whole thing was the fact that she was genuinely innocent and had merely come out for a holiday and to keep me company for a couple of weeks. She was finding it agony being separated from her daughter Emily, who was now being looked after by Nicky's parents. I was adamant that I would do anything to get her released and promised her that she would not be getting sentenced.

The Ecuadorians were concerned about keeping the statistics relating to drug arrests nice and high. That way the press and governments of the world would think they were doing a fantastic job. The mere fact that she was present in that hotel room condemned her. However, the Ecuadorian justice system at the time was suffering a terrible backlog and had come to a virtual standstill. Nicky was going to have to sit it out until we could push the case through the courts.

My lawyer Eva warned that it could take over a year before the case was put before a judge. The only way to speed it up would of course be with money. Nicky kept telling me not to pay as she was innocent and there was no evidence against her. Eva tried to explain that this made no difference in Ecuador. Nicky was in prison now and the only way she would be getting released any time soon would be to pay.

Luckily, at the time of my arrest I had plenty of money, some of which was put aside for a contingency such as this. I instructed Eva to come up with an overall figure for how much it would cost me to get Nicky out. I didn't care about the money; I just wanted her out of there as fast as possible. The weeks were becoming months and Nicky was becoming more and more depressed and homesick.

Eva intended to have the case against Nicky dismissed due to lack of evidence at the first hearing and was in the process of negotiating with the judges and court officials as to how much they wanted in order to release her. This was great news. Things were not looking so good for me, however. In order to guarantee Nicky's release, even with the payoff, the judges were insisting that I plead guilty to the charges of international drug trafficking. There had to be someone convicted for the crime. I would have to change the first statement I had made, in which I had denied all knowledge of the cocaine present in the groundsheet of the tent. Eva set about making the arrangements with the fiscal's office – the South American equivalent of the Crown Prosecution Service – to fix a date for the new interview. I knew I wasn't walking away from this, so why should Nicky suffer as well?

The day of the new interview came and a couple of police officers from Interpol collected me and transported me back to the Interpol offices on the other side of Quito. It was bizarre being driven through the streets where I had walked not so long ago. We drove past tourists wandering around and I wondered if any of them were also here arranging shipments of cocaine.

The colonel at Interpol who had been in charge of the case was there, along with Eva and a fiscal from the prosecutor's office. We got down to business and I gave my new 'version' of events, admitting that yes, I was transporting cocaine back to Europe. I said I was to be the one carrying it, which in fact I wasn't. I had only ever once carried the drugs myself. Mules or passengers would be hired who could do that job for us.

I explained that I had made arrangements with someone in Colombia to package the drugs and then have the tent delivered to me in Quito. From there, I said, I intended to transport it back to mainland Europe rather than Britain. I said this in an attempt to throw into doubt the case in England, which alleged I was transporting drugs to Britain. I stated, which was the truth, that Nicky had no idea what was happening and that she was an innocent bystander with a young daughter who was now without her mother. I reiterated that she had only been in Ecuador for a few hours, during which time she hadn't met anybody apart from me. She hadn't been anywhere apart from the hotel and restaurant so how could she be guilty?

Eva reassured me that would be sufficient to clear Nicky, along with about $20,000 plus $5,000 for Eva's own work. I agreed to the figure and said I would make arrangements to get the money transferred over as soon as possible. We parted company and I was taken back to the prison. I was led up to the main entrance, where I paused for my last breath of fresh air for a while.

It took a couple more months of negotiations and organising money transfers for everything to be set. Eva promised us that she had made all the arrangements for Nicky's release. We were awaiting a date for the hearing at which the fiscal would present his evidence and say who was to be charged and who not. At this point, Nicky would be released and all charges against her dismissed.

Nicky was now much more relaxed. She could see the end in sight. We started looking at flights and informed the embassy that she would be released soon. I had paid a fee to the airline on a couple of occasions to change the return date on Nicky's original booking so that it would not be wasted, as it had cost nearly £2,000. I asked Eva to try to find her a nice apartment in the old part of Quito, where she could stay following her release until all her papers were sorted out. She would need a new passport and various other documents before she would be able to leave Ecuador.

At last a date was set for the first hearing. Some four months had now passed and we were almost in a new year. The anticipation was building and I was feeling nervous and stressed. Nicky was insisting on going back to England.

'I have to go back, Pete,' she said. 'Emily is alone there staying with my parents. She needs her mum and I'm desperate to see her. I can't handle this much longer.' Nicky was almost in tears, the strain showing on her face.

'I'm really worried that if you return to England the police are going to arrest you and try to convict you,' I said.

'But I'm bloody innocent!' she cried out. 'It wasn't fucking me who was smuggling kilos and bloody kilos of that shit was it? It was you! I don't have anything to do with this apart from being your bloody girlfriend.'

I looked into her eyes and could see the anger and distress swirling round in them.

'Nicky, the police in England will arrest you exactly because you are my girlfriend. They know you are innocent but they don't care. They will have a go at you just to hurt me because they can't get to me here.'

I was extremely worried about what was going to happen upon Nicky's arrival back in the UK. A couple of officers from SOCA – the Serious Organised Crime Agency – had travelled out to Ecuador to collect evidence and take DNA samples from me. They told me that it didn't matter where she went – Spain or France or wherever – they would pursue and arrest her and make her stand trial in England. It was clear they were gunning for her and fully intended to arrest and prosecute her upon her return.

Nicky wouldn't believe me and kept saying, 'I'm innocent, I haven't done anything and I'm a mother with a young daughter. They won't arrest me.'

'The police don't care about that,' I said. 'They would arrest you just to get at me out of spite and to bolster their statistics.'

I pleaded with her to fly instead to Barcelona, where a good friend of mine had agreed to her using his beachfront apartment. I said I would have Emily flown over to Spain and they could wait and see exactly what happened with the case in Britain before deciding whether or not she should return. At least if she was in Spain and the British police came looking for her they would first have to find her before attempting to extradite her. But she was insistent on going back to Britain and just couldn't believe the police were interested in her.

On the day of the first hearing, I was collected by a guard early in the morning and taken to a holding cell while they gathered up all the people to be transported to the courts on that day. At this hearing there were three judges, similar to a magistrate's court in England. Nicky was already there with Eva and Martha the interpreter. It was very emotional, seeing Nicky for the first time in several months. She hadn't changed a great deal apart from having a tan and even fairer hair where the sun had bleached it blonde. We got to give each other a long-awaited hug, then had to sit apart while the hearing got under way. Nicky looked drawn with anxiety. God, I hoped nothing would go wrong at the last moment; she would be devastated, as would I.

The fiscal ran through the evidence and, as agreed, announced that they were not going to prosecute Nicky due to a lack of evidence. She didn't understand what had happened at first, but I explained it to her, as she was sat at the table next to mine, and she broke down in tears. She was asking if she was going to be released that very same day as one would be in an English court. Unfortunately not here; you had to go back to the prison until the paperwork was completed and an order of release document called a *boleta de libertad* was sent out to the prison. This was supposed to take no more than 48 hours by law, but often took longer. Eva said she would do her utmost to ensure it took no more than a day for Nicky to be released. I thanked her profusely for her efforts and got to give Nicky one last hug before we all left the courtroom. I was so relieved that she was going free and would be reunited with Emily very soon. I was however still very worried by her decision to fly straight back to Britain without even consulting a solicitor.

Eva was as good as her word and a day later Nicky walked free from the women's prison.

The very next visit day at Garcia Moreno, Nicky arrived and we were reunited properly for the first time in nearly six months. It was very emotional, with both of us in tears while hugging each other. I had rented out a cell on the top floor for the day; it belonged to Jean's Serbian friend Dragan. It was great to be able to shut the door on the prison and spend a few hours in Nicky's company, making love, talking and just relaxing. Now I knew that Nicky was free, all the tension that had built up in me over the previous months seemed to dissipate and for that day I felt at peace.

That peace was shattered at around 4.30pm when the bell downstairs rang to signal that the visit was drawing to a close. All visitors had to have left the prison by 5pm. If not, the police would sometimes cause problems and impose fines on those who were late leaving. If you didn't pay the fine you too could find yourself locked up for the night in the police cells. The police would also sometimes mount a surprise inspection of passports and IDs used to get into the prison, to try to catch people with fake documents or without a visa.

Over the next few weeks, Nicky came in to see me nearly every visit day. Every other Saturday she was able to stay with me overnight in the cell, which was something we both looked forward to very much. She would come in early in the morning, bringing a couple of bags of food shopping. We would then spend until 5pm on Sunday chatting, making love, eating, drinking, watching films and generally having an indulgent time together.

Then Nicky's documents were sorted and she found a flight home, via Holland. I knew that things between me and Nicky had changed as a result of our experiences, and I knew the consequences for both her and her daughter's futures. She had had enough and I couldn't blame her. She hadn't ever become particularly angry with me. She could see I had done everything possible to make sure she went free. I spent a large sum of money to guarantee she was released and had also taken full responsibility for the drugs. She knew I was going to be locked up for many years to come. I was in Ecuador, 5,000 miles from Britain, which meant there would be no contact in the form of visits – or anything much else for that matter. I knew that when she left that was going to be the end of our relationship. I was sad but I had to face the reality of my situation and hers.

We said our farewells the last time she visited. She was ecstatic to be leaving the country where she had been imprisoned for over six months of her life. She had only spent a handful of hours as a free person prior to her arrest on 16 August 2005, a day none of us will ever be able to forget, and finally left just prior to my birthday towards the end of February 2006. But she was also leaving me. I walked her down to the gate at the entrance of the wing, gave her one last hug and watched as she disappeared round the corner. I struggled to hold back my tears until I reached my room, where I sat and wept, engulfed by the sadness and loneliness. My partner, friend and lover was gone.

A week or so after Nicky's departure from Ecuador I received an urgent message from María, who'd shared a cell with Nicky and was still locked up in the women's prison.

'Interpol have been to the prison looking for Nicky. They have been questioning some of her friends in the prison asking if they know her whereabouts. There is an international arrest warrant for her and they are trying to locate her urgently. Apparently she should never have been released. Please warn her and wish her luck.'

This was bad; this was really, really bad.

I picked the phone up and dialled Nicky's new English mobile number and she answered: 'Hi there, how are you?'

'I'm OK but I think you are about to have a problem there. I knew it was a bad idea you going back to England. Interpol have been to the women's prison here looking for you with an international arrest warrant.'

'Fuck, oh no! Shit, what am I going to do? They can't arrest me! I'm innocent, it was you who was being a prick drug smuggling. Fuck. I can't go to prison – what about Emily?' She was starting to panic. 'Surely they would have arrested me as soon as I arrived in the country?'

'I don't know Nicky. Look, the offer of going to Spain is still there. Pack some bags quickly and leave the country with Emily. Drive to Barcelona and my friends will take care of you there. If you're lucky they won't stop you.'

'I can't just go like that,' she said. 'I don't think they will arrest me. I'm a mum with a young daughter and, anyway, I've just spent nearly six months in prison there – surely they aren't going to lock me up again here.'

'Please be careful Nicky. I just managed to get you out of prison here, I won't be able to do the same there. Think about what you are doing. If you need any help call me. I have a very good lawyer in London who can represent you if needs be. Just make sure you call me.'

'OK I will do if I need to but I don't think I will. Speak to you soon. Bye.'

With that she was gone. She never did call me and shortly afterwards the British police came knocking and arrested her. She was charged along with a couple of other people with conspiracy to import over 80kg of cocaine over a two-year period from 2003 to 2005. The police alleged that I was the mastermind behind the whole plot. Nicky was released on bail to await trial at a later date. It was quite some time before the trial took place in Britain so I had to wait and wonder what was going to happen.

CHAPTER TEN
SENTENCIA

Shortly after the first *audiencia*, where Nicky was found to be innocent of all charges after having spent six months in prison, a flustered Eva contacted me. She had received a document with the date of my second hearing, which in effect was to be my trial. It was only two weeks away. Now that I had entered a guilty plea and taken full responsibility for the 7.8kg of cocaine (which was actually only 2kg), this was to be a sentencing hearing. Eva explained that in her entire career she had never seen a sentencing hearing take place so quickly. She had gone to the court to find out what was going on and had been told that the British authorities had contacted the Ecuadorian government and put pressure on them to sentence me quickly so that I didn't have time to organise any proper defence or mitigation.

At the first hearing Eva and I had formulated a strategy to try to minimise the sentence, but it was reliant on me getting documents from England and having them notarised by the embassy in Quito. All this was going to take time. Luckily my friends were already dashing about getting statements and other papers prepared, and Eva had already negotiated with the judges how long my sentence would be and how much this would cost me. SOCA had sent a document to the Ecuadorian police and prosecutor's office, which Eva had acquired a copy of, requesting that I be sentenced to the maximum under Ecuadorian law – 25 years.

The justification they gave for requesting such a lengthy prison term was the ongoing conspiracy case in Britain, plus my criminal record. The British police were accusing me of being the mastermind behind a smuggling operation bringing cocaine into Britain impregnated into the rubber groundsheets of camping equipment such as tents. They were alleging that over a two-year period I, along with several others, had brought over 80kg of cocaine into Britain in this form.

Following the Edinburgh raid, the police had uncovered a number of small laboratories in residential properties where they said we were extracting the cocaine from the rubber using various chemicals. Because I already had a criminal record for drugs, they wanted to give me an extremely high sentence of at least 20 years! Everyone I had asked about whether or not my criminal record would be taken into account here by the judges had said no; that was England and this was Ecuador. I had hoped to be treated as a first-time offender in Ecuador as I had no history there. Alas, this hope was to be in vain.

When I was arrested in May 2000 in England and charged with possession with intent to supply 5,000 ecstasy pills, 2 kilos of base amphetamine, 5 kilos of hashish and 5 kilos of weed, plus a couple of ounces of coke and a sawn-off shotgun, I had got off lightly on account of it being a first offence, as well as my good background and references from some well-respected people in the community.

That doesn't mean I was treated easy – I wasn't. I spent nearly two years on remand awaiting sentence and the first year of that as the only category A prisoner in the whole of

Gloucester Prison. They had me 'on the book', which means they note your whereabouts every 15–30 minutes, 24 hours a day. This means that all through the night they come and open the observation window in your door, and turn the bloody light on, to make sure you haven't escaped. I would get strip-searched nearly every day, sometimes by female officers. My cell would be ripped to pieces nearly as frequently and all my calls were recorded. I wasn't allowed phone cards, all my letters were opened, copied and sent to the police and some of them I never even received. My visits were behind a glass screen, and to begin with, always with a senior officer sitting next to me monitoring everything.

Having finally received my sentence of five years, where did I get sent but to Parkhurst prison on the Isle of Wight? At the time, it was one of Britain's hardest and most secure prisons. They ghosted me there, which means they made a surprise transfer, on Valentine's Day. They wouldn't let me call anyone before I was moved, so Nicky, who was my girl-friend back then, arrived at Gloucester prison for a Valentine's Day visit only to find I had been transferred that very morning to an island in the English Channel!

Back in Ecuador, the British police were doing everything they could to cause me problems. The way they had worded my criminal record, it came across as though I had been in prison 13 times because of there being 13 counts for drugs offences. It was presented in such a way as to make me look like Pablo Escobar.

Even though Eva had negotiated with the judges it made their job difficult as they would be hard pushed to justify a low sentence. I thought they were going to go back on their deal then and there. When I realised this I felt faint and nearly passed out. I turned pale and was shaking. There would be no parole or remission because in Ecuador all these

78

laws were suspended indefinitely. They did give you one month off per year spent in prison, so I calculated that I would have to serve 23 years. Twenty-three years. Fuck! I would be 52 years old when I got released. I hadn't even been 30 when I was arrested. There was no way I could allow this to happen.

In order for the judges to reduce this to 12 years I was going to have to make a hefty payment, but they also needed some sort of documentation from me to be able to justify it. On the other hand, I knew that if I was given a sentence of less than ten years then the British police would call for my extradition to Britain, where they intended to give me 20 years, if not more. So I had to ensure the judges didn't give me less than ten; but also no more than 12 years. I actually had to say to them, 'Please don't give me less than ten years – if you do the British police are going to extradite me to be recharged and sentenced in Britain.'

I hoped that with enough money and the right contacts anything was possible. I certainly didn't intend to serve the full 12-year sentence. The plan was to wait for attention on the case to die down post-sentencing, then, once a year or so had passed, appeal and pay to have it halved to six.

That's where my friends came in. Luckily, being the great friends they are, they got the documents required by the judges to Eva in good time and she was able to take them to the British embassy, who I paid to countersign and notarise them so that it was all neat and official. Eva presented these to the court along with some witness statements and character references and we were set.

The judges had agreed to my and Eva's plan to make an appeal – and pay them some more – to later bring my sentence down to six years. Although the British police were determined that if I served less than ten years in prison they would do all they could to re-sentence me in England, I wasn't too bothered about this as they would have to get me there first, and, once released, I didn't intend to hurry back.

The day of the hearing arrived and I sat before the three judges. Martha, the interpreter from the embassy, was also present to make my defence and so I could understand what was being said. The hearing commenced with the prosecution outlining the charges against me and relaying how I had been captured following a period of surveillance on arrival in the country. The Ecuadorian police officers from Interpol who were in charge of the case and had arrested me in the penthouse of the hotel were also present to give their witness statements and could be cross-examined by Eva and myself.

But I told her to forget it and just to get through the proceedings. We knew what the overall outcome was going to be, having already paid all the judges a handsome sum of money. I was pronounced guilty and told I would be notified of the sentence in due course. It was supposed to take no more than 72 hours but I knew it would actually be several weeks, if not months.

I was taken back to the prison on the bus to await the sentence. I was surprised that everything had happened so quickly. The whole thing had been concluded in less than eight months, in contrast to my two years on remand in the UK. I was kind of relieved to have got it out of the way, as when your future is in the hands of other people you're in a mental stress position. At least I pretty much knew where I stood now. Provided the British police didn't manage to cause more problems, we expected that I would receive a 12-year sentence as that is what Eva had negotiated. So it didn't come as any big surprise or shock when it was confirmed that I was indeed serving 12 years – I just felt quite flat and exhausted.

It took several weeks before we finally received notification of the sentence. It wasn't long before we heard from friends in England that the British police weren't happy and were considering appealing the length of sentence. So I would now have to wait and see if they went ahead. This left me in limbo for a further two months, at which point they decided to leave it as it was. No doubt they had something else in mind, some other way to ensure I didn't go free any time soon.

I now had the task of calling my family and friends to notify them of the outcome. I had done my best to prepare them, knowing the likely outcome. My father and stepmother were the first people I phoned. I explained that the plan was to reduce the 12 years, hopefully to six, after things died down. They were upset, but at least they now knew.

I then had to call my mother, which I had been dreading. She broke down in tears and it nearly killed me. I felt so ashamed and guilty for the grief and anguish I was causing her. She knew to some extent how dangerous it was over here and the thought of her little boy having to endure all that was a lot for her to deal with. I tried to console her but it was so hard to hear her voice and know how upset she was and not to be able to give her a hug.

I was adamant that I didn't want my family to travel all this way to visit me here in these conditions. I tried to paint a much brighter picture for them than it was and excluded the horrific violence I had heard of and seen, and the terrible things I knew could happen in the prison. I remained ever-optimistic that I would be able to get out soon. I kept saying 'within six months I will be out', but the more I repeated it, the more I began to doubt my own words. It's not the despair that kills you: it's the hope.

CHAPTER ELEVEN
MONOPOLY

Over the next few months I settled into the daily routine of the prison. By this time I had become familiar with most of the other foreigners there, as we tended to stick together.

In prison it takes a while to work out who your friends are. As a rule, there are very few people who become genuine long-term friends. I always found that it's best to treat everyone as you would want to be treated yourself. From there you can normally see after a short time who are the ones you want to become friends with.

I have heard people say that you don't, or can't, have friends in prison – and that even if you think you do, none of them will be your real friend. That is untrue. I have met some of my closest friends in prison. The thing is, you are living with a person 24 hours a day, seven days a week, possibly for years, in a very small space from which you can't get away. There are no real breaks apart from a bit of time in the exercise yard, or classes if there are any. No asking for space or a bit of time apart. Because of this you get to learn every last thing about them. When they eat, sleep, go to the toilet, shower and masturbate (although you try to ignore that one! What makes them happy, sad or angry, and every single other mood you can think of). You hear their deepest secrets and get to know how they think. It is unavoidable that some of these people will become lifelong friends. You have to endure extreme hardship, violence and fear together – you witness and experience the most horrendous things. It's a bit like the bond you get in the military. The other side of this, however, is that when you finally get released it takes a long time to readjust. It can be hard relating to people on the outside, who will always find it impossible to understand, especially if you have been through extreme events, because they haven't experienced – and I really hope never will experience – anything like it.

I had recently made friends with an American guy called Andrew who had been in the prison for a couple of years already and lived on D wing. He used to spend his time with some Colombians who were associated with the Colombian terrorist guerrilla group the *Fuerzas Armadas Revolucionarias de Colombia* (Revolutionary Armed Forces of Colombia), known as FARC. They were from an area in the Amazon Basin called Putumayo, on the Colombian side of the river that forms the border with Ecuador in the north. Andrew said he wanted to introduce me to them as they were interested in trafficking some small amounts of cocaine to Europe and were looking for a reliable contact to receive it and pay them. Having me in the prison with them meant there was nowhere to run or hide. I couldn't get away from them in the event something went wrong, as it often did. They were guaranteed to get paid for the coke or I would end up with a very serious problem. I was still wary of getting involved in any business as that was one of the main things everyone had warned me against doing while in the prison, as it could lead to trouble extremely quickly and even end in a slow, torturous death.

But, even with all the inherent risks, I still decided in the end to become involved. I now knew how long I was likely to be here for, and I was slowly starting to accept it. Living costs were high, particularly once all the various bribes and 'fees' had been paid. I knew I would need to create some sort of income to support myself – to ensure my comfort, but also safety. And, of course, it was a case of boredom and wanting something to do. With all the connections I had I felt it would be fairly simple to organise something, make some cash and keep entertained.

It was also a case of making myself something of an asset. If people like these Colombians saw you as having the potential to help them to become extremely wealthy they would look after you. So it was a way of surviving, and, with a minimum of five more years to get through, that's what I wanted to do more than nearly anything.

I had already invested in one planned escapade with my friend Hassan. That had not ended well. I'd lost over $1,500 and our friendship had been damaged as a result. I had given him the money with the plan being that a package would be sent to Britain containing an amount of cocaine to an address I had provided. My friends would then transfer the funds once they had received the package and were happy with its contents. Sounded simple, as it always does but hardly ever is. Everything was going smoothly; the package was prepared and sent. I was provided with a tracking number, which we started to monitor on the internet using a friend's laptop.

At this point, things started to go a bit strange. The website was showing the package as having arrived but instead of being in England it was somewhere in Spain. I confronted Hassan and he made out he didn't understand how this could be and claimed it must be an error – was

I sure? – and so on. He said he would make some calls to get to the bottom of what had occurred. He returned later and told me that the people with whom he was working had supposedly pulled a fast one and switched the delivery address without his knowledge.

Hassan told me there was nothing he could do about it. He did appear genuinely perplexed. I explained that this wasn't my problem as they were his friends and contacts, therefore his responsibility. I had handed the money directly to him so it was down to him to repay me. If there had been a problem at my end, for example my friends not sending the money to pay for the merchandise, then obviously that would have been down to me to resolve. My friends, my responsibility.

I tried to make Hassan see my point of view by asking what he would do if the situation was reversed. He calmed down a little and we reached an agreement that he would pay back as much as he could and try to arrange something else with different contacts. I settled for this as the last thing I needed was trouble with a group of suspected terrorists from the Middle East. I might get blown up by a booby trap in my cell.

After that experience, the thought of now starting business with members of the terrorist group FARC was equally unappealing. I decided to go and meet the Colombians, though, because Andrew was a nice guy and I thought it was unlikely that he would wish to introduce anyone to me who planned to rob me as this would reflect badly on him.

Andrew was also very good pals with a British guy, Mark, on B wing, who had been there some five years. He was a tall, dark-haired northerner (from Manchester or Yorkshire, I never knew which) who had a gruff, stand-offish nature. He was ex-British military and liked to keep his own company. He didn't have time for fools and took no nonsense. This also reassured me – if Andrew and the Colombians were close to Mark they couldn't be all that bad. I knew I needed to be extremely careful if I decided to undertake any business with these guys.

Andrew took me over to D wing to meet the *banda,* or gang, four or five of whom all lived together in the same cell on the ground floor. The door to the cell was open and I could hear raucous laughter as we arrived at the entrance. The cell was full of people, about seven in total, some on the beds, others sitting and a few standing wherever there was space. Andrew and I made nine in a space the length of a bed and a half and in which, if I spread my arms out, I could touch the walls on either side. It was mid-morning and the remains of coffee and bread were on the table along with what looked like leftover fried eggs and rice.

One of the guys was standing up and in full flow, recounting a story of some high-octane adventure in Colombia involving motorbikes, guns, people getting shot or robbed, alcohol, women and cocaine. He was completely reliving the moment with arms and legs flailing all over the place, much to the amusement of his audience. The speaker finally came to an end. He was a short, skinny guy with a wiry physique, tanned indigenous skin and dark hair cut in a military style flat-top – a style popular among the Colombians, particularly the members of FARC as they are (or until recently were) in essence a military force. Many of them regard themselves as political prisoners, soldiers in a war, even if they have been caught with a couple of tons of pure cocaine – *la Reina*, as they call the best of the best in Colombia: the Queen!

We hadn't yet been noticed, apart from by one of the men sitting on the bed. He smiled, his round face lit up with warmth, and welcomed Andrew and me. Andrew introduced him as Mario, the leader of the group and co-owner of the cell along with the storyteller, whose name was Jairo. I had started to realise that virtually everyone in the prison, if they were Latin American, had a nickname. And there were some very peculiar ones. People were named after animals they resembled; body parts that were out of proportion such as big nose or big head; you might get half-cow, tiger, wolf, bull, spider – you name it, someone was called it. Cartoon characters were popular as well, and all manner of birds or plants.

I introduced myself as plain old Pieter from England and we shook hands. Mario reminded me of a laughing Buddha with his round face, bald head and well-padded stomach. Morning was turning into midday and lunchtime was approaching. Colombians, particularly the criminal types, love marijuana almost as much as Jamaican Rastafarians do. It has become part of their culture as well. There are films about marijuana, songs, clothes, artwork – they really do love the stuff. I had noticed that they liked to smoke some before they ate, as it improved their appetites and general enjoyment of the food, which wasn't always up to the highest gourmet standard. A couple of the guys suggested chipping in to buy a packet of weed, which was very cheap. For 50 cents or a dollar you could buy enough for two big joints, 3–5 grams. It was only locally grown or Colombian weed but that's fairly potent. But Mario cut them short, saying that he had business to discuss with Andrew and me. He asked everyone to leave the cell apart from Jairo and two others. The volume of the music was reduced and the door was pushed to, with instructions given to someone to keep watch outside the door so that no one would interrupt our discussion.

We got down to business rapidly. Mario explained that they had a couple of kilos of pure cocaine here in Quito that belonged to them and they wanted to start by sending only small amounts initially in order to test the method and see if everything went smoothly. They had a few members of their family in Quito with an apartment where they would prepare the parcels containing the drugs. To begin with, he wanted to send letters or birthday cards with just 50–100 grams of cocaine in them. The letters were of such low weight that they wouldn't arouse suspicion at either end. Customs were after at least a kilo just to get up off their chairs, otherwise they couldn't be bothered with the paperwork; they knew full well there would be no one at the address and, even if there was, the letter would be addressed to a previous tenant who had disappeared. What could they do about that? Nothing. Therefore, it was of no interest as it in no way assisted their quotas for arrests or seizures and it tied up manpower writing up all the documentation.

I agreed with Mario's way of thinking but cautioned him that technology in Europe was advancing very quickly, so for how long these letters would get through undetected I couldn't say. I knew they were developing machines that could detect the smallest of trace particles on a package, which, if positive, would be automatically pulled to one side on the conveyor belt for closer inspection. I told him I had a friend on my wing who could get as many addresses with names and telephone numbers as he needed. I decided I would make sure I had the cash available to cover any material that reached England so that once it was received I could pay the Colombians immediately. I didn't want them hassling me. It also meant there could be absolutely no problems such as I had had with Hassan.

Mario suggested we purchase a gun for our own protection. He proposed that I should buy the gun and in the event of any *paros* (riots) or other problems he and his group would collect me immediately and protect me. They would also watch my back at all other times and sort out any disagreements I had. For the sum of $400 I thought this was a bargain. Having backup in these places is everything. If people know you are armed and there are more than five of you, they stay well clear. He suggested I might think about loaning money out with interest and they would collect any debts for a percentage. I agreed and we started lending certain people, generally foreigners such as Spaniards and Dutch, $1,000 for a month with $500 interest. This worked out very well with hardly any need to enforce debt collections. People could see we were a strong group and decided it was better just to pay up.

Within a couple of weeks, the Columbians were dispatching a couple of letters or books a week with 50–100 grams of cocaine in each. Some arrived, others didn't, but there were never any repercussions. Doors were never knocked down and no one had any problems. The material was so cheap it didn't matter. A kilogram of cocaine in Ecuador is worth around $2,000. They were getting it for nearly half that as Mario's family had a farm growing the actual coca plant from which they then produced their own product. I told them I would love to one day visit a plantation and jungle laboratory just for the hell of it. They said that was no problem; they would take me.

A few times Mario paid one of his visitors to bring in some cocaine for him. When he and his friends were celebrating a birthday or a special occasion such as Easter or Christmas, they would organise a large party on the wing. They would have a sound system with large speakers or at the very least a powerful hi-fi. Alcohol would be bought or smuggled into the prison, usually with the assistance of the guards, who we would pay around $20 a bottle for the service, sometimes more if the security at the entrance to the prison was particularly tough at that time. The cocaine was easier to bring in as a visitor, usually female, could easily hide a small amount (25–50 grams) in a body cavity. There were no scanners, X-rays or cavity-scanning hot seats to contend with. As a visitor, you would be patted down by a guard and then go through a metal detector and sometimes have to pass a sniffer dog. There were other ways of getting drugs into the prison: paying the guards or one of the office staff, or via the kitchen and food deliveries. This was a good way to get in the alcohol as it could be easily disguised as another liquid.

I suggested to Mario that seeing as we already had the cocaine in Quito and could organise people to bring it in, why not bring some in and I could sell it to the foreigners, who were without doubt the biggest consumers. Not only did they love the stuff, but they were the ones with the money with which to buy it.

Most of the dealers in the prison tended to cut the cocaine heavily with whatever they could find to mix into it. A few of us had been clubbing together and buying a quantity for ourselves anyway, so it was logical for me to source the product and supply it to those who wanted good cocaine and were willing to pay the price for it. I had the capital, the means and the backup, so that's exactly what I started doing and it was extremely popular.

There wasn't really anyone selling coke on C wing, which also made it inconvenient to acquire once the gates to the other wings were all locked at 5pm. You would have to throw your money over to someone waiting at the gate of either D or B wing and trust them to go and buy it for you and throw it back. People would often not see their money again or get very small amounts of drugs sent back and it used to frustrate everyone. I filled this gap. I couldn't have done it without the backing of the Colombians.

The main dealers who currently controlled nearly the entire market in the prison were two Colombian brothers, Jason and Julian. They were serving sentences for drug trafficking and gunrunning and had cornered the market with the help of their fellow countrymen. I knew them both well, having bought both drugs and alcohol from them on numerous occasions after Johann introduced me within a week of my arrival. They were open to doing business, but it was their territory and they would protect it. Before we really got started, Mario and his little group got together with me and Andrew and we all went to meet the brothers in order to discuss what we were going to do. They were reasonably OK about it as long as I also sold their drugs on C wing – the marijuana, base and cocaine.

Between us we agreed the prices at which the different drugs would be sold. A gram of cocaine, $6–8; marijuana $1–2 a pack; base, a matchbox full for $25–30 and individual wraps for a dollar. We agreed not to drop below these prices and so formed a monopoly. Some people preferred to buy the brothers' products as they were generally different. I had no objections, and anyway I couldn't have objected even had I wanted to. That was the only way this would work. Julian, the older brother, explained that now we were working together I also had their protection and backing. This was really helpful as no one crossed them. They had the guards paid off. As long as there were no problems like people getting killed or badly injured, which brought attention, they were permitted to carry on business unhindered. Julian said from now on the guards would have to leave me alone as well, but for that privilege I would need to make a weekly contribution of $150 to cover bribes. We agreed and that was the beginning of the business and virtual monopoly of C wing. We controlled the drugs, sold the alcohol, lent money and I rented cells. Things were looking up. This way I could live very comfortably and have an income during my sentence. Anything else, such as international trafficking, would be a bonus. Everyone was happy, or so I thought.

There were a few foreigners who liked to smoke crack cocaine and no one sold this in the prison as it wasn't very well known by the South Americans; they only knew *polvo*, or base. The Europeans had never heard of this, and as it had an acrid smell and was not as strong as crack, they preferred to buy good cocaine and make their own crack to smoke. For this, the cocaine needed to be good quality in the first place or you would end up with very little crack.

We tried to talk to some good friends who had been buying a lot of coke for this purpose and help them lower the amounts they were taking. It was causing them problems as they were running up large debts to the gangs. One particular friend had been on a crack binge for three or four days. He lived on his own on the ground floor in the penultimate cell. One evening I was standing on my landing on the top floor with some others, looking down the wing. I started to notice smoke drifting upwards from downstairs, near my friend's cell. I joked that he was really going for it tonight. As we stood and watched, the quantity of smoke began to increase dramatically and the acrid smell of burning plastic reached my nose. 'Shit!' I said to the friends with me. 'Quick, come on. I think Mikey's room is on fire.' We rushed down the three flights of stairs and ran along the wing. By now there were one or two people banging on his door. 'Mikey, Mikey! Open the door man.' The smoke was becoming thicker and thicker, the smell of burning plastic choking us and stinging our eyes. We were panicking now: 'Mikey, Mikey! Open the fucking door!' Bang, bang, bang.

I sent someone to get a metal bar so that we could try to force the door open. However, these doors were designed to stop exactly that and Mikey's door was locked from within. We were still pounding on the door and shouting as loud as we could. A large crowd had gathered now. All of a sudden there was the grating noise of metal on metal and the door flew open. A huge dense cloud of acrid toxic smoke came billowing out, followed by a dazed, half dead, black-faced Mikey, coughing and spluttering. 'Jesus Christ Mikey, are you OK buddy?' someone asked.

He was fighting for breath because of the smoke and lay down on the floor to recover. Someone brought him a wet cloth with which to wipe his face and eyes, and a drink of water. We let the smoke clear a little, then quickly went in to inspect the damage. The TV – or what was left of it – was a smoking melted pile of molten plastic.

'Mikey, what the hell happened?' I asked. Mikey explained that he had been awake so late smoking crack that he had passed out, leaving a candle burning on top of the TV. It had subsequently burned down into the TV and set it alight while Mikey slept the sleep of the dead. Which is exactly what he would have been had we not woken him up. The cell had bad smoke damage but was otherwise OK, and Mikey made a full recovery.

One of the other things I cottoned on to was the love of gambling people had here. Those who partook would gamble on anything. A few of the foreigners liked to play blackjack, so we set up a blackjack table and would run a game in the evenings. There was a new English guy on the wing by this point, called Ruben. He was from north London and had a nasal twang to his voice, partly because of his love of cocaine. He was 60-plus, grey-haired and very friendly. He had been a professional bookmaker and had his own spot on a race-course until he took up gambling himself and blew over a million pounds in a year, ending up in prison in the UK for fraud. He had also worked as a croupier in a casino on the blackjack tables. This was great news. He became our croupier, for which I paid him a percentage of the profits if we won. We would normally make between $300 and $400 a night when we played. It was a great little business. All in all, things were going great.

CHAPTER TWELVE
HOTEL GARCIA MORENA

I had been in the prison nearly a year and, now my sentence had been finalised, I knew I would be staying somewhat longer, so I turned my attention to buying a cell. Jean and I were discussing who had a cell for sale. His Serbian friend knew a Swedish guy on the top floor who he thought might be selling. He was an older, very intellectual guy called Sven. He had swept-back, greying hair and glasses. He was well-built, approaching 50 and had the look of a schoolteacher or professor. I went to meet him and he explained that he was due to be released soon. He offered to sell me half the cell for the money up front. I could move in and share with him and when he eventually got the actual date on which he was leaving I would pay him the other half and become full owner. Being on the top floor the cell got plenty of fresh air, and he had kept it tidy.

It sounded like a reasonable deal, so I went ahead and made arrangements to have $2,000 transferred to the person in Quito who he nominated to receive it. We then had to instruct the *caporal* to inform the social workers that I was moving cells so that they could change my location on the roll call. This took a little bit of money and a couple of days to arrange. Living with Sven was OK but he had his peculiarities and would like to get high and drunk every now and then, which he preferred to do alone. I had no problem with this as I respect everyone and their space. I would leave him to it and hang out with my friends until he was ready for me to go back. One good thing about the room was that we had a connection to a guy's satellite dish downstairs so we had cable TV, which really passed the time.

One day Sven baked a chocolate cake but with a secret ingredient – marijuana, and lots of it. This was shared out between his friends and everyone got really high. It was potent. I was going back to my cell with a piece on a plate just as a guard came the opposite way. He was eyeing the chocolatey cake with enthusiasm. I thought it would be funny to give him the cake and see what happened. Luckily, a friend who was with me grabbed it just as I was about to hand it over. He told me if I'd given the guard the cake and he had eaten it the guards would likely have beaten me to death. He probably saved my life that day.

After living with Sven for about six months, things became a little strained between us, as they often can when living in such a small space. I was in the exercise yard one morning doing circuit training when a friend came down to advise me that Sven was in the process of moving somebody out of his cell. At this point we had a big Ecuadorian fella living with us. He was tall and strong and closely resembled the big half-Native American chief, Chief Bromden, from the film *One Flew Over the Cuckoo's Nest*. I had nicknamed him Chief for this reason. I assumed it must be Chief that Sven was moving out of his cell, but my friend said, 'No, he's trying to move you out. He's talking to the *caporal* at the moment to find a space for you in another cell.'

'What the fuck!' I shouted. 'He can't do that. I've paid him for half the cell.'

The mistake I had made was not signing a contract but only having a gentleman's agreement, so on paper Sven still retained full ownership and could decide what he wanted to do. I was furious. I stormed upstairs and confronted Sven at the cell. I asked him what the bloody hell he thought he was doing and reminded him I now owned half the cell. He replied that he was aware of this and that hadn't changed but he wasn't happy living with me. I asked him why and what the problem was but he wouldn't tell me and became evasive. I soon found out he was concerned that because I was involved with several illegal business deals it might cause him trouble, and he didn't need any problems this close to release. That was fair enough and I agreed to find some-where else to live but asked for a couple of days. He reluctantly agreed.

I decided to buy another cell while I waited for Sven's release. It was then I hit upon the idea of buying up various cells to rent out on visit days and for the *cadadas* (sleepovers). On the nights when people's wives or girlfriends stayed over a great many people would be tossed out of their cells and have to sleep like sardines locked in the small gym at the end of the second-floor landing. The guards would still insist that everyone was at least by their relevant door when they came to do the roll call in the morning. It would generally end up being a bloody great party every two weeks. I would rent the cell for the rest of the week to someone who couldn't afford to buy one or just didn't want to. This would give me some extra income so that I wasn't eating into my overall capital.

I approached Riccardo, an Italian-American friend of mine, and explained the situation with Sven and the cell and asked if I could perhaps move in with him. He happily agreed and then offered to sell me the cell as he too was about to go free any day now. I wasn't about to make the same mistake twice and insisted that if I was buying it I should receive all the relevant paperwork and become the actual owner. I could (and probably should) have been buying a semi in Brixton through the Halifax. I told him he was welcome to stay in the cell until he left but it would be mine. He agreed and I became the proud owner of a second cell.

Riccardo was a cool guy to live with and we got on well. He was very congenial and had a big personality. He had a big build to go with it, a shaved head and a round face. Being of Italian descent he was quite fiery and could get very excitable at times. I liked him and we would have a laugh together. He taught me how to cook the best spaghetti Bolognese sauce ever, in my opinion. His girlfriend was a lawyer from Colombia who was doing her utmost to win the freedom of her man. She came to visit on a regular basis and even offered to take a look at my case and see if there might be a possibility of getting the sentence reduced. I said I would think about it, just to be polite, as I was fairly happy with the job Eva had been doing and didn't want to start changing lawyers and upsetting people.

The cell directly in front of Riccardo's on the third floor next to the stairwell had come up for sale. This was Youseff's, the previous *caporal*'s old cell and a fairly good one. He had been released not long after I arrived on the wing. I bought it straight away and decided to completely refurbish it. Neither Sven nor Riccardo had yet been released so those cells were still tied up. I wanted to make this cell feel like my own and kit it out really nicely for the coming years. I was feeling pretty well settled now, had a lot of friends and backup, and some regular business generating income. All I had to do was sit tight, avoid problems and hopefully pay to get the sentence halved very soon and then get released with the 50 per cent rule. Things were going well and I was fairly in control.

I found a couple of Lithuanian inmates who were extremely good builders. You could have whatever you wanted brought in to refurbish cells, the government obviously being quite happy as it maintained the fabric of the building so they didn't have to. Ruben, the older north-London guy, and my Russian friend Sasha said they would be happy to live there while I renovated it, even though it was going to be a mess and covered in dust. I hoped it would only take a month to get it completely sorted.

I had the builders take it right back to the masonry. We stripped out the tiled floor and started afresh. While we were doing this, we uncovered three hiding spaces left by previous owners. One of the spaces – carved into the wall and brilliantly hidden behind a false panel – had been for Youseff's gun. You could even see where they had bored out little round holes for the ammunition. I would have liked to have used it myself, but the guards had to be informed, much to my chagrin. They were keeping a close eye on what I was doing and if they suspected I had made the hiding place it would have been big trouble and probably a transfer to another prison. That I didn't need. We filled the hole in and showed the *jefe de guia* again so that he was happy, and got back to work.

I had all new cabling put in for the electrics, including a new fuse box, an electric shower and spotlights throughout, power points for a fridge, TV, DVD player, kettle, microwave and hi-fi. We made a space for a gas bottle for a cooker. All the walls and ceiling were expertly re-plastered with a fantastic smooth finish. The back half of the cell, where the shower and toilet were located, both of which I replaced, was tiled from floor to ceiling in a beige ceramic marble effect. The other part of the cell, where the beds and seating area were, I had tiled in black porcelain with a white vein. It really looked fantastic. I then had it painted white. I commissioned new cupboards, two chairs, a table and large mirror from the carpentry shop. The chairs I had upholstered in a red damask silk. To top it all off I personally painted the Union Jack in enamel paints on the whole of the interior of the cell door so when it was open everyone could see it. I loved it and without doubt it was one of the best cells in the entire prison. I had brand new orthopaedic mattresses brought in for both me and Sasha, a Sony TV and DVD player, fridge, cooker, fan, small stereo ... I was fully kitted out for my 12-year sentence.

Unfortunately I wasn't to enjoy the cell for a great deal longer.

CHAPTER THIRTEEN
ANOTHER BLOODY SUNDAY

I was in my cell on C wing watching a surfing DVD, wishing I was sitting on that beach in California with bikini-clad girls, soaking up the sunshine. But rather than drinking a tequila with said girls, I was in fact drinking a cup of Twinings Earl Grey tea. It was Sunday and visit day. Midday was approaching and my thoughts had turned to what I might have for lunch from one of the restaurants on the wing. There was Big Ivan the Russian, with his red cafe in the exercise yard, who cooked good homely food – sometimes borscht or other Russian specialities. Then there was Big Boris from Cartagena in Colombia who used to work for Pablo Escobar back in the day, running tons of coke up to Miami and the Florida Keys by boat from the northern Colombian coast. His food was in the Colombian style and very good as well.

A huge wave tore across the screen bearing a little man hanging on for dear life – a feeling all too familiar to me. Suddenly Sasha appeared in the doorway. He was out of breath, having run up the three flights of stairs to get to our room, and looked pale. He was gabbling away in his

Russian-accented English and it took a minute for him to calm down and explain what was happening.

'Quick come with me, come look, they are killing Ruben!' he stammered, waving his arms about and pacing nervously up and down the tiny cell.

'What the fuck! What do you mean they're killing Ruben?' That familiar feeling of icy cold terror spread through my body, the adrenalin kicking in on top of the cocaine from the previous night.

I immediately thought he meant Ruben the Englishman from north London who lived on the wing, and with whom both Sasha and I were friendly. Ruben was forever getting into trouble borrowing money, getting cocaine on credit, running up bills, drinking, gambling and, worst of all, trying to organise drug trafficking business back to Britain. You would never have believed it from a guy who looked like your grandfather. It wouldn't be unexpected if Ruben had a problem. I had bailed him out on numerous occasions and even, unbeknown to him, saved his life a couple of times when the local mafia had wanted to kill him for causing problems. There had been a couple of occasions during the renovation of my cell when I'd wanted to kill him myself, he had annoyed me that much. He had been living there while I was having it refurbished and he would refuse to get up in the mornings when I had people waiting to work on it, and become abusive. Added to that he owed me money at the time and it was proving difficult to collect. He used to drive me mad but I still liked him.

Sasha was virtually jumping up and down on the spot, pacing from side to side. 'Come quick, come quick,' he said, eager to get back to the bloody spectacle.

'Where is this happening?' I asked, trying not to panic while pulling on my shoes.

'D wing, D wing, ground floor. There is blood every-fucking-where. They make big mess, big knife. Ruben is fucked. They going to kill him for sure. Lot of trouble. Come quick.'

I grabbed a ten-inch Tramontina kitchen knife I had to hand, stuck it in my belt and pulled on a jumper to go over the top. I shut and padlocked the cell door as fast as I could. We descended the stairs into the bowels of the prison from the refined third floor. The smells got worse the nearer the ground floor you were, what with the rat-infested, cockroach-teeming drains that stank of raw sewage and rotting food. It used to make me gag sometimes if it was a particularly hot day and everything had putrefied that bit quicker.

We were heading towards D wing, Sasha leading the way, pushing people aside as he went. My heart was pounding with fear and the anticipation of what I was about to witness. A few friends asked what the hurry was as we rushed past them. I didn't have time to stop and reply but shouted out, 'They're killing Ruben in D wing.'

We reached the main gate to the wing that led on to the centre – the circular area where all the wings converged. We passed through and turned to the right, through the unat-tended gate, unhindered by guards who would normally have demanded a dollar. There were two reasons for this, the first being it was a visit day and they generally didn't charge you on these days. The second, main reason was the screams and shouts emanating from within D wing, the gate to which stood wide open as people streamed in and out. As we entered D wing there was a large crowd of men, women and children gathered directly in front of me midway down the wing. People lined the walkways that led to the cells on the upper floors and ran the length of the wing on both sides, watching fixatedly the spectacle below them. I could feel the tension and see the horror etched on the faces of some of the sobbing women who passed us by, carrying their confused and startled young children.

Sasha beckoned me to follow him towards the crowd but also to the cell of his best friend, a Russian Israeli by the name of Lev. As we skirted round the edge of the crowd I caught my first glimpse of the huge pool of gleaming dark red blood. In the centre of this congealing pool lay slumped the torn, cut, bleeding, crying and slowly dying body of someone I thought was going to be Ruben, the grey-haired friendly grandfather. It wasn't, and I was momentarily relieved. Until I saw the figure standing over the dying man with a large blood-covered knife in his hand.

Sasha explained that the dying man was an Ecuadorian by the name of Ruben, which is a fairly unusual name in South America. He was a notorious informant who had been responsible for imprisoning many people. He had more recently been causing all sorts of problems for his fellow inmates by informing directly to the police via a mobile phone supplied by them. He had been reporting details of illegal activity within the prison, in which cells the perpetrators lived and where their stashes were hidden. Unfortunately for him, some of the people he was responsible for incarcerating had ended up on the same wing as him and weren't in the least bit happy about it. Bad enough simply being in the same prison, but the same wing – you just knew what was going to happen. There had apparently been rumours circulating the whole prison that Ruben was about to be killed. Someone had even done him the courtesy of warning him that his life was in imminent danger and he should probably change wings. He had, for some reason, ignored these warnings and said he wasn't afraid of these people and that they could do their worst. That had been a fatal mistake. They had done their worst.

The killer was a thin, unassuming guy in his early twenties and of Ecuadorian appearance. He had emerged from one of the last cells on the right-hand side of the wing carrying a large kitchen knife, similar to the one I had down my trouser leg. I could feel the cold steel pressed against my skin and the thought of that entering my body and virtually passing right through me, tearing and ripping organs and blood vessels as it went, stopped my breath. I had had a recurring nightmare as a kid of being stabbed in the back; I would wake up screaming, arching my back, drenched in sweat. I had always wondered if this was a premonition of my death to come. Would this be the place it happened? People were stabbed here nearly every day.

The crowd were enthralled, waiting for the killer to start attacking Ruben again. We all stood around watching – guards, prisoners, visitors, me – yet no one intervened. I don't know if it was out of fear of being attacked as well or reprisals afterwards for having stopped this notorious informant being killed, but no one moved. The skinny young guy with the large knife circled Ruben like a lion round its prey. He had the wild-eyed look of murder on his face. He was coated in blood. He looked as though he had dipped both his arms in buckets of red paint. Abattoir workers have less blood on them.

'*Ahora tu va moria,*' he kept repeating, 'now you are going to die' – among the profanities he was spitting. Ruben didn't really respond much apart from the odd wheeze and rasp and moan. The killer circled a couple more times, appraising his victim, deciding where next he was going to plunge the 12 inches of Brazilian steel. He struck, driving the knife deep into Ruben's stomach. The crowd groaned, women cried, I felt sick. The killer continued stabbing wildly. Ruben made a few feeble attempts at blocking the strikes to begin with but soon lost consciousness, no doubt from blood loss. A Sunday afternoon in the prison in Quito: children running around playing while a human being was slowly butchered to death in the middle of a wing with guards and visitors looking on. The guards had no doubt been paid to turn a blind eye. Ruben's informing no doubt affected them too – they relied on illicit trade and bribes to subsidise their meagre incomes.

'You want tea with me and Lev? We have good strong Russian chai, not your P.G. Tips,' Sasha said. 'Come, we make tea, you feel better. This horrible, no good.' I agreed. The sweet metallic smell of blood filled the air as it seeped from the puncture wounds all over Ruben's body. It made me want to retch.

I greeted Lev and took a seat in his cell while they went about making tea and chatting away in Russian. I could still hear the killer, inflicting wounds now on a corpse.

'You want something to eat? We have sandwich, cake, biscuits.' Sasha offered a pack of biscuits across the table. He went on to explain that the guy doing the killing was what they referred to here as a *comi muerto*, which translated as 'eat the dead'. They were inmates who had committed multiple counts of murder and were sentenced to 25 years with no parole, or sometimes even whole-life terms. They stood very little chance of walking out alive, so had nothing to lose. You were lucky if you survived five years in one of these prisons, let alone 25.

The gangs or cartel members would pay these *comi muertos* with money or drugs to carry out murders for them, knowing it wouldn't make any difference to their sentence. They would usually jump at the opportunity to earn some extra money. They didn't have to be careful about leaving behind evidence, they would just openly kill whoever was the target. Whoever had orchestrated this killing had paid someone within the prison authorities to have the killer transferred to this wing from the high-security one where he normally lived to carry out the murder. A working vacation in some ways for this guy. A break from the isolation of maximum security to do a job and then back to wait for the next contract to come up. You would have no idea that the quiet, thin guy standing next to you was a half-crazed murderer responsible for the deaths of several people.

We heard later that Ruben eventually bled out after about half an hour of being repeatedly stabbed. The *comi muerto* killer then returned to the cell he had been using, and calmly sat down at the table upon which were arranged his crack pipe, crack, lighter, cigarettes and ashtray. He loaded a pipe and proceeded to smoke it as if nothing had happened. It reminded me of an advert for cigars where the person smokes one while reminiscing on the day's events. He had placed the kitchen knife on the table and was just sitting there smoking. It was only at this point that the guards decided to intervene. The action was over, the task accomplished and the threat to them now minimal. They placed handcuffs on the killer, picked up the knife and led him out of the wing to isolation. He went quietly without protest or resistance and that was that.

I decided I had seen enough and made my way back to my cell before the police arrived with the forensic team and started asking questions. They generally didn't investigate too much. One less criminal in the country, one less inmate burdening the government. They had the killer, the weapon, the body and plenty of witnesses – what more did they need? Case closed.

I wandered back to my cell in a daze, shocked at what I had just seen, with the smell of Ruben's blood lingering in my nose. I sat on my bed and wondered how the hell I was going to survive the next however many years I was destined to be locked up with people who would happily kill you for a one-dollar rock of crack cocaine.

CHAPTER FOURTEEN
PARO!

*The Committee deeply deplores the situation in [Ecuador's]
detention centres and especially in social rehabilitation
centres where prisoners' human rights are constantly violated.
The overcrowding, corruption and poor physical conditions
prevailing in prisons, and especially the lack of hygiene, proper
food and appropriate medical care, constitute violations of
rights which are protected under the Convention (art.11) ...
The Committee notes with concern the allegations that a large
number of prisoners have been tortured while being held
incommunicado.*

U.N. Committee against Torture, 2005.

'Paro, paro!'

Oh no, here we go again! I was standing outside a friend's
cell when I heard the cry. Other inmates started rushing to
the main gate with thick metal chains, guns drawn. The
entrance to the wing was locked. I could see and hear the
same taking place on the other wings. All the guards had
beaten a hasty retreat out of the wings in fear of their lives.
A couple of gunshots rang out. People were shouting, cell
doors banging shut or swinging open. The police were calling
in reinforcements and quickly surrounding the prison,

weapons at the ready, in case there should be a mass escape attempt. After a short while we heard a police helicopter circling overhead. I wondered how many days or weeks this might last. Better start conserving food and water supplies now, just in case, and charge all the phones and spare batteries.

This wasn't the first time I had experienced a *paro*, which would in Europe or America be called a protest or riot. The main difference here was that we generally wouldn't destroy the cells, as we had paid for everything ourselves and would only have to replace it afterwards. Following my arrest on 16 August 2005 there had been numerous protests at the terrible conditions in the prisons – the overcrowding, lack of food and medical care. The laws that benefitted the prisoners were virtually all suspended and had been replaced by secure detention (*prisión en firme*), which basically meant you could be detained indefinitely without trial as long as you had been charged. All cells had to have three people living in them, which was the minimum allowed in Quito, while others had as many as seven or eight. The *comité de internos*, or prisoners' committees, had been organising a series of protests, some of them on a national level, with all prisons locking their entrances at exactly the same minute on the same day.

On a couple of occasions when the gates were locked on visit days, visitors had, in effect, been held hostage some-times for several days. The visitors would quite often be more than willing to act as hostages as it was their family members who were being held, causing them all to suffer. None of them were ever injured as the visitors were viewed as sacrosanct.

I headed back to my cell with a few friends. We would stick together during these *paros* as they could be very dangerous. I collected a large steak knife and waited for

Mario to come over with Andrew from D wing with the handgun I had bought us. I would feel a hell of a lot safer with a gun and a good-sized group of us to fend off any attacks. I could already see little groups roaming around looking to settle scores and collect outstanding debts. People were starting to don long jackets, which usually covered the presence of a machete or shotgun. It was always alarming to see how drastically people's attitudes would change when a *paro* started. Someone who was perhaps friendly before would become very stand-offish and defensive. It made you realise that you had very few real friends in the prison. When any form of control or discipline was temporarily removed, situations that previously might have simmered away would quickly erupt into extreme violence, quite often ending in death or serious injury.

Another inmate told me that during one of the worst *paros* he had seen, bodies were being carried out to the centre of the prison and left there for collection. Sometimes it was just body parts and not the complete corpse. By the end of that particular *paro* there were at least 26 people dead and many more injured.

The protests quickly attracted the attention of the press, who were notified by the prisoners' committee of developments as they happened. People mounted all manner of protests. There were hunger strikes, where people sewed their mouths shut, and crucifixions with people actually being nailed to crosses. There were some extreme scenes, many of which were captured by the press. We would make large banners with messages of protest daubed across them. We would then hang them from the windows or walls of the prison in positions from which they could be seen from the road.

Food and water would start to become an issue after a few days as nothing was allowed to enter the prison.

Buckets tied to a rope would be dropped down over the wall to enable some small amounts of food in. The worst would be when they cut the water off, as clean water would quickly run out and the whole place would begin to smell awful, the toilets couldn't be flushed and no one could wash. The electricity would often be cut both during *paros* to try and make us back down, but also at normal times due to the bill not being paid.

I remember one occasion when the outstanding bill was over $100,000 and they actually discussed trying to charge us inmates for part of the cost! Human rights watch groups became involved with the UN in making a report on the situation. The government of Ecuador came in for a great deal of criticism internationally, at which point they began to pay attention. It wasn't until the government of Rafael Correa was elected in November 2006 that any real changes began to happen. Those changes are still taking place ten years later.

The *paros* were nerve-racking but if not too serious they could sometimes be quite good fun; our group of friends would get together to have a party and not have to worry about the guards suddenly turning up. The worst part would be when the *paro* came to an end, which was usually when conditions in the prison became too dire with no food or water, and the police would come charging into the wing discharging their weapons and firing tear gas.

Everyone would dive into the nearest cell and lock the door from the inside and wait until the police came round, having regained control. This would be particularly scary as you never knew exactly how they were going to treat us. More often than not, we would all be forced to lie face down on the floor with our hands on our heads and the police would then walk around beating everyone with pieces of wood, batons or their guns, and kicking us. I witnessed them dragging people they had issues with into cells and water-boarding them, drowning them and discharging firearms next to their head, as well as severe beatings and strangula-tion. You would hear people screaming, crying and begging the police not to kill them. It was terrifying. When the police were walking down the line of us lying on the floor striking people with pieces of wood you would brace yourself for the impact as you waited for them to hit you.

The worst story I heard about the treatment of a prisoner was told to me by an English friend. The police had gone into Guayaquil prison to conduct a search and were being particularly heavy-handed. When they reached my friend's wing they hauled out the boss of the wing, who was a noto-rious gang member, and dragged him down the stairs to the exercise yard while his wife and daughter watched. They started to beat him and then forced him to kneel on the ground. The police officer in charge said, 'We have had enough of your bullshit. It ends here tonight. It's over, you are finished.' The guy was begging for his life, and his wife and six-year-old daughter were screaming and imploring them not to kill him. The officer took his handgun out and shot the man in the back of the head and twice more in the body. The wife and daughter were in hysterics. A barbaric scene. The body was removed and that was that.

We were often terrified that after a severe problem in the prison, for example a gunfight, the police would come in and just execute us all, as had happened in some other countries in South America. To make it out of here alive I knew that I not only had to survive the gangs and all the violence, but also the police brutality and torture.

CHAPTER FIFTEEN
ESCAPE, PART 1

Anyone who's ever been locked up will have spent a good deal of time thinking about how to escape. It is your natural instinct. In prison you tend to have two groups. There are those who would rather sit there and quietly do their time and get out when the given date arrives. The others would prefer to attempt escape and live with the consequences. It tends to be people serving longer sentences with little to lose who are more inclined to attempt escape. If you only have to spend six months behind bars, why risk being shot dead trying to escape?

If you are successful you have to go on the run, continually looking over your shoulder. If you're recaptured you face the prospect of a lengthy sentence being added to your original one. If you have a life sentence or anything over ten years then it might be worth a go. This is particularly the case if you intend to leave the country in which you were imprisoned and not return any time soon. However, in that case, having escaped you're then faced with a whole other set of problems. You need to get ID to travel. You need money, shelter, clothing, food and water. In order to acquire most of these you'll need to interact with society (when you possibly don't speak the language). This inevitably means running the gauntlet of security cameras that capture our images hundreds if not thousands of times a day. Communication becomes difficult as the authorities will be monitoring all forms of electronic contact. With facial and vocal recognition, biometrics and satellite tracking, it's hard to run and hide virtually anywhere on the planet. Any contact with family or friends is almost impossible as this is the first place they will look for you. Yet, even taking all this into account, risking all for freedom can still be better than spending years rotting in a prison cell and trying to survive in a dangerous environment.

I had always vowed that should I ever receive a sentence of ten years or more I would spend every day trying to escape. I knew that the British authorities were making attempts to extradite me to face the charge of being the head of a group who had imported nearly 100kg of pure cocaine to Britain worth an estimated £4.5 million. If they succeeded, I would likely be pulled from my cell in the middle of the night and flown back to Britain in handcuffs to face a lengthy trial. If found guilty, I would receive a long sentence, most of which would be spent as a category A prisoner in England's hardest prisons. As SOCA had already made a request to the Ecuadorian judges that I be sentenced to the maximum of 25 years in prison, which is what they told me I would have received if I had been sentenced in Britain, I knew what I was facing if the extradition was successful. In a UK prison, there would be no visits in your cell three times a week, nor any sex, drugs, alcohol and whatever food you wanted brought in along with all your mod cons. It was this and the prospect of a much longer sentence that encouraged me to consider escape – and the thought of trying to survive at least ten more years in the prisons in Ecuador.

In Garcia Moreno, there was only one obvious route out of the place and that was over the rooftop of the prison itself and down the other side of a very high perimeter wall to the street and away. There was one big problem with this idea. The roof was almost constantly patrolled by guards and police armed with shotguns and M16 assault rifles. Needless to say, I ruled this out quite quickly.

During my time in Quito there had been a couple of escapes from A wing, which was supposedly the maximum-security wing. We were certain they had been assisted as both times they used a ladder to climb up on to the roof and escaped across part of the prison that used to be the chapel and had a pitched roof, so no security on it. At one point, a very famous trafficker from Ecuador by the name of Oscar Caranqui tried to escape out of A wing dressed as a police officer. He had paid the entire squad of police officers on duty that night somewhere in the region of $250,000 to supply him with a uniform. They walked him out the front door when they changed shift in the morning at 5am. For some unknown reason, Oscar decided not to cover his face, even though a lot of the officers wore balaclavas at night as it was so cold. As he was being led out of the prison dressed as an officer an off-duty prison guard coming in to work spotted him and raised the alarm. Everyone, including the police officers, was arrested. Oscar soon had his previous jail-keepers as next-door neighbours on the wing. About eight police officers were arrested and convicted of assisting an escape attempt. Unluckily for Oscar, he didn't have too many years to live. He was transferred to another prison where he was killed not long after.

Garcia Moreno had a long history of escapes, from single breakouts to as many as 40 or 50 at a time. People had simply walked out along with other visitors using fake ID or dressed as women, or they had dug tunnels, crawled through the sewers, shot their way out of the main gate, got over the roof and walls using ladders, escaped from the court, hidden in the rubbish and even dressed as guards and police officers – and of course they'd paid bribes to walk out the front door. When I heard all of these stories I was happy and relieved that it was definitely possible to escape. I would go to sleep each night plotting different ways to get out and then make my way to Colombia, where I had friends who would help me out. I also liked the idea of going all the way down the Amazon River into Brazil, where I knew there was no extradition treaty with Britain.

I decided to talk to a couple of my friends about escaping to see if they had any ideas. I first discussed it with Sasha and a very good friend of mine from Rome by the name of Stefano. Between us we came up with many different ideas; some highly improbable but some more than feasible. Sasha wasn't particularly interested in the idea of escaping as he was nearing the end of his sentence and it just wasn't worth the risks involved. He was more than willing to assist us in any way he could, though, which was appreciated. He was a true friend who was there when you needed him.

I also spoke to Andrew to see if he had any ideas as to how we might be able to get out of this place. He suggested I dress up as a girl, get a copy of the security stamps they put on the visitors' arms, walk out the door and collect the ID of someone who was inside visiting. I would have to pay the girl whose ID I collected as she would be in for some fairly intense questioning. I came up with another level of subterfuge to add to this. We were able to obtain liquid latex, which the prison used in some of the art classes. I had seen the latex masks they created for special effects in films and wondered if we might not be able to find a make-up artist in Ecuador who was good enough to do the same, and was willing to help out for a nice chunk of change. The plan was to find someone reasonably similar in appearance to me and get them to come in on a visit along with the make-up artist. Over a period of time, the artist would make as good a copy as he or she could. Once the mask was ready the willing victim would come in to visit someone. I would take his clothes, tie him up so that it looked like he had been forced to cooperate, put on the mask, duplicate the security stamp on the arm and casually walk out of the prison, collecting the guy's ID on the way. I would of course pay the poor guy for helping out. I still think the plan would have worked brilliantly had we been able to find a make-up artist willing to help. We couldn't.

A simpler version of this plan entailed finding someone who resembled me as closely as possible. It would then be the same idea: they would come in on a visit, I would tie them up and leave, collecting their ID. We thought it would be good to leave with a group of visitors. I considered trying to walk out among a large group already carrying a passport, so that when the others retrieved their IDs I could mingle with them and then make out I had just collected mine as well. This might have worked but there were too many things that could go wrong. If it had gone wrong the police could have done almost anything from beat the hell out of me at best to execute me at worst, and all manner of horrible torture in between those two extremes.

Another idea we came up with, though this one was somewhat costly, was to hire a helicopter and pilot, then kidnap the pilot mid-air and get him to fly over the prison and airlift us out from the large exercise yard in B wing. This would have cost somewhere in the region of $50,000 in order to do it properly and I couldn't raise that money quickly enough.

Shortly before I arrived in the prison a group of heavily armed inmates succeeded in shooting their way out of the main entrance, and several of them managed to escape. There was a running gun battle between the inmates, guards and police that left at least four inmates dead and many more seriously injured. They had opened fire firstly in the centre where all the wings converge and worked their way down the narrow passageway that leads to the main entrance. They had then forced the door open and shot their way out of the prison. I met a few people who bore the scars of that day's gun battle having been caught in the crossfire at the OK Corral.

Andrew mentioned to Mario and our friends the Colombians that I was interested in planning an escape. All of them were pretty keen on getting out of prison and excited about helping out however they could. They told me that they could hire some friends who were members of the Colombian guerrilla force FARC to come down to Quito and blow a hole in the perimeter wall of the prison using an RPG (rocket propelled grenade). They would have several men with them to lay down covering fire with machine guns to fend off the police and guards should they intervene. This sounded feasible and I had heard of a successful escape using this method from one of the prisons near the Colombian border in the north. I told Mario to make some enquires to see if it could be organised and how much it would cost.

The next idea we came up with was digging a tunnel out of the prison and/or using the sewer system that ran below. Various people had told me about numerous escapes involving tunnels that had taken place over the years. On one occasion as many as 30 people had succeeded in escaping. Mario told me it was like a rabbit warren under the prison and if you dug one tunnel you would be sure to come across two or three more in the process of excavating. There was a well-documented case of a garbage truck being driven over a tunnel that went under the road and collapsed under the truck's weight. Mario knew of a half-completed tunnel that ran from the far end of B wing, which was adjacent to the perimeter wall, out towards the street. The people who had started it had been transferred to another prison. He proposed we purchased a cell as near to the end of B wing as we could and put some of our friends in it. We would then break into the tunnel, complete the job and make our getaway.

I liked the sound of this. A few days later we bought the penultimate cell on the right-hand side of the ground floor of the wing. I funded a loud party on a visit day to disguise the noise of hammering as we set about breaking the concrete floor to create an entrance to the tunnel. We had sand and cement from the renovation work on my cell in C wing. With this we formed a concrete lid to cover the entrance. The party was a great success, as were our engineering works. We now had an active tunnel complete with lid. Mario's guys got to work excavating, disposing of the soil and rocks as best they could down drains, in the exercise yard and in the rubbish. We had to be careful as the guards employed inmates to regularly check the rubbish for evidence of tunnels (and body parts).

Mario estimated the work was going to take a good three or four months to complete. He suggested we rent one of the houses that lie just outside the prison wall on the hillside and pay someone to start digging inwards as well. He told me he could get some ex-miners to come and do the work if they were paid well enough.

The tunnel proceeded. The first section was fairly easy, as we could just follow the line of the wall from the wing above. We had the concrete and tarmac of the exercise yard as the ceiling. I let them get on with the work and stayed well away. I planned to take as many people as I possibly could. There was a good chance we could make an escape down this rabbit hole but I was concerned that too many people were now aware of our plans. This was a constant worry as people loved to talk and spread rumours. It would only take one person to say the wrong thing and we would all be in big trouble.

CHAPTER SIXTEEN
GHOSTED

I lay on my bed in the darkness, staring out of the window at the Pichincha volcano behind the prison. I was restless in the heat of the night and couldn't sleep after the lines of coke Sasha and I had taken earlier while watching a film. Thoughts kept racing through my mind about my family, friends, the case and how much longer I was destined to be locked up. My mind kept gravitating back to a feeling that something wasn't right. I couldn't help thinking that something was about to happen. Was I going to be extradited to Britain? I kept trying to suppress it and tell myself it was the cocaine making me paranoid, but it just would not go away. I could hear Sasha was awake too, on the bunk above me.

'Sasha? Sasha? Are you still awake?' I asked quietly.

'Da, I'm still awake,' came back the heavily accented voice. 'What's up?'

I paused for a brief moment, unsure whether to mention my thought or not. I didn't want to come across as being paranoid.

'Sasha, I'm worried I might get transferred to another prison, or extradited. I keep getting this feeling like something's wrong.'

'Ha! You being paranoid. That coke is strong, huh?'

I bloody knew he'd put it down to that, I thought, as he laughed.

'I knew you'd say that, Sasha, but that's not it. I just keep getting this idea in my head. You know, like an instinct.'

Sasha went quiet. He knew me well and that my instincts were good.

'Listen, my friend,' he started. 'No foreigners ever get transferred out of this place. You have to be real big asshole for them to do that.' He was trying to reassure me. He had been in the prison nearly a year longer than me, so he knew what he was talking about.

'Oh thanks, Sasha. Don't tell anyone what I said please.'

'I won't. I won't. Don't worry my friend. You not going anywhere soon. Ha, you got 12-year sentence remember?!'

Great that he was finding this amusing, I thought. 'Yeah, thanks for reminding me.' I eventually fell asleep but the thought stayed with me even after Sasha's reassurances. He was probably right. Why would they want to transfer me? I was slipping all the guards a few dollars every week and not doing anything too crazy that would draw attention. Where would they transfer me anyway?

Everyone told me I needn't worry about extradition as I had now been sentenced and would almost definitely have to finish that sentence before the Ecuadorian government would even consider looking at the documents. I wasn't so sure, but I did have to agree that extradition felt unlikely. There was nothing I could do about it anyway but wait and see.

It was a Wednesday and visit day. I was in my cell with the door locked, not feeling much like seeing or talking to anyone. I wasn't expecting any visitors, so I was watching a DVD and dozing when there was a loud knock on the door, the kind that normally only a guard made. I snapped awake and quickly hid my phone in a secret compartment in the leg of the bed.

Bang, bang, bang. '*Abre la puerta! Abre la puerta!*'

Shit! The guards. Just what I needed, and on a visit day when they normally left everyone alone. I opened the door and sure enough there was a guard who I really didn't like, carrying a length of wood. What the hell was this?

'*Que pasa?*' I asked. He told me I had to come down to the office of the *jefe de guia* immediately because he wanted to speak to me. I was worried. This sounded like trouble or a shakedown to squeeze money out of me. I certainly hadn't done anything to warrant the aggressive approach. I locked the cell, and luckily Sasha arrived just as I was being led down the stairs to the wing entrance. I gave him the keys to the cell and told him to find Nizar, the *caporal*, as something was obviously wrong and I didn't know what.

I reached the *jefe de guia*'s office and immediately asked what was wrong. '*Te vas traslado*', he replied: you're being transferred. At first I thought he was joking and they were playing some kind of prank on me, perhaps to squeeze me for a few dollars. But he was insistent. What the hell? So I had been right. I couldn't believe it – I had actually predicted my own transfer and vocalised it to Sasha.

I asked the *jefe de guia* if I could please be allowed back on to the wing to collect some of my belongings. '*No!*' There was no way I would be allowed back there; this was it. I stood there in just my tracksuit bottoms, fleece top and trainers, with no money, none of my belongings and I felt the colour drain from my face.

A couple of people from the wing passed me and I asked them to tell Nizar that I was being transferred and could he please grab some of my clothes and phone numbers. Under the bed was the large black holdall with which I had left France that fateful day two years ago. Nizar arrived with it and some of my other belongings a short while later, for which I was very grateful. I asked him to talk with the *jefe de guia* to see if we could perhaps work out some sort of deal to take me off the transfer list – I was willing to pay him. The *jefe de guia* wasn't having any of it and told me that my own embassy had requested the transfer, which baffled me. I started to panic. Was this the dreaded extradition? Nizar reassured me there was no way it could be extradition as that was a complicated procedure that took a while, and papers had to be served by the British government.

I asked the *jefe de guia* where I was going. He seemed reluctant to answer. I finally persuaded him to tell me. It was absolutely the worst possible outcome. The Penitentiary Litoral de Guayaquil. No, there must be a mistake. He checked and double-checked. Yep, the infamous 'Peni'. At the time this was the fourth most dangerous prison in the whole of South America. Completely gang-controlled, with multiple murders every week, frequent gunfights – a place no one wanted to go.

'Who else is being transferred?' I asked, looking around the reception area, where sat only one other person.

'Just you and the Dutch guy,' the *jefe de guia* told me.

Special transfer. Jesus Christ! This really was serious. I vaguely knew the Dutchman, who was called Kelvin. He had run into problems here in the prison and had a death sentence hanging over his head from one of the gangs. His embassy had made a lot of noise and managed to get him a transfer as far south as you could go, to the town of Machala on the Peruvian border. He looked quite happy to be going. I, on the other hand, was not at all happy. Just when I was really getting on my feet and organised here, they'd pulled the rug from under me. Surely they couldn't know about the tunnel? Was this how it was going to be from now on? Just like in Britain – regular transfers to stop you getting settled and forming friends.

I sent messages with a couple of people who passed by to any of my friends who I knew were well-connected to the gangs in Guayaquil, asking them to phone ahead with a recommendation for me so that I would be well-received and not be a victim of extortion as a new arrival would normally be. At this time, I had been exercising with Sasha in the gym for two hours every night and had become quite muscular and very strong. At least I would be able to put up a hell of a fight if they wanted to go down that road.

Nizar kept saying to me, 'Put me in charge of your cells. I will collect the rent and send it to you in Guayaquil.' I thanked him for the offer and said I would make contact once I was there and had decided what to do, but it made me immediately suspicious that perhaps this transfer was a big ruse in order to take control of the three cells I owned on C wing and the one on B wing, along with all the contents. This totalled more than $15,000 and was more than enough for someone to be interested in robbing me. For the moment there was nothing I could do. Whoever had instigated this had the upper hand and I was on the back foot. Until I was able to start taking control of the situation again, I just had to go with the flow.

We waited nearly an hour for the arrival of the guards who were to escort us on the 350-mile journey south, through the Andes mountain chain. They were armed with handguns and shotguns and were prepared for trouble. Kelvin and I were searched and then each handcuffed to a guard. We were led out of the main entrance, past the visitors waiting to come in for the *cadada*, and down the road to where a minibus with police lights its roof was waiting, along with a police patrol vehicle with four policemen armed with M16 assault rifles. All this security was for me, as the Dutch guy Kelvin had requested his transfer, so was going voluntarily. Did they think I was preparing to break out or something? I'd had no warning, no idea it was happening. There was no time for me to organise for a team to break me out. Kelvin looked at me and asked, 'What the fock have you done man?'

I shrugged my shoulders because I really didn't know the answer to that question.

CHAPTER SEVENTEEN
THE ROAD IS LONG

We travelled through the city of Quito and were soon ascending the roads that led up into the Andes mountains, following the highway south, winding its way around the hillsides like a boa round a tree. On we went, higher and higher, the cloud engulfing us and the air temperature dropping rapidly so even the guards complained that it was too cold. We went through towns and villages where I wondered how people survived and why they would ever choose to live in such an inhospitable place.

Kelvin and I were handcuffed to one another with arms interlinked – very uncomfortable and very romantic! We found it amusing for about the first ten minutes until the handcuffs started to dig into our wrists and cut the circulation off. We asked the guards, who sat both behind and in front of us in the minibus, to loosen them or take them off altogether but our requests fell on deaf ears.

We spent a good couple of hours up in the mountains and I was closer to the sun, moon and stars than I had been for several years. I was so anxious about what lay in front of me at the new prison that I wished we would perhaps end up lost and just driving around in these mountains aimlessly – which is how I kind of felt anyway. I was lost to my family, friends and anyone else for that matter in a never-ending nightmare in the Ecuadorian prison system.

As we travelled further south, we started to descend into the valleys, the air becoming humid and warmer. The vegetation changed from cloud forest and woodland to denser, more bushy canopy, with flowers and lush green leaves. This all seemed beautiful and new to me after two years spent in the concrete corridors of Garcia Moreno. We seemed to be following the course of a river flowing south out on to the plains that form the southern and western half of Ecuador, heading out towards the Pacific coast.

The roads were surprisingly well-maintained, and we raced on, dropping ever lower, the air becoming ever warmer. We would come up behind a line of traffic and, rather than waiting, the driver of our minibus would just switch on the sirens and lights to clear a path through for our little convoy, occasionally picking up another patrol car as we went that would guide us through their area and then fall away. At one point we hit a small town in the mountains that was in the midst of its annual carnival and we got stuck behind a procession winding its way along the main street. We became almost a part of the event as the locals stared at this strange group, two foreigners, a load of armed guards and a police patrol – hardly an everyday occurrence.

We were now travelling through the plains, one of the more fertile areas of the country. The road was bordered on each side by large plantations of bananas and fields of maize. The large leaves of the banana trees made quite an ominous wall of green, with just darkness beneath them. There would be a break every now and then for an entrance into a plantation, at which point we would get a glimpse of the workers' houses, which were little colonial affairs, almost like large dollhouses. Somehow they didn't quite look big enough for people to actually live in, but then I suppose you would think the same of a prison cell. The entranceways were gated and armed guards sat around smoking, making sure only the right people came in and out. I had seen places like this in the north of Colombia where the guards do actually have to protect the estate against FARC or paramilitary forces who would come raiding for cattle or to kidnap the owner.

We sped onwards and hit a small town, where I heard the guards discussing where to buy some bread. We stopped on the main drag near a mechanic's shop and three of the guards got out. Kelvin and I were really hoping we would get a chance to stretch our legs, which had gone to sleep now after four hours on the road. This didn't happen, so we just sat, dazed by this sudden burst of reality after two years behind walls.

I leant across to Kelvin and quietly suggested we should make a break for it, but in jest. I knew we would only get 40 or 50 metres and then be cut down by a hail of lead. I was sure this is what the guards were secretly wishing for, too. 'Go on, try it and see what happens, gringo.' They were keeping a close eye on us, with their trigger fingers ever ready. One of them returned with some freshly baked bread for us, still warm from the oven, and a bottle of Sprite, which took the edge off the hunger and thirst. The guards climbed back on board, changing their seating positions, and off we went again towards Guayaquil.

The plains we were now crossing were more populated than the mountains we had left behind, and we were passing through towns with greater frequency. The sun had turned to a blazing pink as it began its descent towards the horizon, casting an amazing colour over the flat country below it. Back in Quito, I never really saw the sun set as it would just drop behind the mountains. Sometimes the night sky would light up behind them, but then darkness would descend rapidly.

Our trip now became monotonous as the beautiful sunset had quickly turned through shades of grey to darkness and there was nothing to look at apart from the oncoming headlights and the towns we went through. A lot of people had now begun to emerge on to the streets as the coolness of the evening replaced the oppressive humidity and blazing heat of the day. The restaurants and bars were starting to fill as the dinner hour neared. Every now and then I would catch the smells coming through the open windows on the breeze and tell myself that I would one day be sitting on those restaurant terraces enjoying such pleasures I could now only watch pass by the window. I tried to close my eyes and sleep a little but this was virtually impossible while I was handcuffed to someone, surrounded by sweaty armed guards and feeling hot and worried.

On and on we sped towards a destination that seemed to grow no closer. Perhaps they would just take us to the border and say 'bye bye, nice knowing you, you're free to go', or maybe they would pull over on a quiet back road and put a bullet in the backs of our heads and say we had tried to escape.

Eventually I started to see Guayaquil appear on the road signs and we reached the outer edge of a city. The driver spotted a garage and decided to pull in to refuel, but didn't know on which side the fuel cap was. This turned into a comedy sideshow for a moment, which brought me and Kelvin some light relief. The guards all piled out with handguns drawn and shotguns at the ready, much to the bemusement of the forecourt attendant. Passers-by started to gather to see what was happening. The guards told me and Kelvin to get out so we could use the toilet at the garage and stretch our legs a little. This came as a huge relief after seven or eight hours handcuffed arm in arm in a cramped minibus. I fell out of the door pulling Kelvin with me, bringing the place to a standstill as the locals stared at the two foreigners cuffed to one another.

We were escorted across the forecourt to a dark toilet surrounded by the guards, and told to use the toilet while handcuffed together. 'They must be joking,' I said to Kelvin. To wind us up the guards suggested we help each other. Kelvin went first and managed the task in hand, but as I was wearing tracksuit bottoms without flies and with an elasticated waist it was impossible. The guards found this even more amusing. At this point I snapped and blew my top. They realised it wasn't a joke and thankfully uncuffed me so I could relieve myself. When I was done they put the hand-cuffs back on us and it was straight back into the minibus.

My Spanish having improved somewhat in two years, I found out from the guards' conversation that we were first going to Machala, which is way past Guayaquil, to drop Kelvin off, and then I would be dropped off on the return journey. It seemed to me a rather roundabout way of doing things as we were passing close to Guayaquil. Why not drop me and then continue on to Machala? But no doubt they did it this way round to earn more overtime.

We travelled for several hours more and arrived in Machala around midnight. The driver eventually found the prison, having first had to stop and ask for directions. We got out and finally Kelvin and I were separated. I wished him well in his new home and watched him go, disappearing through a set of high steel gates. I was now standing in the street with only a couple of guards and the police escort as the others sorted out the paperwork for Kelvin, but I was certain they could sense what I was thinking. Could I make a run for it? How far would I get? But the guards were starting to get a little edgy; I was instructed to get back into the minibus. I sat there waiting until we were ready to go, but then the guards decided they had had enough of driving for the moment and asked me if I would like some food with them.

'Sure thing, that would be great,' I replied. We set off through the empty streets of Machala and before long found a restaurant that was still open. The proprietor agreed to let us eat there and the guards set up a cordon around the restaurant, taking turns to eat so I was always surrounded. It all seemed a bit dramatic just for me. A couple of the waitresses gave me lovely smiles as they served the food, which made me wish all the more that I was free. For the first time in two years I was sitting in a restaurant on the street eating a meal. It felt so good to be away from prison – away from the incessant noise of people and doors and locks and keys – even if only for a short while. I listened to the cicadas and felt the warm night air as I tried to imagine again being free to walk out of a door and go somewhere without first asking permission.

Back in the minibus I managed to fall asleep, now I didn't have my companion wrapped around me. I awoke to the sound of cobbles under the tyres of the minibus. Outside were rain-streaked streets lit by sodium bulbs. We had reached Guayaquil and were lost. I was slightly dazed and confused until my senses returned and reality kicked back in.

The prison lay to the north of the city, up the coast road towards the airport, although it took the guards a good while to find it. Tall walls with razor wire stretched into the distance on either side of the gatehouse. I had arrived at the Penitentiary Litoral de Guayaquil, known locally as La Peni. This place looks big, I thought to myself.

We all climbed out and I was escorted to the reception area so that they could sort out the paperwork. It was now about four in the morning and it still felt warm. We were very near the coast.

I sat in the reception area and contemplated how much harder and more complicated everything would now be as far as fighting my case was concerned. My lawyer was in Quito, my case was in Quito, the embassy, the court, everything I needed was in Quito and now I was in Guayaquil about to have to start afresh in a hostile environment. *Que bueno.*

CHAPTER EIGHTEEN
LA PENI

As daylight began to spread rapidly, and the grey concrete dust-covered edifices began to take shape, the grim reality of my predicament was revealed. Dark holes became barred window and doors. I couldn't believe this was a functioning prison. Had it not been for the presence of police and guards I could have easily mistaken it for a building site.

I wandered in and out of what was supposed to be the holding cell, located just inside the main gate at the front of the building that contained all the offices, including that of the governor. No one paid me a blind bit of notice. I started to wonder whether they had forgotten me as the hours crept by and the prison slowly came to life.

A well-built guy, aged about 30, came up to me and in American-accented English asked my nationality. He introduced himself as Eduardo, from the Dominican Republic but resident in New York. He explained that he had been sentenced to 16 years for trying to smuggle four kilograms of heroin to the United States. He had been in the prison for a couple of years already and had assumed the role of looking after newly arrived foreigners. He outlined the way the prison functioned – i.e. gang-controlled and totally corrupt. I was shocked when Eduardo told me how much the gangs tended to demand of people like me. The *ingresso* (entrance fee) alone, he lamented, was going to be between $2,000 and $10,000, according to how much they deemed I was worth and what they could squeeze out of me. I had expected it to be quite a lot but not this much, considering that in Quito it was $60! What would happen if I refused to pay it, I asked. Eduardo's face changed markedly from one of smiles to one of world-weary mournfulness. He lowered his voice and glanced around nervously to make sure he wasn't overheard. 'You really don't want to do that.' He went on to explain that the gangs here were very adept at extorting money from people; they colluded with the guards and even the director, who were paid to turn a blind eye. Basically, you either paid or you were going to go through hell: tortured with beatings, drownings, electrocution, hanging, strangulation; with knives, guns, bats, machetes and all other manner of horrific methods. In short, Eduardo explained, if you got on the wrong side of the gang then you were in deep, deep shit and could quite easily end up dead.

Fuck! I tried not to show my fear and anxiety but my mouth had dried up and my stomach was turning inside out. Oh well. I would just have to pay. I would just have to hope that those calls I had been promised by my friends in Quito to ensure I was well received at Guayaquil had been made. Eduardo reassured me that as long as I played ball but didn't roll over I would be OK. I already had the experience of two years in an Ecuadorian prison dealing with these types of people, so at least I was better prepared than someone who had just arrived in the country.

Eduardo headed off, leaving me to mull over all the information he had imparted. He had told me that two heavily armed gangs controlled the prison with regimented brute force and violence. There were regular gun battles between the two gangs, often resulting in multiple deaths. The place was out of control and the authorities basically left them to get on with it, merely containing everything within 15-foot-high walls patrolled by armed police who would shoot to kill. Whoever had instigated this transfer really wanted to fuck me up. In fact, it felt as if they wanted me dead.

Directly in front of me there was a large wrought-iron gate, which I guessed was the main entrance to the prison. I could not see very far into the ominous darkness beyond it. To the right of this there was another part of the building that looked semi-derelict, but in which I could see movement. People kept coming to the gate to look out across the dusty dirt road that appeared to encircle the place like a no man's land. A few of them called over to me and asked where I was from. 'England,' I replied. Upon hearing this they became quite animated and started beckoning me to come over to the doorway. I was wary of getting into trouble for leaving my supposed holding cell, but then I heard a definite English accent, and south London at that, call out to me. I looked across to the entrance of the building to the right of the main gate and could make out the pale, bearded face of a well-built, middle-aged man with wavy brown hair. He was beckoning for me to go over to him and shouted out not to worry about the guards or police.

I decided to risk going over to see this Englishman. I crossed the dusty dirt track that seemed to run all around the prison. As I did so I realised that I was surrounded by a high perimeter wall topped with razor wire. The wings were inside another wall running parallel to this outer one on the opposite side of the no man's land – a rectangle within a rectangle. I reached the wrought-iron gate from where the Englishman had called me and asked a guy who was standing there watching the world go by (as best I could) for the Englishman.

'Hello mate, how are you doing?' he greeted me. We shook hands. He introduced himself as Simon, and I explained who I was, why I was in prison and about my sudden transfer from Quito. I discovered that this dusty, empty building site was in fact the hospital wing. If this bombed-out-looking building was the hospital, which you would expect to be the most sanitary of places, then what the hell was the interior of this prison going to be like?

Simon asked why I had been transferred, a question to which I had no clear answer at present. All the way from Quito the night before I had been asking myself the same questions: who had requested the transfer, what implications would this have for me in the future and, primarily, how the hell could I get back there as soon as possible? Anything was possible in this country, I told myself, if you threw enough money at it and were persistent.

Simon had never seen a Brit transferred from Quito or Guayaquil in the four years he had already been locked up out of a 25-year sentence, which was for trafficking 400kg of cocaine to Britain hidden in the digger arms of heavy plant machinery. I remembered reading about the case when I was still in Britain. Simon hadn't been caught with even a trace of cocaine on him and wasn't in either country when the alleged offences had taken place. They still gave him 25 years, the maximum for drugs, following heavy pressure from the British authorities.

I thought back to the British police arriving in Quito a couple of times to collect evidence in my case and to ensure I wasn't going anywhere soon. The words of the *jefe de guia* rang loud in my ears from the night before, when he had said my transfer was at the behest of the British. I must have really pissed them off this time. They seemed intent on me dying in this hellhole. They knew how bad these places were and the strong likelihood of ending up either sick or crazy by the time you finished your sentence – if you were lucky enough to make it that far.

Simon explained that he was living in this building site as his life had been threatened by one of the gangs within the prison. This had occurred after a business deal went wrong, leaving him indebted to murderous, ruthless thieves who only cared about one thing – their money; *dinero, plata* – and would go to extreme lengths to recoup or extract it. As we both knew, there was no escaping a debt here and Simon knew it was only a matter of time before they got to him, unless he negotiated his way out of the mess.

No one seemed the slightest bit interested in who I was or where I was supposed to be. This suited me fine. The longer things weren't fixed, the more chance I had of manipulating the situation to my advantage. I persuaded a guard to let me into the wing with my bag. Simon and I spent the rest of the day talking about our cases, the other British prisoners in the system and the way in which we had both been royally stitched up. He let me use his mobile to place a couple of calls. The first I made was to my family, who were shocked that I had been transferred and terrified about where I had ended up. I then called some friends in Quito to see if they had spoken to anyone down here and ask them to perhaps to put in another call. I asked them to make sure my things were being looked after so that the embassy could collect some of them and bring them to me.

I spent that first night sleeping fitfully on the floor next to Simon's bed in a building site, and I awoke the following day cold, stiff and tired from a bad night's sleep. Not long after the morning count, a guard came and shouted for me and took me back over to the holding area I had disappeared from. I left my bag with Simon so I didn't have to heave it around with me. The guard told me to wait in there. At this time the prison service wasn't really computerised and all records were kept in paper form including fingerprints and photographs. When you were transferred your *carpeta*, or folder, was supposed to be sent with you along with your photos. I sat there as the heat just built and built, increasing slowly as the morning went on.

I just managed to get some lunch as they went around serving the meagre prison food. I was hot, tired, hungry and thirsty so was thankful for the bowl of soup and the plate of rice with some chicken in a sauce that tasted pretty good right then. The food here seemed to be a lot better than in Quito. Just after lunch I saw an Ecuadorian beckoning to me from the main gate to the prison. He called over, 'Are you Pieter? Have you just come from Quito?'

'Yes' I replied, my spirits lifting but also my nerves kicking in.

He was smartly dressed and accompanied by two equally well dressed guys in crisp shirts. They seemed to command a degree of respect from the other people crowded around the gate, who had made space for them to come through to the front. These were quite obviously not your run-of-the-mill inmates; most of the other people around them were dressed in clothing that looked as if it had never been washed. I guessed that this was going to be my first contact with the gang that controlled this half of the prison.

They told me to come over to the gate to speak to them. There were a couple of guards sitting at the entrance in the shade, controlling who came in and out. The three guys were conversing with them quite freely as if they were friends. This seemed quite strange to me, as in a British prison you didn't talk to the guards unless you wanted something. If you were seen being friendly with guards there, you would be classed as a grass. I waited a second, unsure whether to go over or not until one of the guards beckoned to me. The main guy told me that he had been sent by Coyote, one of the bosses.

I had met Coyote a couple of times in Quito. He was being held in A wing, the maximum-security unit, on firearms charges. He was in fact a reasonably high-level international trafficker. He had been transferred to Guayaquil six months prior to my move in order to finish off his sentence closer to his family. I had liked him when I'd met him before. He was a relaxed, calm guy to whom you could talk freely about business or day-to-day matters. He was friendly and genuine compared to some of the people you met here who were only interested in what they could get out of you. I felt reassured that Coyote had been contacted and had sent people to find me. My friends had obviously done their job. The guy said he would go back and let Coyote know I was here, and they would sort out which wing I would be allocated and then return later in the afternoon to collect me.

I wandered over to tell Simon what had just happened and he immediately warned me to be careful and, if possible, avoid going into the main prison. This compounded my fears and left me feeling even more unsettled.

Eventually, at around three o'clock a large group of very well dressed guys sporting heavy gold chains and chunky watches turned up at the gate. This was obviously the gang. They looked like something out of a rap video. Evidently these were the bosses, as they were giving out orders to people around them and receiving phone calls. All this was taking place in front of the two guards stationed on the gate, who almost appeared subservient to the men behind the bars. They were looking and gesturing towards me and I spotted the guy from earlier on talking to one of the bosses. I was feeling pretty bloody nervous now. Here we go, I thought.

After a short exchange the guards opened the gate and out streamed a large group of over 50 gang members – bosses and bodyguards. I was quickly surrounded with people on every side.

'You're Pieter?'

'Yes.'

'Your friends from Quito have called, you've been highly recommended. Nice to meet you.'

We shook hands while the others milled around, keeping an eye out. Various members of the group were on their phones and I caught glimpses of the butts of guns tucked into the belts of shorts. Jesus Christ! This was insane. These guys were wandering around as if they owned the place. Even the guards on the gate were unarmed. The gang seemed to have complete immunity.

Two policemen walked by armed with M16 assault rifles and gave this group a wide berth, a wry smile and a nod of the head. The boss, who introduced himself as Olea, produced a phone and asked if I would like to speak to my friends in Quito. Without waiting for a response, he dialled the number. I wasn't quite sure who he was calling, as in the midst of my hurried departure I had asked several people to please call ahead.

He handed me the phone and it was Nizar, the Syrian *caporal* from C wing. Nizar told me he had spoken to the bosses of the gang and that I would be well looked after. He also raised the subject of me signing my cells in Quito over. I was becoming more and more suspicious as this was the third or fourth time of asking. Could Nizar have instigated my transfer? He and I had had our differences over the last two years and I'm sure he felt his position was threatened. I was now suddenly worried that he had arranged this reception party with a view to extorting me out of every last penny I had. Oh God! I felt like a gazelle among a pack of lions, about to be torn apart. There wasn't a lot I could do really. Talk about out of the frying pan into the fire!

The boss concluded the meet and greet by telling me I would be well looked after. He explained that they would organise everything with the guards so that I would go to one of the best wings in the prison where a large number of them lived. They would protect me and make sure all was well. I wasn't sure quite how to take this. It could all be a ruse to lull me into a false sense of security, to get me to drop my guard. At this point, however, I had become fairly good at reading people and he was coming across as genuine. I was still nervous, but felt kind of respected now that such a number of people had come to greet me on the word of my friends in Quito. I doubted very much whether this happened with many other foreigners. I could see the other inmates wondering what was going on. Who was this newly arrived gringo that the whole mafia came to greet?

This was my initiation into, and first contact with, the notorious Los Cubanos gang. A gang who not only controlled half a prison with a population at that point of nearly 8,000 inmates, but also a large part of the south of the city called Guasmo. I was now well and truly in their hands, and my future and very survival depended on how the next few hours and days went.

Simon had watched this take place, along with quite a few others from the wing he was on. I went back over to speak with him, emboldened by my new feeling of security. He warned me to be very careful and not to get involved with the gang as they regarded all outsiders as merely an opportunity to make money, normally by stealing or extortion. They specialised in playing mind games, he went on to tell me. This they called *cerebro*, which means 'brain'. It was a favourite pastime of theirs and they were very good at it. I was glad of the advice and promised myself I would treat everything with suspicion. Simon also told me not to accept any gifts or make any promises as they would ask you for five times what they had given you and you would be obliged to give it. Any promises, no matter if made flippantly, would be expected to be fulfilled.

Later that day Eduardo came to find me. He introduced me to a Chilean lady who helped foreigners in the prison. Her name was Margarita, and she greeted me with a lovely smile. I immediately took to this motherly lady who was helping people from the kindness of her heart without asking for anything in return. She explained that she was the accountant for a local evangelical church and had first become involved with the prison when she came to the aid of a couple of Chileans imprisoned in Guayaquil. It transpired that she not only knew the honorary vice consul of the British embassy in Guayaquil but was very good friends with her, and she said she would call her directly once she left the prison. She offered to help in any way she could with, for example, collecting money transfers or bringing in shopping, clothing, medication or pretty much anything else that was needed – providing it was strictly legal. Being a devout evangelical Christian she was totally against drugs, and alcohol as well. I was relieved that I had encountered someone who would be able to help me with money transfers, as this was vital here. I knew that any day now I would have to make some payments to the gang either for my *ingresso* or to buy a cell.

After the last count, a guard came looking for me. He started to hustle me along, saying he was taking me to the wing that the gang had arranged for me to live on. I said goodbye to Simon for the time being and promised I would try to come out and visit him whenever I could. Off I headed into the bowels of the Penitentiary Guayaquil, not knowing when, or even if, I would emerge alive.

CHAPTER NINETEEN
ATENUADO ABAJO

The heavy iron gate crashed shut behind me. In front of me, as far as I could see, was a long, dark passageway some twenty feet wide, intermittently lit by strip lights. We hadn't gone far when we came to a gateway on the left, the entrance to a wing called Atenuado Abajo. There was an inmate standing outside the gate with a guard, both drinking cans of beer, and another smoking a fat-looking spliff of marijuana. We stopped outside the gate while an inmate inside the wing produced a set of keys and unlocked a hefty padlock that secured a thick iron chain wrapped around the gate. The guard was then free to open the lock to let me in. This place was insane.

As I walked through the gate, the half-drunk inmate made a grab for my bag, but I had seen it coming and swung around, giving him a solid backhander in the face. This he was not expecting and he fell backwards, landing on his arse, much to the amusement of everyone there. I followed the guard to a cell on the right-hand side where he stopped, knocked and called out, 'Olea.' The heavy wooden door swung open to reveal a pretty fucking opulent cell for a Third-World prison. Olea was sitting on a plush double bed bathed in cool blue backlighting, watching satellite TV on a large screen. There was a fridge, cooker, furniture, rugs on the tiled floor and pictures on the walls. Not a bad set-up. The cool air from an air conditioner circulated, bringing relief from the oppressive evening heat.

Olea passed the guard a $20 note over and he disappeared. Olea offered me a chair. He told me that normally a newly arrived foreigner would be charged at least $2,000 *ingresso* to come on to the wing. However, because I had been transferred from Quito and came highly recommended, he was going to make an exception and only charge me $300. I sighed a breath of relief – thank goodness for that. My friends from Quito had obviously managed to call the 'right' people and had secured me a reasonable welcome. Perhaps my doubts about Nizar were ill-founded?

Olea asked if I might want to buy a cell in which he said I could live on my own. I could have whatever I wanted and they would make sure I was well protected and that no one bothered me. The idea of being able to live on my own again after two years living in a cell with two other men sounded like paradise. And how much would this favour cost me? I was quite surprised when Olea said $800. A fully equipped cell in Quito was over $2,500.

Olea explained that the other half of the prison was controlled by another gang, Los Rusos. His gang was in charge of this half of the prison, not the authorities, so whatever I needed it was best to ask him first. He also said it would be a good idea not to get into debt, to pay my bills, keep my word and not to start taking loads of drugs as that was frowned upon. A really big no-no was to start selling drugs in any way, as this was their business and me trying to get in on it would likely result in a rather gruesome death. Foreigners weren't really permitted to have any kind of business at all as the locals viewed this as taking money from them and their families. It reminded me of people in Britain saying that immigrants were taking their jobs.

I was told that the *guardia* (a fund used to bribe the guards and director to turn a blind eye to the gang's activities) and food had to be paid each Sunday, collection day for everyone on every wing. The *guardia* and food were each five dollars weekly, irrespective of whether or not you ate the food. There were also sometimes what they called 'collaborations' to raise funds for things such as Christmas, painting the wing, general repairs and so on. These were also compulsory. Olea stressed again the importance of paying all of these as this money went directly to the gang and it would cause problems if I didn't pay.

Olea said that there were several cells empty on the wing at the moment and I could take my pick and move straight in. Yes! He carefully wrote down his girlfriend or wife's name and passed it to me. I assured him that I would have the payment organised in the next few days and asked from where I could make a phone call. Simon had told me the previous day that making phone calls here was a bit of a pain, as there was not a single pay phone, or *cabina*, in the whole place and the authorities had erected towers with antennae that blocked the phone signal to try to prevent the gang from controlling their business in the street. However, the gang had seen this as an opportunity to control the market in calls by restricting who could have phones and setting up their members to rent minutes on mobiles at high rates.

Two of the previous directors had been gunned down when they failed to cooperate with the gang's activities within the prison. Several guards had also been murdered for refusing to help the gang bring in drugs, guns and alcohol. I could now appreciate why the guards were so friendly with these guys and treated them with a lot of respect. Half of them had grown up in the same neighbourhoods and knew each other and their families. Not only that, a guard's monthly salary was only $400 or $500 and the temptation to earn ten times that in a week bringing in drugs was just too much. Simon had told me that there was a whole bunch of former guards imprisoned here in their own little wing, and that quite often once they were released they would get their old jobs back and carry right on as before.

Olea made it clear that I had protection here now and that I would be escorted by a couple of guys wherever I went, to watch my back. They would take me to make some calls in the morning and I could even use his phone to do so. He then called for someone to show me the cells on offer.

The cell I was shown was dark inside as there was no light bulb. The guy I was with explained that I needed to buy a light bulb from the shop on the wing, which I duly did. The cell was completely empty, devoid of bed, TV, cooker, any fixtures at all. Everything of value had been stripped, obviously down to the light bulb! What the fuck?

I went back to Olea and explained that I would much prefer to buy a cell that was fully equipped and pay more, say $1,500 dollars, rather than have to go through all the hassle of trying to get everything brought into the prison by bribing guards. I asked if I could stay with one of his friends for the time being until something was arranged. He agreed to this and sent somebody off to fetch whoever it was I was going to stay with.

A few minutes later, a well-built, chubby guy with a friendly face and glazed, stoned-looking eyes came to the door. Olea explained the situation and my new room-mate, whose name was Chorito, took me to his humble abode. He instructed me as to his cell rules and showed me a kind of mezzanine level with a stepladder leading up to it, built of

wood, where I could sleep on a mattress. He slept in the
hammock he had erected on the ground level as it was cooler.
The cell was fairly basic but it would do for the time being
until I got myself sorted out. I was glad to have somewhere I
could finally have a proper sleep and shower after the last
few days. The only other things in the cell were a small
14-inch portable TV and Chorito's beloved hammock.

I immediately detected a strong smell that was familiar
to me but which I couldn't quite place. As the evening
progressed, it became apparent what the odour was. Chorito
was in fact the drug supplier for the wing and the smell was
polvo, the drug similar to crack that they loved to smoke,
usually mixed with marijuana or in a pipe. There was a
fairly constant stream of clientele. I sat watching the TV and
chatting to a few people, explaining why I was there, my
case, who I knew in Quito, the usual prison banter. I was
slightly concerned that I was now living with the wing drug
dealer but in other respects it could mean that I would be in
some ways viewed as one of them.

I asked how many foreigners there were on the wing and
was told there were about ten or more. There were two
Bulgarians, Canadians, a couple of Spaniards, a German
and then a few Colombians, Chileans and Peruvians. I was
surprised that none of them had come to introduce themselves. In Quito whenever somebody new arrived we would
give them food, clothing, a bed, whatever they needed until
they managed to get themselves sorted.

I decided that if they weren't coming to me I would have
to go to them. Chorito pointed the way to a couple of their
cells and sent me on my way with a parting word of caution.
Some of the foreigners were heavily into cocaine and Chorito
warned me not to get too friendly with them as they were
seen as junkies. I decided to follow his advice.

I went first to the cell of the Bulgarian he had said was a good guy. I knocked on the door and a voice enquired from behind the wood, 'Who's there?'

'I'm a new guy on the wing and British. Could we have a chat?'

There was silence for a second, then, 'Hold on a minute.'

I guessed perhaps he was putting something away he didn't want me to see. A moment later the door opened and there was a tall, good-looking, clean-shaven, muscular guy of about my age. He didn't invite me in, so we had a brief conversation in the doorway, in which he said he had to be careful as the gang would be watching me closely until I paid my dues and my being too friendly with him could cause him problems if I didn't pay up. His name was Vasil. He reiterated what most people had already said: don't get into debt, be very careful of the gang, don't take drugs and stay healthy. I immediately warmed to him.

I left and walked across to the next cell and knocked on the door. It opened up after a short time to reveal four guys playing cards. I could smell alcohol and cigarettes and one or two of them looked wired, I guessed from taking cocaine. The cell belonged to a German whose name was Dieter. He welcomed me in with a big smile but the other three weren't so friendly. One, a Spaniard, said hello, as did a somewhat nervous-looking guy who turned out to be the other Bulgarian, named Pico. The fourth guy was a Canadian called Karl. He was middle-aged, perhaps 45, and had a military look about him, with short black hair brushed to one side and the strong, wiry physique some men end up with after service. He wouldn't look me in the face. He was fidgeting and twitchy and it made me feel decidedly uneasy. I didn't know what was going on and put it down to the effects of cocaine.

I felt it best to leave them to it and bid them all good evening. I don't smoke and the cigarette smoke from four people in a small room is quite overpowering. I left the room feeling generally unsettled by the reception I had received from all of the non-South Americans. They'd been very stand-offish all round and I realised that here there was not much unity between the foreigners – apart from the Colombians, who all stuck together as ever.

I spent the next few weeks settling into the new routine and customs of this prison. Every prison functions slightly differently, has an individual heartbeat and momentum. The trick as an inmate is learning how to adapt to that rhythm, fit in and then turn it to your advantage. I therefore sat back and watched the comings and goings while at the same time organising what I had to in the way of payments to Olea and the gang, or mafia as they preferred to be called. I was having to use the telephone daily to call my family and friends in Quito and Britain to arrange first the *ingresso* and then the buying of a cell. I was also trying to salvage what I could of all my belongings that had been left behind in the hurried transfer.

The embassy in Quito appeared to be as baffled as me by the move and wrote a formal letter of complaint to the Ministry of Justice, requesting that I be returned to Quito at the first opportunity. That letter was never even acknowledged, let alone replied to. On my departure from Quito the head guard had kept on telling me the embassy had requested my transfer, and yet they appeared to be completely unaware of it. The honorary vice consul Isabel had contacted the director of the prison in Quito several times, and the director had told the embassy that under no circumstances would I ever be transferred back there as I was a high security risk and had supposedly been in the midst of planning a massive escape of more than 16 people. That made more sense as there was a degree of truth in what he said. I had indeed been planning an escape and had made good progress on the tunnel down which we were going to disappear one fine night. I'm sure there were other elements that had contributed to the move, such as my owning four cells and controlling a large percentage of business on the wing.

Nizar had heard that I was suspicious of him having arranged the transfer and asked that I call him. During the conversation, he swore blind that he had not done a thing and that I was his friend and why not put him in charge of the sale of my cells and contents, totalling around $15,000 or $20,000. I declined the offer and thanked him for clearing the air. I had hurriedly placed Ruben in charge of selling them as he was British, and the embassy were in regular contact and could to some degree ensure he did what he was supposed to. Or at least I thought so. I also asked three other good friends, Mikey the Canadian, Sasha my Russian room-mate and Alejandro the shopkeeper, to watch what was going on and make sure things went smoothly. Ruben and I had had our differences but I thought he would help me out with all this

Apparently a few people had made moves to take over the cells, but Sasha and Mikey had fended them off. They had managed to bag up most of my clothes and personal possessions and handed them to the embassy. I wasn't particularly worried about the material items; it was things like my letters and photos from family and friends, which were irreplaceable, that I really wanted.

I planned to use the money from the sale of the cells to pay Eva to see if she could finally get me released from this prolonged nightmare that seemed in some ways to be getting worse. I called her, and she told me that, as per our original plan, she had managed to arrange a deal with the judges in my case to reduce my sentence to six years. The cost was going to be $20,000 but none of it had to be paid up front. As long as I could show them the money was here in Ecuador in an account or cash, they would go ahead and reduce the sentence. I would then pay them once I was happy with everything. This sounded great. I already had $10,000 but needed the other $10,000 from the sale of the cells. This was my freedom we were talking about: surely Ruben wouldn't get in the way of that.

Not having a phone was proving both difficult and costly. I wondered if I could pay the gang to be permitted to have my own. My father was very worried about my having been transferred to this notoriously violent gang-controlled prison, and daunted by the prospect of having to shell out a few thousand dollars again to sort me out down here with a cell and everything while my cells in Quito were 'on the market'. I asked him to please cover the *ingresso* as that was the most pressing. I knew that once I had paid that promptly they would have faith and trust my word and I could buy myself time to get the money for the cell.

A couple of days later I presented Olea with the Western Union money transfer code. He was happy enough but now he had scented money he immediately enquired as to when I would be paying for a cell. He hadn't actually shown me a fully equipped cell yet. He told me to follow him to a cell that would probably be OK if I wanted it. Halfway down the wing, which was the bottom half of a two-storey building, he opened the door to a cell on the right. This was his 'office', he told me. It had everything in it: a large fridge-freezer, 32-inch TV on a wall-mounted bracket, a reasonable-looking mattress. It was also designed for one person to live in so, as he had previously explained, I could live on my own. When could the money be arranged, he asked again. This guy was persistent. I tried to explain the situation without giving too much away. We parted company, me feeling very much under pressure again. I now knew I was totally committed to buying this cell and that it needed to be asap.

I started spending time with the Bulgarian, Vasil. We would exercise together in the morning and evening with home-made weights – bars with concrete cast on to each end. I couldn't keep much in the cell I was living in because it would almost certainly go missing, so Vasil offered to look after anything I wanted kept safe. He told me of some of his experiences of massive gun battles between the police and the gangs, murders and all manner of torture. I was to some extent accustomed to such stories, but this was a whole new level of madness.

I would return to Chorito's cell to sleep but it was difficult with people knocking on the door 24/7. Chorito kept a rucksack full of drugs in the cell that you could smell from outside the room, it was that pungent. There was certainly nowhere to hide it. I thought, what do we do if the police come in to conduct a search? We are going to be in some serious shit if that happens. I didn't much fancy another sentence on top of the 12 years I already had, particularly not for something that wasn't mine. It was quite normal here for everyone who lived in a cell where contraband was found to be sentenced.

Chorito had by now grown to trust me and would send me on errands delivering large packages of *polvo* to the dealers on other wings. I would also help him with the selling in the evenings, sometimes to the wing upstairs, where a lot of foreigners and wealthy prisoners lived.

Los Cubanos' key bodyguards were mostly experienced contract killers on the street or ex-military, and nearly all of them had firearms training. They were frequently sentenced to 25 years without parole for murders, so didn't care at all about killing again. In the event of a murder, sometimes multiple murders, quite often it would have been sanctioned by the gang, so the guards were aware it was about to happen and would have been paid off in advance to turn a blind eye. If not, they would certainly be paid afterwards, with the added threat of their families and themselves being brutally slain should they decide to talk. One of the gang's favourite ploys was staging a suicide.

Olea wasn't in the gang's top tier, which was made up of three brothers, but as one of the main bosses he would usually be accompanied by ten to 20 gang members of his choosing from our wing. He would never leave the wing unless his group was with him. Even on the wing he would almost always be accompanied by three or four of the gang, all armed with guns and knives. At any minute intense violence could erupt without warning. I started to become attuned to the tension in the place; it was a feeling of anticipation that something awful was about to happen. And it was.

Every wing had spotters on the roof, one on each corner, again armed with handguns. It was their job to keep a close lookout for any members or groups of the opposing gang encroaching from the other half of the prison. The two gangs would exchange shots across the no man's land that separated the two halves of the prison on an almost daily basis. I think this was to some extent out of boredom rather than anything else.

The spotters also kept an eye out for the police in case they mounted a surprise search of the place. The gang prohibited anyone other than their members from going up there. It was also extremely dangerous because the police had the right to shoot you as it was viewed as attempted escape. I would quite often hear warning shots being discharged over the heads of people who had strayed too near the edge.

Not long before I arrived a prominent member of the gang had been shot dead on the roof by the police. This had sparked a 16-hour gun battle and siege, inmates against the police. I had seen the reports on the national news. Every single wing had chained shut the entrance gates and barricaded them with whatever they had to hand. They had then opened fire down the long passageway that ran the length of the prison. They unleashed everything they had. The battle only stopped when there was no more ammunition to be fired. The police dropped tear gas bombs from helicopters above the prison. Miraculously, no one was killed although several were injured. Vasil told me that when the police finally came in, he and his friend were petrified that they were just going to summarily execute everyone to make a point. They didn't, but they beat and tortured nearly everyone.

Because of their relationship with the guards, the gang members were also allowed off the wing they lived on when we were otherwise supposed to be locked in. The gates would officially be opened up just after the first count, which took place between 7.30am and 8.00am every day apart from Sunday, when it was 9.00am. You then had to be back on your wing at 5.00pm for the final count, after which they locked the wing but the cells were left open all night. We were of course supposed to be locked up in our cells but the gang had put in place an arrangement with the guards and director so that we were left alone. This applied to all the wings in the prison.

On the whole I saw very little of the guards. All they did, basically, was the count in the morning and the evening. They wouldn't intervene to break up a fight as it was just too dangerous for them. In fact, it was not unusual for them to assist the gang beating people and even go so far as killing them. I viewed them on the whole as other members of the gang, just with keys and uniforms.

There was no one to turn to for help in the event of a problem. If you complained to your embassy they would only call the director of the prison, who was being paid by the gang, and he would notify them that you were causing problems and tell them to silence you. However, sometimes trouble comes looking for you.

CHAPTER TWENTY
EXODUS

In January 2007, when I had been in prison for nearly eighteen months, Ecuador's newly elected president, Rafael Correa, took office. In his election campaign, he had promised to introduce various prison and law reforms in an attempt to sort out a system that had essentially come to a standstill.

The prison system had been placed in a state of emergency, thus giving the president executive powers. He reintroduced automatic release on bail if not sentenced within one year of arrest; the reintroduction of two for one, which basically meant you were released automatically after having served half of your sentence; and the reactivation of the *pre-libertad* system, which was akin to early release on parole – this could be applied for after having served two fifths of the total sentence.

The most important change for us foreigners was the introduction of the badly needed *indulto*, or presidential pardon, which was one of the very first things Correa did having gained power. The *indulto* would apply to anyone, foreign or national, who was captured with two kilograms and under of any drug, be it heroin, cocaine, cannabis or ecstasy. It would mean immediate release for those to whom it was applicable. Many foreigners would benefit from this and everyone was eagerly waiting to see if they might be able to go free much sooner than they had anticipated.

For the *indulto* to apply you had to be sentenced and the sentence had to be confirmed and executed. You couldn't be making any sort of appeal or awaiting repatriation. You had to have served ten per cent of the sentence and be a first time offender. The *indulto* only ran for one month and if you missed the time limit that was it. The lawyers were having a field day processing applications, charging anything from $200–$1,500 to complete the paperwork and file the application in the court. There was some flexibility with conditions such as the weight limit, as long as there were a few banknotes to back your word up. An example would be if the police had weighed the drugs in the packaging or wrappers. I saw a few cases where people had drugs weighing a total of 2,200 grams but still managed to get the *indulto* by saying the extra weight over the two kilograms was due to the packaging – and of course paying the judge.

I discussed with Eva the possibility of my being released on the *indulto*. In my case there were no drugs weighed as they were impregnated in the groundsheet of the tent. The police had weighed the whole tent instead of extracting the drugs, which I had wanted to do myself. If I had extracted the drugs and not listened to Eva then I would have gone free with the *indulto* after only two years as I knew there was less than two kilograms of cocaine within the rubber. But by this point the tent had been destroyed so it was no longer possible. I felt sick knowing that I was legally eligible to go free but couldn't. I had to sit and watch as hundreds and hundreds of people walked through the prison gates to freedom. There was nothing we could do. That decision not to extract the cocaine was to cost me so very, very dearly.

In total some 2,300 people, half of whom were foreign nationals, were released as a direct result of the 2007 *indulto*. Many of my friends were released. Some of the lucky ones had only been in prison a little over six months but fitted the criteria, so went free. There was a fantastic sense of optimism throughout the prison population. Nearly everyone felt as if they stood a good chance of going free. As far as the other laws went, towards the end of 2007 thousands of inmates were suddenly released within a month or so. Along with the 2,300 who went free with the *indulto* there were probably over 5,000 more who went free under other laws that came into force at the same time. This was almost half the prison population going free.

I finally moved into my cell on Atenuado Abajo in the Peni at the end of 2007. Nearly every afternoon ten to 15 people would be collected from nearly every wing, taken to reception and released. We went from having some 150 people on the wing down to 65 or fewer. It was quite eerie, as if I had been forgotten. Overall the prison went from 8,000-plus inmates down to under 3,000 in a matter of months. At the end of this mass exodus the eight cells to the left of mine and five to the right were completely empty. I didn't have neighbours for three months! The wing, which was usually quite busy with people wandering around, was now completely dead and almost silent. I would stand there with the song 'Ghost Town' by The Specials running through my head.

I was walking down the long central corridor that ran the full length of the enormous prison connecting all the cells when I suddenly heard someone call my name. I turned to meet eyes with the face of none other than Tigre, with whom I had nearly had the serious fight with shortly after arriving on C wing.

'*Hola* Pieter. Remember me?' he asked grinning.

The grin vanished from his face instantly and I saw the look of a *sicario* appear in its place. 'Aw, no hard feelings my friend. I know it wasn't you who had me transferred, it was some other son of a bitch.' He offered me his hand so I took it and we were once again friends.

Tigre, it transpired, had been transferred all over the place as he just couldn't stay away from trouble.

'I am the boss's bodyguard now.' As he said this he raised his t-shirt to reveal the pistol grip butts of two handguns protruding from his jeans, much like a gun slinger in the wild west. 'Fuck me, Tigre. You want to watch you don't blow your own balls off with all the fire power you have there,' I joked.

Tigre laughed and all was good between us once more.

'You get any trouble, and I mean any, you call me straight away. No one can touch you here or they have Tigre to deal with.'

'Thanks my friend, that's really appreciated.' It was good to know I had backup if it was needed, and particularly from someone high up in the gang as well.

There was a great deal of debate about the effects of the law reforms within the country, with opinion divided. It certainly alleviated the overcrowding problem for a while. The president continued with his reforms, clearing the courts of a lot of the corrupt judges and officials, and training large numbers of new ones to replace them. His programme of prison-building won approval and the construction of an entire new prison estate began that was to replace all the old ones. The regional prisons were born. They were similar in design to prisons in America and extremely modern with a great deal of security. There were separate security zones from supermax secure through high, medium and low. The security was going to be handled by the police with the guards becoming mere custodians. Correa certainly stuck to his word and saw through the projects he had promised and reforms he had proposed. Ecuador slowly but surely began to improve as a country under his leadership; everyone was affected by the changes in one way or another. The rate at which people were leaving the prison began to balance out and the prisons slowly began to fill again; many new faces and a few of the old came back again. It wasn't long before overcrowding began to be an issue once more.

CHAPTER TWENTY-ONE
THE LAST SUPPER

Something wasn't right in the wing. I had now spent enough time living in Ecuadorian prisons that I had begun to get a sense of when a problem might erupt. The normally buzzing wing was virtually deserted. Doors that would usually be open were shut fast. The only people I could see standing around were members of the Los Cubanos gang. Pairs of them could be seen talking in lowered voices and pointing at various doors. Some were gathered around the entrance gate. They were planning something.

I went to the shop to buy ingredients for the spaghetti I was cooking. When I returned to my cell a couple of the gang were standing by the concrete bench in front of my room chatting. I jokingly asked them what the deal was: '*Que pasa?*' In response I received a cold stare and silence. This was unusual as they were normally quite talkative. Now I knew for sure there was a problem.

My cell was midway down the wing on the right coming from the central passageway that separated the 26 wings down the middle, 13 each side. There were about 125 inmates on the wing at this time. Even though it was run by Los Cubanos the power structure was complicated by the presence of some 30 members of another gang called Los Choneros.

This infamous gang originated from a small town called Chone, near the port of Manta in the Manabí province, hence the name. They ruthlessly controlled the area and had done for many years. The gang had come into existence after blood feuds between families spiralled out of control, leading to hundreds of murders and disappearances. They were also renowned contract killers. In particular, they worked as 'cleaners' for the police, contracted to kill criminals, or for opposing gangs and drug cartels to carry out assassinations. For years, their area of control had been expanding and had rubbed up against other gangs in neighbouring cities impinging on their turf, leading to battles for control of the drug trade, prostitution, arms dealing, robbery, extortion and basically any form of crime.

The city of Guayaquil in which the penitentiary sits is the largest city in Ecuador, with a bigger population than Quito. It is the country's principal port and thus also the main exit route for the tons and tons of cocaine heading all over the world by boat and container. These shipments are destined for Central America and countries such as Spain, Holland, Russia and Britain. The drugs are often concealed in shipments of bananas or other tropical fruit, which Ecuador produces in vast quantities. The battle for control of this trade and the exit route is fierce and ruthlessly enforced.

The city is controlled by several street gangs from different areas and this was also reflected in the prison, with the power roughly split in half. One half was controlled by Los Cubanos and the other by Los Rusos, along with a couple of smaller gangs. Los Cubanos were headed by three brothers, one of whom, the head of the gang, was nicknamed

Cubano. The other two brothers were Caiman and Matria. They originated from an area in the south of the city called Guasmo. This is a notorious and extremely dangerous gang-controlled area over which they held sway even from behind the walls of the prison.

The Rusos (none of them are even vaguely Russian) were headed by two brothers. They also controlled a swathe of the city, an area in the north called Duran. These two gangs were deadly enemies who often clashed over control of turf for the sale of drugs. These clashes would frequently result in deaths, and the daily papers would usually dedicate their first eight or nine pages to the carnage and aftermath.

Into this volatile mix in the Atenuado Abajo wing landed the 30 Choneros, following their arrests on murder charges. I arrived shortly after them.

Los Choneros were almost looked upon as guests by Los Cubanos into whose territory they had involuntarily strayed. Los Choneros were not interested in becoming involved in the politics of the prison or the business deals of the two gangs – a sensible decision.

However, as usual with money or power, trouble was in the post. The tension had been slowly building up between Los Cubanos and Los Choneros over a period of months, caused mainly by the inter-gang killings that had taken place in the streets. Certain members of the different gangs were seeking revenge.

At this point one of the bosses of Los Cubanos, the man I knew from Quito, whose name was Coyote, was due to be released. Coyote had a great deal of influence in the prison as he was a large-scale international drug trafficker and also came from Guasmo, the same area as the three brothers who headed up Los Cubanos. The brothers ran their half of the penitentiary in conjunction with Coyote's help, as he was their main supply of cocaine for the prison and most likely a good deal of the other drugs coming in as well. He had decided that it would be a good idea if the power was split between Los Choneros and Los Cubanos.

Of the three brothers only Caiman remained in the prison in Guayaquil, as Cubano had been transferred to Quito in a bid by the authorities to weaken the gang's control. Divide and rule. Matria had managed to escape from the penitentiary some years before in a daring plan that saw 16 people flee. They did so using speedboats to travel down the river that passes the prison and then out to sea and away into the night.

The job of securing the gang's interests in the penitentiary thus fell to Caiman. He did not like the idea of his fiefdom being split and of perhaps ultimately losing control of the entire place. He set about secretly planning the murders of the heads of Los Choneros in order to eliminate the threat once and for all. Caiman's principal target was the leader of the gang, whose name was Jorge Luis Zambrano, or JL as everybody called him. He then intended to murder JL's brother Carlos and a couple of the others who were key members.

I was very friendly with JL's brother Carlos, who lived in the cell directly in front of mine. We spent quite a bit of time together talking about all manner of things, from politics to football, just having a laugh in general. He loved to cook so we would prepare meals between us, him showing me Ecuadorian recipes and me showing him European ones. At the weekends, we would quite often have a few drinks and a party, which was always a welcome break from the stress of being confined in a ticking time bomb. His brother JL was also a great guy (at least with me), though more aloof and somewhat cold and emotionless. When he was arrested at the age of 26 it was reckoned that JL had killed more than 85 people.

One day I was sitting in my cell talking on the phone to a good friend of mine in England when in walked one of Los Choneros, whose nickname was Tiny. He was of course the size of a silverback gorilla. I explained to my friend that Tiny had just walked in and that he was a member of a gang of contract killers. My friend, who had spent time in prison in England, asked me a couple of questions about the crimes the gang were alleged to have committed. Tiny was all too happy to elaborate on what they had done and confirmed that JL had indeed killed 85 people, an astronomical number, with his own hands. He had also given orders for the killing of many more.

It was noticeable that Los Choneros were well-educated individuals, generally from good backgrounds. In comparison, Los Cubanos were still basically a street gang and tended to come from poorer backgrounds. They were more thugs and thieves who didn't have a lot of style. The clash between the two brought new meaning to the phrase 'class war'.

For a couple of weeks in the lead-up to 9 October, a group of guys had been gradually moved on to our wing from another wing called C Alto. This was where practically all the drugs coming into the prison would be processed, packaged and distributed. All of these new guys were fiercely loyal members of Los Cubanos, virtually all of them serving sentences of 16 to 25 years with no chance of parole. Most of them had been sentenced for multiple murders, manslaughter and armed robbery. Nearly all of them smoked crack or sniffed cocaine daily, which made them very wired and aggressive. This was seen as a move to re-establish control and influence over the wing – which was now effectively being run by Los Choneros.

I had been warned that there was quite possibly going to be an attempt to kill JL and several other gang members in one go. I was told to be very careful and remain alert to anything strange, especially as I was living smack bang in the middle of the wing and directly in front of JL's brother Carlos. Los Choneros had put me in charge of selling all the cocaine on our wing and the wing upstairs. I had the sole licence to deal coke, and worked in conjunction with Los Cubanos, who supplied the cocaine already packaged. This meant I had the backup of Los Choneros but also to some extent Los Cubanos. My friendship with both groups put me in a unique position. On the one hand, I was a foreigner and not viewed as a threat to anyone. I was also generating money that was going into their pockets. So, as I was an income stream, to some extent this meant they would protect me. However, it also placed me in the middle of the conflict. I was aware that I walked a tight-rope over the raging rapids of gang warfare.

We had been having quite a good time of it doing what we wanted and in a fairly relaxed atmosphere under the influence of Los Choneros. They had stopped the extortion, which used to happen a lot while Los Cubanos were in charge. The wing had become generally more ordered and calmer, which made it a lot more bearable. All this was about to change drastically.

My German friend Dieter and I were drinking a few glasses of home-made wine while we cooked spaghetti Bolognese in my room. I commented to Dieter that it was so quiet, with so many cell doors closed, that it felt strange, but he seemed not to have noticed and shrugged it off.

By around 9pm he and I were feeling fairly cheery, the Bolognese was simmering away smelling lovely and all seemed well. I popped down to one of my Los Choneros friends Gato's cell to get a plate as I'd promised him some food. As I approached the room, seven or eight of Los Choneros were clustered by the main entrance, sitting on the benches in front of the shop. There was a new boss on the wing who Caiman had placed in charge, following the release of Olea, supposedly to assist JL. He was a tall, well-built black guy whose nickname was Polilla, which in Spanish means moth. I had also become friendly with him since his arrival on the wing with the other new men. As I approached them and the shop, Polilla, who was sitting in the middle of them all, raised his arm and called out hello, along with a few of the others. All very friendly, but everyone here wore masks.

I knocked on the door of Gato's room and he answered as normal, cheery as ever; he was a friendly type, always smiling and joking around. He was just passing the evening with a couple of friends watching TV. He invited me in and went to get a plate from the kitchen. When he came back he showed me a picture of *The Last Supper* by da Vinci, which he had just had framed and now took pride of place on the wall of the cell. The frame was made of teak carved with a floral design and then waxed and polished to a high shine. I asked if he could introduce me to the person who made it as I wanted to commission one for Margarita. Even though she was evangelical and they weren't supposed to have images of Christ I knew she would still like it as a gift.

Ten minutes later I was walking back to Gato with his plate of spaghetti. As I approached I could see Polilla and his group were still sitting by the gate. I knocked on Gato's door with my back to the gang. Gato opened the door and thanked me for the food and I turned to head back to my cell. As I turned there was an explosion from my right and Gato's head snapped back. The plate of spaghetti flew into the air, covering the walls, along with Gato's blood and brain matter as he collapsed backwards into his cell. In a split second my legs were propelling me towards my cell as further shots rang out and the adrenalin surged through me. I hurled myself through the doorway and into the room.

Dieter was on his feet with a look of shock on his face. He was a veteran of several gun battles and assassinations and went to stick his head out the door to see what was happening. Unbelievable I know, but gunshots were so commonplace that you almost became used to them. I grabbed him back from the doorway and had to reach out in order to pull the door shut, as they all opened outwards, thus exposing myself to gunfire. By now all hell had broken loose. I didn't even look, I just grabbed the handle of the wooden door and slammed it shut, bolting and locking it from the inside. It was a reasonably thick, solid door and I judged that it would withstand most bullets. Many of the doors on the wing had a space directly above them, which was there so you could install air con. However, I had made sure mine was bricked up and concreted over in order to stop anyone getting into the cell this way, as I had seen it done before. I had witnessed hand grenades and petrol bombs being thrown into cells through the gap as well. You can imagine the effect a hand grenade has on anyone in such a small and confined space. The intention of a petrol bomb was to force you out of the cell so you could be attacked.

Now that we were locked in the cell I grabbed the largest kitchen knife I had, my Tramontina 12-inch blade, and put my back to the wall to the left-hand side of the door facing into the cell. I figured if anyone broke through the door I would swing the knife back at exactly chest height as they entered and hopefully score a direct hit on the heart. I told Dieter to get behind the low dividing wall that separated the seating area from the kitchen/shower area in case any bullets came through the door and told him to keep an eye on the window, which was very large, so horribly vulnerable to attack. In quite a few cells people had built wooden shutters that they would drop down at night or even in the day in case of attack. Mine were raised at this point because of the heat from the cooking and I didn't feel like risking moving in order to shut them.

By now there were dozens of gunshots ringing out, from all different calibres of handgun. We could make out the repercussions of several 9mms, a couple of .38s and one or two .45s that sounded like cannons going off in such a confined space. We could hear the footsteps and cries of people running for their lives up and down the wing. Obviously, no one would open a door in the middle of all this. I pitied the people trapped out in the middle of the gunfire with nowhere to run. There was the occasional crash of the fridges and freezers dotted about the wing hitting the ground as they were turned over to use as barriers. It was terrifying listening to this cacophony of destruction taking place just the other side of two inches of hardwood. Even more terrifying was the fact that we had no firearms in the room at the time with which to defend ourselves.

After 45 minutes of almost continual gunfire there were signs that the pandemonium was beginning to calm. Then we heard JL shouting from the chapel/kitchen end of the wing.

'You motherfuckers, we've got your motherfucking black boss now and we are going to blow his fucking brains out. You're nothing without your black cunt of a drug-addicted boss.'

There were two gunshots and we could hear Polilla crying out in pain, begging for his life, saying he had a family and two young kids – both of whom I had met on visits. This went on for a good half an hour with more shouting and screaming between the two factions as they insulted each other and their families.

171

I then heard JL's voice cut through the din: 'That's it, this motherfucker is a dead man. You're nothing without this piece of shit.' Polilla was crying and begging JL not to kill him, that he was sorry. Two more shots rang out and then silence for a moment. Polilla's suffering was over. The moth had flown too close to the flame and was burnt.

'Now you see you cocksuckers, your boss is dead. We got your black cunt of a boss and now he's fucking dead just like the rest of you are going to be. We're going to kill all your families outside in the street and then you last so you see your families die while you're locked in here with us,' JL shouted.

The gunshots carried on, interspersed by the detonation of the odd hand grenade, which in an enclosed space is indescribably loud and truly terrifying because they are so indiscriminate in the damage they cause. My door started receiving impacts that sounded like bullets hitting it, or possibly the debris that was flying around – or someone trying to get into the room. The walls in the corridor were lined up to halfway with ceramic tiles, many of which I could hear falling off and smashing on the floor as they were hit by bullets.

In between the repeated bangs on my door I could also hear voices directly outside discussing trying to kill someone, and then the sound of guns being reloaded. I was numb with fear, and Dieter looked it too. I really started to think that my time on this earth was severely limited and that my contract with my maker was well and truly nullified. Then there was the unmistakeable rapid-fire staccato sound of an Uzi machine pistol being discharged, quickly followed by rapid footsteps as people ran for cover. Whoever had the Uzi let go three or four clips of ammunition in volleys of bullets that sprayed the wing with lead.

Where the fuck were the police, you're probably saying. Let me tell you: I was saying exactly the bloody same thing. When was this going to end? When would they intervene? This had already been going on for over an hour. How much longer could it possibly go on for without the authorities getting involved?

By now it had died down a fair bit and we could only hear the voice of one guy, Santiago, nicknamed Monta la Burra. He was an ex-marine imprisoned for the murder of three policemen and extremely dangerous. He was the right-hand man and bodyguard to Caiman. Santiago was now walking up and down the wing discharging a revolver, probably a .38, while shouting insults. We could hear the empty shell casings tinkling on to the floor as he reloaded the gun and then started shooting again. He was screaming and shouting.

'Fuck you Choneros, this is my wing now. You killed Polilla you motherfuckers but you couldn't kill me, fuck you. Come out and I'll kill all of you cocksuckers. I killed your friend Gato. Come out JL, you pussy, and I'll fucking kill you too and your fat fuck of a brother.'

It was at this point that I worked out what the banging on the door had been. It had been caused by Carlos in the cell opposite hurling pots, pans, plates and anything else he could out of the space above the door in an attempt to hit Santiago in the head. He must have run out of ammunition and was literally throwing everything but the kitchen sink at him.

After more than two hours we finally heard the crackle of police radios from the exterior of the building as they encircled the wing. This was equally bowel-churning, if not more so because there was no way of avoiding what was coming.

173

We knew what sort of treatment we could expect at the hands of the police. At the very least all the inmates were in for a beating; at worst some of us would be tortured or even executed on the spot.

Up until now Dieter and I had both remained uninjured, amazingly enough, apart from a loss of hearing in my right ear from the sound of the first shot that had destroyed Gato's head in front of my eyes. We knew from the conversations we could hear that at least two people were dead. People were calling over from the wing behind ours, which was where Caiman lived, asking what was happening, and people in our wing were giving them a running commentary and body count. Caiman's soldiers were shouting over progress reports to the commander of the gang. Basically it was one corpse a side with a lot of injured as well, but the main target of the attack, JL, was unscathed. The attackers were none too pleased about that as he was one they really wanted dead. They also knew that they had stirred up a hornets' nest that would never again sleep.

We heard the guy in the cell to the right of mine enter his room, lock the door and start breaking up a gun to dispose of it before the police arrived. After he'd broken the pistol down into the smallest possible pieces, we heard him getting rid of it down the drain that ran under the back of all the cells. He was one of the killers who had been brought in to carry out the assassinations. To look at him you would never have guessed he was a cold-blooded killer, but then the most unassuming inmates were quite often the most dangerous. As he was breaking the gun up he was shouting to another guy, who was in the cell to the other side of me, telling him who he had shot and what he planned to say should the police pull him out for questioning.

I set about hiding items such as my knife, iron bars, and other bits and pieces in preparation for the entrance of the police. We were now going to have to open the door to a scene of devastation and carnage, plus I knew that as the police would view everyone as a potential threat and would not hesitate to shoot anyone who flicked an eyelid, they were going to be highly strung. One wrong move could mean death.

The police entered the wing, shouting, '*Abre las puertas, todo por afuera, al piso, al piso*' – 'open the doors, everyone out, on the floor.'

I opened the door slowly and Dieter and I emerged into the wing hesitantly. I first looked left towards Gato's cell. Wall tiles and debris were scattered all over the floor, as well as pots and pans outside my door where Carlos had been trying to pelt Santiago. I could see Gato's feet sticking out of the door way.

There was another shape lying in the entrance to the wing by the main gate, which later turned out to be that of a guy nicknamed Tropico. He was one of the most unhinged, psychopathic men I have I ever had the misfortune to meet, and I met a few in my years of prison. He had once spent the weekend in a tomb complete with skeleton, smoking crack, taking mushrooms and communicating with the dead. It later emerged that he had been stationed at the gate where he acted as a lookout for Los Cubanos in order to alert the wing if the police were coming in to do a search. He also held the key to the padlock that secured the chain around the wrought-iron gate in order to delay the entry of the authorities in the event of a raid. Los Choneros had a serious grievance with Tropico after he slashed the cook, who happened to be one of their friends, with a large kitchen knife.

I later found out that upon hearing the shots that had killed Gato, JL had come bursting out of his cell with a 9mm in one hand and a 45mm Colt automatic in the other. The first person he shot was Tropico, as he was the nearest and a very real threat. The bullets had ripped right through his emaciated torso, taking a good part of his colon and spleen with them. Tropico lay bleeding on the floor for the whole two hours of the gunfight. JL had then, with the help of Manuco, another Choneros, between them engaged nine or ten of Los Cubanos in a running battle up and down the wing. They had somehow managed to corner or capture Polilla, the boss of Los Cubanos on our wing, in the entranceway to the exercise yard, which was basically a space the width of a cell but open, with a barred gate leading to the yard. They had shot him twice in the stomach and disarmed him, which is the point at which we heard JL shouting that they had captured him and were going to kill him. They finally did so after 45 minutes of Polilla begging for his life. A further two shots to the head silenced him for ever.

Within seconds of stepping out of my cell the police were on me, screaming and shouting, forcing me to the ground as they were doing to others. They had also begun to kick and punch people while waving their M16 assault rifles around and brandishing handguns. It was a case of lie down on the floor and cover your head as best you could and wait for the inevitable beating, which they had already started meting out to the people on the ground nearer to the mess that used to be Polilla.

People were crying and begging the police not to torture or kill them. The police were screaming at everybody, asking them who had been in the gunfight and who was responsible for the two corpses. I could hear someone being tortured in a cell by some police officers, who were subjecting the man to a *submarino* as the locals called it. Drowning in a bucket of water, or whatever was available. I could hear the police telling their colleagues to hold the guy under for longer and to 'kill this motherfucker'.

The beatings were progressing systematically from the far end of the wing, working down in our direction. The police liked to use of a piece of wood, or the metal Stilsons wrenches used to cut locks or chains. These could inflict serious injury and even kill you if you were caught on the head too hard or at the wrong angle. There were police officers marching up and down keeping everyone under control and telling everybody to look down and not to move unless they wanted a kick in the head.

I was surprised to hear one of Los Choneros get up and start pointing out the members of Los Cubanos who had been responsible for the attack. I suppose, when you think about it reasonably, they had only defended themselves whereas Los Cubanos had proactively tried to kill them, and Los Choneros wanted to get the hell off the wing. One of their good friends had been slain right in front of me. They couldn't very well stay on the same wing as the people who had just tried to kill them all. It was now open season; war had officially been declared.

When the police got to Santiago, who had killed Gato, they dragged him screaming and crying into a cell, telling him they were sick of his shit and were going to execute him then and there. We heard a couple of heavy-calibre shots come from the cell and assumed that was it, but we then heard him crying again as they dragged him off for questioning at the fiscal's office. The police had reached where Dieter and I lay on the floor. We were both searched roughly for weapons or phones and then kicked a few times in the ribs. I also caught a boot in the back of the head. It could have been worse.

After more than an hour face down on the cold floor I was starting to shiver and ache from the beating and from lying prone with my arms up around my head. We could hear the crime scene analysts discussing what had happened and recording evidence. They were collecting up the guns and shell casings they could find, and prising bullets from walls and doors.

They dragged Gato's body, and then Polilla's, out of the wing by their legs, right past our heads, along the length of the wing. I will never forget the sound of the bodies slick with blood sliding past, disturbing the debris on the ground as they went. I looked up briefly as Gato's body was dragged past, the guy who had a couple of hours earlier asked me for a plate of spaghetti. His eyes were at funny angles in his frozen face and his arms dragged along the floor behind him, leaving a trail of dark blood. One of the policemen commented on how big and fat a guy he was, as if they were moving the carcass of a cow.

'*Levantate! levantate*! Get up! Get up! Everybody move it.' After two hours the police were moving us. We didn't know what was going to happen next or where we were going. They pushed, shoved and herded us towards the exit to the exercise yard and I thought we were being taken right out into the yard, as had happened so many times before during searches. I was wrong on this occasion. I reached the exit, where there was a congealing pool of Polilla's blood some two centimetres deep, dark red, with the light reflecting off the surface. The police were forcing us all to stand in this tiny space meant to accommodate two people. Everyone already in there was trying to avoid standing in Polilla's cooling pond of blood but it was starting to get full. At this time, there were some 130 people on the wing and the police wanted us all in this space. I walked into the gore, standing there while my friend's blood slowly soaked into my trainers and through

to my feet. The rest of the people coming in followed suit –
they had no choice. They crammed all 130 or so of us into
this blood-drenched space. The metallic sweet smell filled
everyone's lungs.

I thought, this is it, we are going to be slaughtered in this
small space on this warm Ecuadorian night, that now felt so
very cold. The police began shouting at us again. I expected
bullets to start ripping through us but instead people started
filing out and breaking into a jog while the police stood there
with a cat-o'-nine-tails whipping as many of us as they could
hit, as we darted out like frightened cattle. We went into the
area of the wing that was used as the chapel and kitchen. As
I entered this area I could see men's faces in shock, wild-
eyed, looking at me. I actually smiled and laughed in – slightly
deranged – relief that the nightmare was over. I felt bad for
smiling but I couldn't help it. But what I hadn't realised was
that it wasn't over yet.

The head of the guards came into the chapel and told us
all to sit down. What had happened had happened, he said,
and it was over now and he didn't want any repeats. So did
anyone want to leave the wing who maybe had 'a problem'
with Los Cubanos? At this point the remaining Choneros
stood up and left, about ten of them. He then asked if anyone
felt unsafe; if so they could leave as well. I thought about it for
a minute as I had been very good friends with Los Choneros
and wasn't sure how Los Cubanos would now view me, but in
the end I thought, fuck it, I'm going to stay. I sat tight.

CHAPTER TWENTY-TWO
THREE BLIND MICE

Los Choneros were gone. They had all been moved to the largest wing in the prison, called San Maritano. We were all put in our cells and told to close the doors and stay there. Dieter, my German friend who had sat through the drama with me, returned to his room, leaving me alone with my thoughts. The only people permitted to be outside their cells on the wing were those members of Los Cubanos who remained, the rest having been taken either to the police station for questioning or to hospital with bullet wounds.

The bell rang at around 8am as usual and everyone emerged from their cells somewhat cautiously, half-expecting people to start trading lead for breakfast. The wing was a scene of devastation. Fridge and freezer units still lay where they had been used as cover, and broken wall tiles and smashed plates littered the floor and crunched underfoot as we walked down the wing. There were bullet holes all over the place in the doors and walls.

With the count completed, the gang members called everyone around them. They explained that they had 'bravely risked their lives fending off Los Choneros who were bad people, hell-bent on killing us all.' I held my tongue but was seething underneath. They were talking about my friends, who I knew very well were much better people than any of this lot. Now Los Choneros were gone the wing was going to revert to one of extortion and bullying by the gang members. They instructed everyone to go back to their cells and stay in them until told to do otherwise. Whenever this had happened before it usually meant something bad was about to take place and they didn't want anyone to witness it. I knew there was going to be a backlash from the gang members and that they would use this as an excuse to even scores and target people they didn't like. I returned to my cell and bolted the door shut from the inside and waited.

It didn't take long before I heard the first door being banged on and then raised voices, followed very quickly by the noise of someone being hit. The gang members were shouting in Spanish, 'Get him out of here, off the wing, off the wing.' Oh God. That didn't sound good. I sat there waiting for them to reach my cell. I knew I would be seen as a target by Los Cubanos, firstly because of how friendly I was with Los Choneros and secondly because I was a foreigner. A couple of people told me to watch my back as well so I was really on edge. There was a knock on the door but not the hard one I had been anticipating. I hesitated a moment, wondering whether I should just ignore it and pretend to be asleep and hope they left. But then I took a deep breath and shouted, *'Quien es?'* – who is it?

'Soy Margarita,' came the reply.

My heart leapt for joy. I opened the door tentatively and there stood Margarita, as if someone really was looking down on me and had sent this angel to protect and watch over me. I welcomed her into the cell and quickly explained what had happened the previous night in the gunfight. She had seen the aftermath on the news – Gato's wife and family arriving at the prison to collect his body, absolutely distraught. As we were sitting talking, there was a very loud knock on the door and I could hear voices. Sure enough, there stood the skinny, nasty-looking member of Los Cubanos that we had nicknamed 'the Worm'. This guy was pure evil – just horrible. I stared him hard in the eye and asked what he wanted, letting him see that Margarita was in the cell. He paused and peered round my shoulder. I told him I was busy with a visit as he could clearly see. He thought twice about pushing his way in, then turned and looked at the rest of the group he had with him, who all reluctantly shook their heads. They walked off towards the next cell they intended to target.

The inmates respected the visitors highly and would generally not harm them, although there had been a couple of instances of people having been caught in crossfire and killed. Margarita was well aware of the politics of the gangs and had pretty much been guaranteed by Caiman and Coyote that she would never be harmed. I was ever so grateful that she had come to see me that day. She is very religious and would say that it was divine intervention, and it certainly felt like it. Thanks Margarita.

The Cubanos men went on their way, going round all the cells where people lived who had anything whatsoever to do with Los Choneros or came from that area on the coast, Manabí. They were kicking them out of the wing, stealing all their possessions and reselling their cells. They were like a pack of wild dogs descending on a half-dead animal. I'm certain that had Margarita not been there that day then I would have lost my cell and all my belongings. They were looking for the smallest excuse to rob people. I was so angry.

Margarita was well used to the bloodbaths that occurred with alarming frequency in the Peni. And the city of Guayaquil as a whole has a very high murder rate, and violence and gunfights are a daily occurrence. But she was still very brave to have come straight in the day after the shoot-out.

After Margarita left I came out of my cell to survey the scene and find out what was going on. I walked around, looking into the cells of my friends who had left or been thrown out of the wing. Everything of value had been stripped; doors stood wide open to now silent cells. I walked past the spot where Gato had been slain and also the exit to the exercise yard where Polilla had come to a bloody end. I recalled the gruesome images of the night before and it made me shudder. I was so lucky to be alive.

Later that day Santiago, aka Monta la Burra, arrived back on the wing, his arm bandaged and in a sling where he had been shot in both the shoulder and the hand. He was now in charge of the wing with the Worm, Pedro the 'priest' – who wasn't real priest but called himself one – and Cholo, his acting deputies or lieutenants, all of whom were thoroughly horrible people. Added to these key figures on the wing were many others helping them out running errands, delivering drugs and guns, providing security for the wing and filling many more roles. Tropico was not in fact dead, but in hospital in intensive care hovering between life and death. All those others injured were walking wounded, having been shot in the arms, legs, fingers and shoulders.

I went up to Santiago straight away to have a chat and see where I stood, as I didn't want any surprises popping up. I had always been on reasonably good terms with Santiago. As an ex-marine he had a large strong build. He told me how he had used me as cover to kill Gato when I had knocked on the door to deliver his plate of spaghetti Bolognese. I felt sick. The whole gunfight had begun basically because I had taken my friend a plate of food, thus costing him his life. Santiago confirmed what I had suspected – that had I entered the cell he may well have shot me in the back to get at Gato. I could tell he was watching my reactions in order to gauge with whom my loyalties lay. I played along and tried my best to convince him that the whole situation had come as a complete surprise to me, and that as a foreigner I really wasn't involved or a member of either gang. This was basically true, as I had friends in both gangs, but I had become far closer to JL's brother Carlos and thus the Choneros gang.

I asked Santiago outright whether or not they had a problem with me staying on the wing. He laughed and said that it was fine for me to stay, absolutely no problem at all, but I could see a couple of the other gang members exchanging looks between one another that made me wonder just how welcome I really was. I told Santiago I would be willing to help them out if I could, perhaps selling the cocaine on the wing or maybe some other role. He said he would think about it and let me know once the tension had died down a bit and things had returned to normal – or at least his idea of normal.

Over the next few days it became clear that the atmosphere on the wing was far more oppressive. Under Santiago's leadership the extortion of newly arrived foreigners became worse. Upon arrival, foreigners would be split up and allocated to different wings across the prison. The gangs had contacts among the guards and staff working in the offices, who would notify them when people arrived. They wanted to make sure they got the wealthiest foreigners allocated to their wing in order to extort the greatest amount of money possible from them. For this they would pay them a few hundred dollars, depending on how much they managed to squeeze out of the person.

The *ingresso* charge used to be a couple of thousand dollars for Europeans, North Americans, Canadians and anyone from rich countries. However, if there had been a lot of attention from the media and it had been reported that you were involved in a case with either large quantities of drugs or money, then they would target you and charge even more. The money would have to be sent by Western Union or MoneyGram to someone in the family of one of the gang members, such as a wife or girlfriend. Once collected, the money would be split, some going to the boss of the gang, a percentage to the prison staff and the remainder would be pocketed by the wing boss, with some also going to those who had assisted him in extorting the unlucky victim.

It was horrible seeing and hearing people being heavily tortured, particularly as you couldn't do much about it, as to interfere would mean you taking responsibility for that person's debt. The unsuspecting new foreigner would be greeted with great bonhomie and welcomed into a cell where a group of the gang would be waiting with guns, knives, machetes, iron bars, barrels of water, electrical cables and a rope tied in a noose. The door would be closed behind him and a few people stationed outside to prevent anyone entering or leaving.

The group would quickly make it very clear that they expected the victim to call their family, using the phone they provided, to arrange to have whatever amount of money they were being charged transferred over to the given name. This is where the problems would begin. Most people would just outright refuse because they had no way of paying. The whole reason they had ended up in the prison was because they had acted as a mule, carrying drugs, and they would only have been paid after delivery. They would have been doing this in the first place because they had no money and neither did their families. So how were they going to be able to pay the gang? The gang members didn't understand this and assumed that all westerners had huge bank balances and were loaded. They simply couldn't comprehend the fact that there is a great deal of poverty in Europe as well.

At this point the gang members would usually start by hitting and slapping the victim, threatening them with knives and machetes. If this didn't work, they would become progressively more violent. Their favourites were drowning, waterboarding or simple strangulation. The reason for this was, if it went too far, as it did on numerous occasions, and the person died, they could easily stage a suicide by hanging them up. When this happened, the police would come in, take a few photos and generally that would be the end of it. It was extremely disturbing being on the wing and knowing someone was being tortured just metres away. One morning a noise woke me at around five o'clock. I soon realised it was the sound of a guy from Slovakia being tortured by the Worm and a few others in a cell at the opposite end of the wing. It was chilling hearing it and makes me feel sick just remembering it. They had been torturing this guy for nearly a week, day and night, taking it in turns. There was nothing we could do. I told the British embassy but they said they were powerless. You couldn't talk to the guards or the director as they were all involved, and if you interfered you ran the risk of at least being tortured as well, if not killed. It was a horrendous situation.

One Spanish inmate who had just arrived was being tortured and he had broken free somehow and was running up and down the wing screaming for help, asking the guards at the gate to please help or take him off the wing. They just laughed and carried on watching as he ran up and down the wing, shouting, crying and begging. There was no escape and no help – no one was coming and there was no way out. Sometimes people killed themselves rather than endure the torture – they knew there was no way they were going to be able to arrange the money. The gang were relentless. Human life meant nothing to them. Their only interest was money.

It was so, so awful when things went wrong and someone ended up dead. They would sometimes chop the body up and dispose of it in the rubbish, down the drains, in the sewers, buried under concrete, fed to dogs. They would pay the guards to remove the person's name from the list so it was as if they had never existed. One gang member I knew was killed for trying to bring in drugs on the side, strictly against gang rules. They stabbed him to death and then dismembered him in a room in which I witnessed the bloody mess and the terrible smell. They then decided to try to burn the body in the same cell. All night a horrible, stinking smoke billowed out of the window and door as they slowly fed parts of him to the fire. It was like a horror film, except it was real and right in front of me. I will never forget it.

I tried to keep a low profile and stay off the radar as much as I possibly could. This did not work at all and in fact not only did I reappear on the radar, but I became a huge glowing beacon and the absolute focus of Santiago's attention. The reason behind this was crack cocaine.

No one in the prison was selling crack. Nowhere in the entire place. Like in Quito, they only sold *polvo*, which they liked to smoke in a joint with tobacco and marijuana – a very toxic combination they called *maduro*. I saw a huge opportunity to create a new market with all the foreigners as I had in Quito. I had tried to talk to Caiman and had also tried to explain my idea to the head of the drugs business. He took it on board and liked the idea as it signified large profits. But for some reason, unbeknown to me, they decided against the sale of crack, which I viewed as madness considering they were already selling *polvo*.

The problem that arose for me was with Santiago, who of an evening loved to smoke copious amounts of *maduro*. Santiago had imposed a curfew of 9pm on the wing. By this time everybody had to be in their cells with the doors shut and locked. A select few were allowed to remain out, usually just the other gang members. Everyone else had to remain in their cells until the following morning. If they needed something like drugs or alcohol then a runner, usually whoever was acting as security on the gate, would procure it for them at a small cost. Santiago liked it this way because of the extreme paranoia the combination of drugs he was consuming could frequently induce. I became involved in this because someone had whispered in Santiago's ear that I was a master chef when it came to cooking crack cocaine. He came to visit me early one evening, not long after taking control of the wing, and asked me whether I could prepare him some crack if he paid me in either drugs or cash. My door would also remain open all night and I was under his direct 'protection' in return for doing him this favour.

At first I thought this was a good deal. I very quickly realised though that I was in for a very nerve-racking next few months, or however long he stayed in charge of the wing. The problem was that Santiago consumed an incredible quantity of drugs every single night. Once everyone was locked up, he would come to my cell and hand me six or eight bags of cocaine that he wanted converted into crack cocaine.

He would then mix the gram or so of crack this produced into his joint. I remember the first time I watched Santiago prepare this. He would join together two rolling papers to make it larger, then break a cigarette into the papers and mix in three or four grams of marijuana. Next he would sprinkle three or four packs of the vile-smelling *polvo* into it. The final ingredient of this mammoth drugs cocktail was the gram or so of crack cocaine I had prepared. When I saw the amounts of each drug he was putting in I assumed he was going to share the joint with at least four or five other people as they normally did. But Santiago intended to smoke this all by himself.

He left the cell with his killer joint and I thought that I wouldn't see him until much later on, or maybe the next day, as this quantity of drugs would last the average person most of the night. But an hour later a sweating, shaky Santiago was at my door again with five or six more bags of cocaine, wanting me to make more crack. I couldn't believe it. I cautioned him that this was a lot to be consuming so quickly and explained that the crack I was making him was extremely strong and could easily cause him to have a heart attack. The fact that he was mixing it with huge amounts of other drugs would only exacerbate the risk. I now started to worry a great deal. I couldn't refuse to make it for him as he would turn on me and have me either tortured or thrown off the wing. If he became ill or died I would be instantly blamed and very probably killed shortly afterwards by the gang. I was in a really precarious position. Santiago would start smoking at ten o'clock every night, once everybody had been ordered back to their cells. He would then carry on right through until 3 or 4am and I would have to prepare him crack every hour. This lasted for nearly six months until he was transferred to another prison. Every time he left my cell with a handful of rocks I was worried he would die. It was six months of pure anxiety.

However, I now saw an opportunity to take revenge on Santiago for Gato's death. I had vowed never to teach anyone how to cook crack cocaine if they were a user, as this was the ultimate recipe for total disaster and personal destruction. In the past I had shown the recipe to a couple of people after they drove me mad pestering me. I still regret it to this day and feel very bad for having done so, as those people went on to become serious drug addicts, sold all their belongings for drugs, and ended up either dead or destitute. I hated myself for having been the direct cause of this. I therefore reserved this especially for my enemies. I would show Santiago and let him be the agent of his own destruction.

Of course, Santiago kept on hassling me to show him the process of making crack cocaine. I pretended to be reluctant and even explained why it was such a bad idea. I kept this up for a few weeks, but eventually 'bowed to pressure'. After all, I had warned him – it was his choice. I showed him exactly how to do it, hoping that once he knew how to cook it, he would make it for himself. I thought that his knowing how to do it himself would either lead to his death from a self-inflicted overdose, or else cause him to mess up the running of the wing and thereby land him in big trouble. If he dropped dead from an overdose it would also relieve me of my responsibility. However, I was wrong and he preferred me to keep on cooking the crack for him, so on went my own little nightmare as well.

It proved to be the latter – he messed up and became a turncoat, betraying Caiman's gang to join another one. I believe in fact that he joined Los Choneros, even though he had slain one of their members. Many others followed suit as they saw Los Choneros becoming ever more powerful in the country and Los Cubanos slowly disintegrating, as the prison authorities kept transferring all the bosses from the wings, including Santiago, and the upper echelon of gang members along with them to other prisons.

With the transfer of Santiago, the three gang members directly below him assumed joint control of the wing. I called them the Three Blind Mice. One was the Worm, the skinny guy I narrowly escaped from when he came to my cell after the shoot-out when Margarita was visiting me. The other two were Pedro the pretend priest, who would pray to God for forgiveness and lead services, then hours later be torturing some poor person just for the sake of a few hundred dollars and killing others who he disliked. The third was Cholo, who was particularly nasty and vindictive. He had no friends and was brutal and psychotic. I knew that everyone's life on this wing was now going to become a living hell, mine in particular as they really disliked me and viewed me as a possible threat. I would have to be extremely vigilant to avoid falling foul of one of the traps, the ones they called *cerebro* – mind games.

The Three Blind Mice called a wing meeting shortly after Santiago was transferred. At this meeting they told everyone they were now in charge of the wing and everybody had to respect them and do as they said or face severe punishment. The first changes they announced were the doubling in cost per week from five to ten dollars for both the *guardia* and the food, which was in fact provided to them for free. That meant that every Sunday, after the visitors had left, each and every person on the wing, nearly two hundred people, unless you were part of the gang, had to pay $20 without fail. Those who didn't or couldn't pay would be locked in the space that led out to the exercise yard until they came up with something or had to call their families. I would often bail out friends who didn't have money at that particular time as it was just so horrible the way they were treating their fellow inmates. If someone hadn't paid for several weeks they would be taken into a cell and subjected to torture for hours on end.

The next scheme they struck upon was that of charging everyone to 'help' them carry out improvements to the wing such as painting the walls – they got the paint free of charge but it would cost each of us a minimum of $20. Another was the replacing of the electrical cabling that ran the length of the wing on both sides. The most costly one was the purchase of a 50-inch plasma screen TV for the wing. Each person was expected to chip in $40 on top of the weekly $20. We got to watch the TV for less than a month before it mysteriously disappeared, only to materialise in Caiman's, the boss's, cell in the adjacent wing. He had knocked down the wall between two cells, forming one large one just for him. On the same wing he had also created a discotheque, by knocking down the wall between two more cells. It was complete with large speakers, a set of decks and a mixer, disco lights, a glitter ball revolving above a dance floor and a pole for pole dancers to perform on. Every weekend they would have raucous parties, drinking dozens of bottles of expensive whisky and consuming vast amounts of cocaine and marijuana. They would often bring in a group of girls with whom to party.

In the exercise yard they had constructed a quite impressive cockfighting ring in which on visit days inmates would pit their prize birds against one another. I used to see large wads of money being bet on fights and recall Coyote pulling out a bundle of some eight thousand dollars from his pocket and betting a thousand dollars on a fight against anyone who could match him. There were easily 50 cockerels in the exercise yard that people would treat better than their children.

They used to keep me awake at night cock-a-doodle-dooing every hour on the hour. First one would pipe up and I would bury my head in my pillow as all the rest joined in.

They called these joint collections 'collaborations', and the next one they applied to all the wings. They decided to buy large paddling pools that were a metre deep and you could easily fit 30 or more people in. Everyone was asked to pay $30. The pretence was that they were for the children who came in on visit days, so they could swim with their friends or parents. A lifeguard was appointed to keep watch over the children in case the parents wanted to spend some intimate time together in a cell. It did work well and proved to be very popular. The pools would be cleaned out and refilled before each visit day. On the intervening days the gang members would wallow in them while virtually everyone else, the ones who'd actually paid for the pools, were banned from using them.

I must admit though, there were a few occasions when I got to relax in one of the pools and it was very good in the intense heat of the equatorial sun. Once or twice I spent time in them with a couple of beautiful girls in bikinis while drinking whisky and having a party. It almost felt like I wasn't in prison for that brief time. I love being in water, especially with the sun warming my skin. Amazingly coloured dragonflies would buzz about overhead catching insects and sometimes land on my shoulder. We used to get swarms of them, into the thousands, flying around over the exercise yard, the most I have ever seen at one time. It was awesome to watch. It made me want to be one and fly away free.

Then, one afternoon, I was napping in my cell when I heard screams from the exercise yard just outside my window. I jolted awake and carefully crept to the window, which had a screen covering it through which I could see but not be seen. The yard that I overlooked was that of the opposite wing and was the key stronghold for the gang. At this moment some of the gang members were busy trying to drown a couple of youngish-looking inmates who must have done something to annoy them. There were two guards standing there, watching, laughing and even helping. This carried on for about half an hour until the gang members finally got the information they were after out of one of the inmates and they were dragged off to who knows where.

There were fairly large trees in most of the exercise yards that not only provided shade but also fruit, which you could eat if you were quick enough to get it before someone else. In our yard we had a large avocado tree some 10–12 metres high with lovely dark green leaves that provided a respite from the intense sun. It bore fruit twice a year and people awaited these seasons eagerly. We also had in other exercise yards orange, lemon and lime trees, and even a mango tree and a banana palm. There were various other tropical fruit trees too, which I was not familiar with, but they made the place somewhat more bearable than if it was just barren acres of concrete.

There was a large area of no man's land between the inner wall that enclosed all the wings in an elongated rectangle and the outer perimeter wall, of perhaps 300–400 metres in width. I thought this would be an ideal space in which to set up gardening plots where the inmates could cultivate vegetables, fruit and even keep a few animals. The growing conditions in Ecuador are amazing, almost perfect, with sun virtually all year round, rain, and fertile volcanic and fluvial soils, particularly in the sierras running down to the coast where I was now imprisoned.

The British ambassador, who lived in Guayaquil, owned a very successful agricultural company supplying the whole country. I knew the company would all too happily provide us with seeds, fertilisers, tools and pesticides to get the project going. It would have provided good work for the inmates, many of whom had agricultural backgrounds and were extremely knowledgeable. Furthermore, it would have meant we were producing a large percentage of the food needed by the prison, thus saving the government money and providing us with a much better diet. I spoke to Isabel, the honorary vice consul from the embassy, and she said they would certainly back me if I could get permission from the governor of the prison. I wrote up a project plan and summary and submitted it along with the signatures of well over 200 inmates in favour of the project, with a covering letter from Isabel voicing her support. That was the last I heard of it. I tried to follow up the proposal but just kept receiving the same answer: 'Wait, we are busy and will answer you soon.' This country ran on the motto 'relax, don't rush, we'll do it tomorrow'. *Mañana, mañana, mañana.* I used to find it so frustrating being told 'tomorrow' all the time. It appeared to us that the prison service was not really interested in the rehabilitation of inmates. We all found it very demoralising and somewhat depressing.

The fact that there weren't any courses, education or work exacerbated the problems within the prison tenfold as it meant the inmates had nothing to do other than occupy themselves doing what they knew best: crime and drug-taking. Due to having no other distractions, a lot of people easily fell in with the gangs as it provided them with work, excitement, an income, protection, the possibility to provide for their families and a host of other benefits. What would you do to survive? The prison system was in a mess and failing horrendously.

Now that Santiago had been transferred and the Three Blind Mice were in charge, I knew my days on the wing were numbered. I had to get out before they concocted some way of causing me trouble. I explained to my English friend Simon, who lived upstairs on Atenuado Alto wing, what was going on and asked him to speak to the boss of his wing about the possibility of my moving up and buying a cell there. I knew I would have to forfeit my cell down in Abajo wing but I was past caring. The final straw had come when they tried to extort money out of me.

I was sitting in my cell on a visit day with the door open when an attractive girl whom I vaguely knew came to the door and started talking to me. I was instantly suspicious as the gang regularly used girls as entrapment. She asked to come in and talk to me. We chatted for a while, various friends of mine called by and she left.

Shortly after all the visitors had gone, a group from the gang came to my cell and started trying to say I had kissed and touched the girl and even suggested I had slept with her. I instantly knew they were trying to extort me. Luckily I had seen it coming and had kept the door open and made sure that numerous people had seen we were not doing anything – we didn't even sit next to each other. The gang were insistent and it started to get heated, at which point I said I would involve the boss of the gang – Caiman at the time – whom I knew. This sent them into a panic and they wouldn't let me go near the gate to send a message. They started to back off a bit, knowing I could create serious problems for them. In the end, however, I had to call my family to send over some money just to put a stop to the situation, which was causing me a lot of stress. Thank goodness I was already set to transfer up to Atenuado Alto. The Three Blind Mice were powerless to do anything to stop the move as I had spoken to and paid the right people.

CHAPTER TWENTY-THREE
CHANGING PLACES

Mid September 2009. I bought the new cell upstairs in Atenuado Alto with the utmost caution as I didn't want the Three Blind Mice creating more problems for me.

I had spoken directly to the boss of the wing, who was nicknamed Media Vaca or 'Half Cow' because of his size and large head. He was quite friendly and all too happy to sell me a cell for $2,000. The cells on this wing were the best in the prison, like small penthouse suites with an en suite shower room with toilet, a kitchen and a cloakroom where you could hang your clothes and keep your bags, shoes and other belongings. Over a period of a week I had been slowly passing my smaller belongings upstairs to Simon for safe keeping. The larger things, such as the TV, air-conditioning unit and the mattress, I had to leave until last. I also didn't want the gang noticing that the room was emptying.

When the day of the move arrived, Media Vaca organised a couple of guys, as well as himself and Simon, to come down and help me move, but also to give a little support in case there was any trouble. I had to pay the *jefe de guia* to switch me over on the list and also to be present on the day. For this 'favour' I paid him $250. They all arrived outside my cell along with a few of my friends from downstairs. They had brought a trolley. I had arranged my belongings by the door ready to go, so we loaded them on quickly and I disappeared, much to the chagrin of the Worm, who arrived just as I was leaving, looking most upset indeed!

As we set off, the *jefe de guia* asked me who I was, and where exactly I had come from and when. It transpired that I was not listed on a single roll call of any wing or anywhere in the prison at all. The *jefe de guia* said he had no record of me in the prison – not photos, fingerprints, prison history, absolutely *nada*. With a sick feeling I realised that, had I known, I could in theory have just walked out of the place on a visit day. If I'd been challenged I could have said, 'Well show me my prison record, sentence and offence,' which of course they wouldn't have been able to do. It would have been worth a go. But it was too late. The *jefe de guia* said that at a future date he would have me brought over to the offices in order to be photographed and to sort out my file. I had been in this prison for two years they hadn't even known I was there. The place was so far out of control and in such disarray it was incredible.

I was warmly welcomed on to the new wing by several of the other foreigners with whom I was already acquainted. I immediately felt much more at home and far more relaxed. It was really great having Simon just a couple of doors down from me and various other English-speaking foreigners, with whom I was already friendly, nearby in other cells.

I would cook most evenings with groceries that Margarita brought in for me. Several of my friends would do the same so we often swapped food with each other, giving us plenty of variety. I would wander around visiting various people, having a chat for a bit, then moving on. I felt so much more at home on this wing and that omnipresent threat of the gang was far less up here.

However, good times never last long. The gang would sometimes come up in the day, ten or 20 of them, to check things were running smoothly or to mete out punishment to someone who had done something to upset them. The tension started to build after a while. There was a little group who had moved over from an area of the prison known as 'the Kitchen' after the three people were killed there. They wanted to take over the wing, or certainly the sale of drugs and alcohol.

One of the key players from the Kitchen was a guy nick-named Power. He was kind of Indian-looking with long dark hair, and quite unfriendly. He sold cocaine, *Polvo* and weed at lower prices and better quality than the gangs so naturally a lot of people began buying from him. Los Cubanos did not like this. They couldn't let this guy just do as he pleased on their turf. Power was defiant and took no heed of the stern warnings from the gang downstairs. There was talk of a gun battle coming, or even an assassination. People started to become wary of strangers on the wing or rooftop. There were open spaces near the ceiling that let in air and light, but could also be used by the gang to mount an attack on the wing by either firing guns through there or dropping hand grenades. The tension on the wing was tangible now as everyone knew an attack was imminent. No one would go near Power for fear of being caught in the crossfire.

The day the attack happened I was outside in the exercise yard, getting a bit of sun and fresh air, doing circuits of the yard. Power was also out there doing much the same. I was behind him and as he reached the steps that led up to the wing entrance I saw some movement on the roof. By now Power was roughly halfway up the stairs to the wing and I had carried on around the yard. Shots rang out at close proximity and I saw Power running with his hands over his head up the rest of the steps and another man who was behind him collapse on the steps. I felt something hit me in the back as I ducked. The shooter on the roof was lying stomach down, with his arm extended out over the steps, holding the gun and firing blindly without even looking where he was shooting.

I felt something warm on my back and thought, surely not, I can't have been shot as well. I gingerly ran my hand up under my T-shirt and felt blood. I followed up to around my shoulder blade, where I found the injury. It wasn't a bullet, but something had definitely hit me. Fuck! I waited until I was sure there was no more shooting, then went to the steps leading up to the wing. Here I encountered the man who had been behind Power. He was slumped on the ground with a pool of blood around him and, as far as I could see, gunshot wounds to the chest and arm. He was still breathing but had lost consciousness. I went on up the steps and found Power lying just inside the wing, with gunshot wounds to the arms, one in the stomach and another by his ribcage. He was still breathing but he too was unconscious. People were cautiously emerging from their cells now, to see the aftermath of the shooting, and some came to help. Someone had summoned the guards and police.

I said I thought I had been hit too and stripped my T-shirt off. A couple of people had a look at my back and confirmed it looked as if I might have been hit by a bullet fragment where one had ricocheted off the wall. A friend cleaned away the blood and pressed into the wound, which hurt a bit but not too much. He said there was something in there we would have to get out. I didn't want to go to hospital so had decided to get Carlos, a friend with some medical training, to remove the fragment for me. I told someone to get a pair of tweezers and some alcohol, not only for the wound but to drink, and three or four bags of cocaine to numb myself up a bit. After I'd drunk a good amount of whisky and sniffed several bags of coke my friend sterilised the wound with medical alcohol, which hurt more than the actual impact. I braced myself and he began fishing around in the wound trying to locate the bullet fragment. It didn't take long before I felt him slowly pull the fragment out and sterilise the wound once again.

Power was taken to hospital and then transferred to another wing. The second guy to be shot behind him had a miraculous escape. One of the bullet wounds to his chest had missed his heart by a matter of millimetres and passed out of his back without damaging any organs. The second bullet had lodged in his forearm. He was back on the wing the same evening, bandaged up. I couldn't believe it. His family took the prison authorities to court and in exchange for their silence he was quietly released a few months later, so it proved to be a blessing in disguise, even if a rather painful one!

After this event, virtually all the dealing stopped on the wing other than that authorised by Los Cubanos. I was in charge of selling the home-made alcohol distilled in the prison using sugar cane, yeast and rice. They called this *chambar* or *huanchaca*. I would buy ten or 20 gallons, which I would then decant into half-litre water bottles and conceal in the large hiding place I had in the closet. The previous owner of the cell had fitted a false ceiling in there and to access the space you swivelled the light fitting. You could fit some eighty bottles of whisky into this space, which was so large you could also hide drugs, phones and chargers, guns and other weapons. It was incredibly useful and had survived various thorough cell searches by the police.

It was really good being able to have my own phone once again and I kept it switched on 24 hours a day. The only place I could locate a signal in the cell was within the closet against the wall, where there must have been a reinforcing rod running through it that acted as an antenna. One morning at about 6.30, I was standing on a stool in the closet talking to my sister in Scotland when I heard a rumbling sound similar to that made by a plane flying low overhead or an approaching train. I knew what was coming and I asked my sister if she could hear the noise as the first shock waves passed through the building, nearly knocking me off my stool. It was a huge earthquake, measuring 7.2 on the Richter scale.

Earthquakes are a frequent occurrence in Ecuador, as it has numerous fault lines running through the country where tectonic plates are colliding and being forced upwards, creating its mountain ranges. There would normally be a couple of small tremors every month, measuring around 4.0 on the Richter scale. If these didn't occur, you knew that pressure was building up somewhere below your feet and would be released suddenly when the plates finally slipped with a huge jolt.

The strongest one I experienced was at 9.30 one evening when we were all locked in our wings with no way of getting out of the building. The guards were all outside the prison in their office, where they tended to pass the nights. As the first shock waves hit, travelling across the cell from right to left, my chair was rising and falling by a considerable amount. It felt like a fairground ride! All the lights went out and people came pouring out of their cells in a panic and shouting at the gate for the guards to get us out of here. Of course no one came. The guards weren't about to risk their lives for us. The power remained off for about two hours. We liked to imagine that there'd be a strong enough earthquake one day to split the prison in two, destroying the watchtowers and exterior walls, enabling everyone to escape into the night. I had heard of one instance in Peru where a town was destroyed by a strong earthquake. The prison literally split wide open and some 900 inmates managed to escape. Many, however, were also killed when the prison collapsed, and the majority of the escapees were soon recaptured.

Over a period of six months to a year quite a few corrupt police officers, military, politicians and one regional governor were allocated to our wing as it was viewed as a lot safer for them up here. I didn't like the fact that I was now on a wing with a whole bunch of ex-police and military. In British prisons, ex-police officers, corrupt or not, had to be placed on the protection wing as they weren't tolerated on ordinary wings. Their mentality and way of thinking is inherently different to that of most inmates. They tend to be of the general opinion that they have not committed any sort of criminal offence and still view the inmates around them as criminals to be looked down upon. It is of course complete hypocrisy for one criminal to look down on another because his brain is hard-wired to think like a policeman.

The ex-police and military combined on our wing numbered over 40. They started grouping together, dividing the wing, trying to take over and make our wing independent from the rest of the prison. The first steps they took were to inform on anyone they disliked, even fabricating lies in order to get them transferred either to other wings or out of the prison altogether. Anyone they suspected of having strong links to the gang they really targeted. The next step was trying to ban anyone from selling drugs that originated from the gang downstairs. I thought this was suicide considering what had happened to Power. They even went so far as trying to enforce an exercise regime and make everyone, including the foreigners, stand in the exercise yard while they raised the Ecuadorian flag, and sing the national anthem. This was a step too far. I point blank refused to sing the national anthem of Ecuador and also to salute their flag. This was becoming more of a dictatorship than a democracy. It was as if we were demonstrating the politics of Ecuador in a microcosm. A lot of people started to take umbrage at the behaviour of this merry band of men.

My patience completely snapped when a particular ex-policeman arrived on the wing from a horrendous case known as 'el caso Fybeca' only to be greeted by his fellow ex-policemen as a hero. The man in question was a captain of police who had been linked to the murders of eight inno-cent bystanders in the case of a robbery at a pharmacy and the disappearance of three others. The police had opened fire indiscriminately, killing several members of the public. He was also found guilty of carrying out contract killings and robberies. The part that really got me was the repeated rape of his 12-year-old daughter and a couple of other girls of similar age. He immediately started trying to lay down the law about how the wing should be run and to cause all manner of problems. At the count one morning, I overheard him talking to some of the other ex-police, bragging about the things he had done, and I lost my temper. I squared up to him and quietly told him, while staring him straight in the eye, that if he didn't shut the fuck up and stop causing problems I would kill him. A few of the others with him started to get involved and I said they would all get dealt with if they wanted a piece of me. I was livid.

They backed down and of course ran straight to the guard, who they told I had threatened them with a gun and that I should be taken off the wing. The guard came over and started giving me grief, but the *caporal* who was a friend of mine stepped in and got rid of the guard. From that day on I was pretty much enemies with most of the ex-police. They tried numerous times to create problems for me but never quite succeeded.

Their real aim was to take over the drugs trade in Atenuado Alto. It wasn't long before a couple of them were getting their friends in the police force to bring them in cocaine and weed. By now Los Cubanos were so weakened by the loss of their members who had been transferred to other prisons that they were having a hard time maintaining control. They decided it would be easier to negotiate some kind of deal, rather than lose the wing altogether. The gang had a meeting and agreed that our wing would from now on be independent. This meant people could bring in their own drugs but we weren't supposed to sell to people from the wings downstairs that were controlled by Los Cubanos. On the other hand, Los Cubanos still had the right to sell drugs and alcohol on our wing. Obviously, people from downstairs and other areas of the prison came to buy from us, but that was their choice. As long as we didn't actively seek customers from the wings controlled by the gang it was OK. It was a kind of peace treaty. Things were changing in the prison as a whole new era was coming.

CHAPTER TWENTY-FOUR
DIVISION OF THE GANGS

The government had realised that Guayaquil prison was completely out of control and they were no longer able to keep a lid on it and stop the public from finding out. I didn't tell my family much about what was going on to avoid worrying them. I never told my mother what I had been going through. I had hurt her enough already, so I painted a picture of a safe environment where the conditions were good.

The president himself, Rafael Correa, ordered the prison governor to regain control, split up the gangs, heighten security and restrict any goods whatsoever from coming into the prison in a bid to prevent contraband, and in particular firearms and ammunition, from coming in. This really didn't make much difference as it was the guards themselves, and sometimes even the police, who would drop off a couple of handguns and boxes of bullets in order to make themselves a very healthy profit. I recall the bosses displaying their new toys to me, such as Glock 19s with enough bullets to kill half the wing.

Finally, after another gunfight in the prison left two people dead, the prison governor acted. One evening hundreds of police officers and some military descended on the prison. They had a list with the names of all the key gang members on each wing including the boss, the main drug dealer and the gang members directly assisting the boss. The police went from wing to wing and dragged out all those named on the list. These people were handcuffed and led to waiting buses, then driven to a secure holding centre near the airport. All of this was being filmed by the press, who had been invited along.

Caiman, the remaining Los Cubanos brother and boss of the gang in the Peni, was number one on the list and was taken with all the others. The authorities had chartered a military aircraft to transport everyone to Quito. They broadcast pictures on the news of all the gang members on the plane handcuffed, shackled to the floor with hoods over their heads and ear mufflers on so that they couldn't speak to one another. There were a large number of military personnel on the plane, heavily armed. They flew them to Quito because they were absolutely certain that if they went by road the convoy would be attacked in a bid to set the gang free or possibly kill them. When they arrived in Quito they were transferred to the maximum-security wings of A and F in Garcia Moreno. Cubano, who was the overall head of Los Cubanos, was already on A wing, so they put his brother Caiman on F wing to keep them apart.

Around this time, a couple of people filmed a number of the guards receiving bribes and dealing drugs in conjunction with members of Los Cubanos. I saw them with a 'handy cam' in a cell on our wing. On the film, you can quite clearly see numerous guards walking up to a table where a gang member hands them various amounts of cash and one guard even hands a package of what is presumably drugs to an inmate. This recording was shown on the news in Ecuador and can still be found on YouTube. It resulted in the arrests of over 30 guards on corruption charges. Many more were questioned and several went on the run, fearing they were about to join the inmates on the wing but this time as prisoners.

This double whammy really rang the bell for Cubano's gang. Not only was nearly everyone worried about getting transferred to another prison miles from home, but the guards were now reluctant to bring in drugs and guns, not knowing if they would be the next ones to be filmed. The governor saw that his actions were beginning to have an impact so tightened the noose a little more by heavily restricting the flow of goods into the prison, such as food shopping and soft drinks, along with virtually everything else. This was annoying as it meant Margarita couldn't bring in shopping for me apart from on rare occasions.

The government had commissioned the building of a new super-high-security prison virtually next door to the penitentiary, intended to hold just 50 of the most dangerous prisoners in Ecuador. It was designed to be escape-proof and monitored everywhere by camera. It was quickly nicknamed 'la Roca' or 'the Rock', after Alcatraz in San Francisco Bay, which was supposedly unescapable.

I knew straight away that this was a recipe for disaster, having witnessed similar ideas put into practice in other countries. If you place the top 50 most influential and powerful criminals together in a tiny prison with guards who are notoriously corrupt, you will have fireworks eventually. Many of them were not only sworn enemies who loathed each other but also competitors in the drugs and firearms trades. The most notable arrivals were members of Los

Choneros, including JL. There were 20-plus of them, so they occupied nearly half the entire place. Then you had two of the Los Cubanos brothers, Cubano and Caiman, along with perhaps 15 to 20 of their gang. Oscar Caranqui, who I knew from Quito and who had tried to escape dressed as a police officer, was transferred there as well.

This did have the desired effect on the gangs, who were very much weakened by the loss of their leaders. It also served as a strong deterrent to anyone else who decided to pick up the reins where the others had left off. There were several articles in the country's press and bulletins on the news denouncing the poor level of human rights and basic standards in the Rock. They spent 23 hours a day locked up in the cells with just one hour of exercise in an internal covered courtyard with no natural light. There were no payphones and pretty much nothing was allowed in the cells. However, before long, the scent of dirty money wafting down the landings proved all too alluring for the guards' senses. Within six months of opening there had been several gunfights in this tiny toy prison. Cubano and Caiman were hit by bullets but survived. Oscar Caranqui was killed by an assassin with a gun. Both of these events made headline news throughout the country.

One evening I was in Simon's cell when a shock wave blew in the wooden shutters on the window, followed shortly afterwards by the noise of the explosion. Word quickly spread through the prison that someone had just launched an attack on *La Roca* in a bid to break out some of the inmates. There was a buzz of excitement as we heard the police sirens and the helicopter circling overhead. Everyone was rooting for whoever had managed to get out, hoping they got away. Unfortunately the huge explosion had only blown a hole in the exterior wall, not the interior one, so no one got out. We saw the news the next day with pictures of a gaping hole in *La Roca*'s wall and rubble strewn about all over the place. They had used either an RPG, as I had proposed in Quito, or plastic explosives.

A couple of brothers on the wing by the name of Martinez were big players in cocaine trafficking and had serious connections to FARC in Colombia. The deputy minister for defence, who was called Chauvin, was arrested in connection to their case but later cleared of all charges. He did however spend a good six months on the wing with us. The brothers Martinez were also in favour of making our wing completely independent. The final break from the control of Los Cubanos gang came with the arrival of a Colombian by the name of Esteban. He was alleged to have been involved in the supply and shipment of tons of cocaine to the Sinaloa cartel of Mexico, headed by Joaquin 'Chapo' Guzmán.

I had spotted an article in the reputable broadsheet newspaper *El Universo*. The article covered an entire page and explained in great detail how this Esteban was an informant working for the United States DEA (Drug Enforcement Agency), and was responsible for bringing about the arrests of several hundred people in villages in Peru involved in the growing and production of the coca paste that is then refined to make cocaine. This paste is transported by the ton up the jungle corridor that runs through Peru all the way up the edge of Ecuador on the eastern side to Colombia. It terminates in the Amazon jungle in Colombia, deep in FARC territory. In these lawless borderlands, the cocaine is refined in large laboratories hidden by the dense jungle canopy. From here it is transported to seaports in neighbouring countries such as Ecuador and Venezuela for onward shipment to nearly every country in the world where there is a market.

Esteban, as you can well imagine, was somewhat paranoid that his life might be cut short at the behest of his employers in the Sinaloa cartel before he caused any more damage with his loose lips. He undertook works to beef up the security of the wing using some of the money he had stashed away before his arrest. He had rolls of razor wire installed along the top of the wall that ran between our exercise yard and that of the wing downstairs. The gang now had to go past the guard on the gate to come into the wing and Esteban began paying them to not let anyone in who didn't live there. He also blocked all the spaces around the top of the wing with metal grids so no one could drop hand grenades or shoot at him from the roof. He was very careful when going outside the wing.

CHAPTER TWENTY-FIVE
TB

'**V**acunas, vacunas!'

Vaccinations. They would occasionally do mass vaccinations in prison. A team of healthcare workers from the Ministerio de Salud – like the UK's National Health Service, except nowhere near as good and hardly ever for free – would arrive and just inject everybody. It wasn't obligatory but there was a lot of pressure put on you to have these injections. I was extremely wary of these 'vaccinations' because you didn't really know what they were injecting you with, whether it would work or if you even needed it.

Many of the South Americans would be queuing up as they thought that anything for free was worth having, and many of them had never had vaccinations or inoculations against anything. I would normally refuse to have the injections, which would quite often result in heated arguments with other inmates of the wing, who viewed my refusal as a risk to them. They believed that if I didn't have the injection, whatever it may have been for, I would become ill and infect them. Of course I never did, until the one time I gave in and agreed to having an injection against tuberculosis, under threat of being expelled from the wing. This would have meant losing my cell and probably my possessions.

I was sure that coming from a European country I would have been vaccinated in childhood against such diseases as this. I tried to explain this to the *caporal* and others who were complaining about my refusal but they were having none of it.

'You either have the injection or face ejection!'

'Oh fuck it, go on then.'

I still intensely regret those words. In fact, I will do so for the rest of my life, which has undoubtedly been cut short as a result of having that one injection.

The healthcare staff asked if I was in good health and I said I was. At the time, I was fit and well built, weighing around 90kg. I couldn't remember the last time I had had a cough, let alone been seriously ill. The injection left a lot of people feeling a bit sick for a few days afterwards, which is probably normal. I thought nothing more of it and carried on with the daily fight for survival in the war zone that was the Peni.

About three months later I developed a cough, which I thought might have been the result of my occasional smoking of drugs (I have never been a cigarette smoker) so I immediately cut that out, but the cough intensified and I began to produce phlegm that wasn't the usual consistency. You know your own body and you know when something is wrong and something was definitely wrong this time. I bribed my way over to the healthcare centre and paid to see the doctor. Yeah, I know. Paid. Nothing was free in this place.

The doctor said, 'Oh, no need to panic. You have a throat infection. Nothing to worry about.'

He wrote me a prescription, which Margarita took to a pharmacy outside. In the meantime, the cough proceeded to worsen and the phlegm I was now struggling to cough up was strand-like with small balls in it and very hard. It smelled disgusting. This is a sign of serious infection. I was really starting to panic now as my famously large appetite was well below par and I was rapidly losing weight. I was also having terrible fevers or night sweats where I would wake up drenched after every sleep, be it daytime or night-time. These fevers were unlike any I had had before.

In the next six months, I probably lost 20kg. By now I was finding it difficult to walk upstairs without getting breathless. It was a nightmare. When I was young, I had been in the top five cross-country runners in my year at school, captain of the cricket team, hooker in the rugby team and a keen cyclist. Since then I'd kept up my fitness with years of gym training. I had been in good condition, and to now struggle up a set of stairs was destroying me. There was no way I could run even two steps. What the fuck was wrong?

Not only was my breathing now chronically bad, but my leg had also begun to swell up massively, from the ankle up, and also my foot. At first I thought it was an insect bite, as only one leg swelled, breaking veins in the process, but then the other leg started to do the same. I didn't have a clue what was happening to me and it seemed nor did anyone else. Surely after all these years of prison I wasn't going to die of a disease now?

The doctors didn't seem to be interested so my family, and the angelic Margarita who had seen the state I was in, put pressure on the embassy to act. After their repeated inter-ventions I was finally diagnosed with chronic and highly contagious TB. Had this happened in a British prison, I would have been placed in isolation immediately. Not in Ecuador. I was packed off back to my cell after being placed on an ever-growing list of prisoners infected post-injection. The healthcare centre informed me that I was lucky as the government had just started making the expensive TB medication free to all those infected. On one of my trips to the clinic I saw box upon box of medication piled high, so there must have been a large number of cases.

Just getting to the clinic was a real effort now as I could hardly walk because my breathing was so bad, added to which was the complication of both my legs being swollen to the size of an elephant's. I was refused a medical visit in my cell so it was an agonising battle to make my way there, choking and wheezing all the way, with someone supporting me.

The guards could see I was having problems getting about, so they would just count me in my cell from the doorway to save me from coming out. My friends undoubtedly saved my life on one occasion, when my fever ran out of control and I became incoherent and was hallucinating for three or four days. They kept me cooled down with ice packs and damp clothes. If they hadn't done that I would surely have died.

At the lowest point my weight dipped to just under 50kg, 40kg less than I had weighed previously. I didn't know where to turn or what to do. I felt trapped in my own personal hell within the living hell of the prison. I didn't want to talk to my family as I didn't want to worry them. I tried to make light of the situation, but I knew I was close to death. I was so certain my days were numbered that I wrote letters to my family and friends saying goodbye and apologising for all the trouble and anguish I had caused. I addressed them and gave them to the embassy to send in the event of my death.

My breathing deteriorated to such a point that I would wake up suffocating. I had to have a constant supply of inhalers and a loaded syringe of dexamethasone by my side at all times to open up my airways so I could breathe. I had taken to sleeping sitting upright to avoid choking, as every time I tried to sleep horizontally I would literally wake up dying because my bronchia were completely clogged with TB. I would be sitting on my bed in my cell alone, suffocating from the phlegm blocking my airways, unable even to call out for help. I had to will myself not to panic, to control my breathing and not die. My bladder and bowels would release uncontrollably, much the same as when someone is about to be killed. My body shook, all my muscles taut and my face blue, sometimes for hours locked in this battle between life and death, while everyday prison life carried on the other side of the door. This was worse than being shot, tortured or beaten.

The medication they gave me finally began to have some effect, although it was sporadic at best. I was given the correct retroviral pills maybe only three days a week. Sometimes I didn't receive them for weeks on end. This resulted in my developing a strain of TB that was multi-drug resistant. They increased the dosage from eight to 12 pills a day. These pills were some of the most disgusting I have ever taken and caused dizziness, aches, nausea and disorientation. During the worst period of my illness I didn't leave my cell for a year – not once: 365 days in a cell.

My lungs are scarred for life, I have been left with a post-TB cough that I will probably never get rid of and there is always the chance that the TB may flare up again. Being continually that close to death for such a prolonged time has really made me appreciate being alive, being able to breathe, walk, eat, talk – things most people take for granted. I am very much aware of how precious and delicate our lives actually are.

I still wonder whether we were used as test subjects to trial TB drugs on as the medication changed at least four times during the years I was taking it. The fact that so many people contracted TB after supposedly being inoculated against it was incredibly suspicious. Surely that's not right? I will never know or be able to get to the bottom of it, but I will forever live with the consequences – unlike several of my friends whose lives it claimed.

CHAPTER TWENTY-SIX
THE MOST PAINFUL LOSS

'Something's wrong. I can feel it.'

We always had that kind of a bond, she and I. We would call at exactly the same second, having not spoken in days. We would think of the same things, randomly, and come up with identical comments in conversation. She often knew if I was sick even when I wasn't around, and vice versa. So it was that day. Both my sister and I tried to phone my mother and, getting no answer, phoned her former long-term partner within an hour of each other, even though I hadn't spoken to him in years. He had rushed her to hospital that afternoon with a perforated stomach ulcer.

'But how is she?' I stammered, waiting for those dreaded, life-changing words to be uttered. They didn't come this time. She was alive. I wept tears so long held back. She's alive! I hardly heard the next sentences through my tears. He repeated them. She had received treatment very quickly, which is what had saved her life. They had operated and repaired her stomach. That wasn't the problem now.

'So what is it?' I cried, the cold fear rushing back through me, twisting my stomach. She had vomited while unconscious and had inhaled a large amount of vomit into her lungs, choking her. Again the doctors fought to save her and again they did, but she was now in an induced coma and the doctors were not hopeful that she would survive more than three or four days as she was so weak and her organs were shutting down. My world collapsed. I hardly dared ask the question, knowing what the answer was going to be. It always was the answer.

'Had she been drinking?'

'Yes.'

'And is that why she vomited and the cause of the stomach problem?'

'Yes.'

So it was the fucking alcohol that was killing her. It was always going to be linked to alcohol abuse in one way or another. She had had a drink problem for years, her preferred drink being whisky. She had started on this path to oblivion when I was young, five or six, maybe even earlier. She would change quite dramatically if she had been drinking, so much so it was almost as if she became another person. This other woman was not a happy individual, nor did she have much patience or sympathy. She would often become aggressive, even physically violent. She was angry and tearful, but worst of all were the horribly hurtful things that she would shout and scream at my young sister and me. We knew it was this other person ranting and that she would doubtless not remember those words the next day, but we could not forget. There they stuck like a painful thorn from a beautiful rose.

The person she really was cared for us both immensely, and would have done anything for us, and we in turn adored the real her. That was who we wanted to be with. The beautiful Cumbrian woman with long brown hair, so kind and caring. She loved to read and write, paint and draw. She used to love long walks in the countryside, but not so much lately; the damage from heavy smoking and drinking had made that difficult for her.

My sister Sarah had been on holiday with her boyfriend in the house in France when she heard the bad news, so she flew back as soon as she could to be at her side, to talk to her and hold her hand; to watch the woman we both loved so dearly slowly slip away. I wanted to be there too, so very, very badly. I was nearly due to be released, or so I thought.

I had submitted my parole application and the result was due any day. A sure thing, everyone said. I was already passed the date at which I could apply for it by some six months. Six years was enough surely, to keep me in this hellhole. I was costing their impoverished country money, there was no rehabilitation, so what was the point in keeping me longer? At the very least deport me, kick me out of the country, but just let me out.

It had been my worst fear that someone very close to me might die while I was in prison. All I wanted was to be there for her, to help her out and look after her, provide for her so she no longer had to worry or struggle or feel obliged to anyone. But I wasn't there. I was 5,000 miles away behind steel bars and concrete walls. It was tearing me apart, the thought that she was dying and I hadn't seen her for over six years. Why? Why now, when I was due to be released any day? I prayed, pleaded, begged, offered my life for hers; please don't let her die, please!

My dear friend Margarita came in to see me, having been told by my family what was happening. We sat around the small table in my cell and she prayed and consoled me as I wept uncontrollably. If there really was a God, then why did He seem to keep taking the good people from me? I had already lost countless friends, starting at the age of 14 when one of my best friends died suddenly. Then a very dear girlfriend was killed in a car crash when I was 17, and another died a few years ago in Quito.

So very many good people had died around me. My friends called me the 'Grim Pieter'. If only it had been a joke. Everywhere I went people died. I had been surrounded by death nearly my whole life. When I was released from prison in England, within six months my stepbrother, with whom I lived in the family home, killed himself. It had been just me and him in the house that day. Four weeks later his cousin did exactly the same, so both my stepmother and her sister lost their firstborn in the same month. This had followed the death of their mother, also in the family home, three months earlier.

Sarah called me from the hospital once she arrived at our mother's side. I could hear the heart monitor bleeping out the rhythm of her heartbeats. The doctors had reiterated their opinion that she probably wouldn't survive more than three days. I refused to believe it. There must be a slim chance she could recover, surely. No, they said. I discovered later that they had put her in this induced coma just to keep her alive long enough for my sister to come and say her goodbyes.

Sarah asked if I would like to say anything to her. She could hold the phone to her ear and I could talk to her from 5,000 miles away. I wanted to be there so badly, not only for her, but also for my sister, who was having to deal with this on her own. Through my stupidity and selfish actions, I had ultimately let down the two women in my life I most cared about. I told my sister I would have a think about what I wanted to say and call her back later on. For the moment, she held the phone to my mother's ear just so that I could say hello and send her my love and tell her to keep fighting, and not give up. I tried not to cry, to be brave, but I couldn't help it. I thanked Sarah and told her to call me should there be any deterioration. With that the line went dead and I was alone again in my tiny room.

Memories kept coming to me of happier days when all was good and nothing went wrong. They were distant memories though, followed by many sadder ones. A couple of friends called in to see if I was OK, and to offer words of support. I washed my tears away with cold water and told them I was fine and that she had been ill for a while. I couldn't say that alcohol was the cause: it just hurt too much.

I phoned Sarah, having prepared some things to say. I asked her to watch the heart rate monitor as I spoke to see if there was any reaction as I spoke to her. This I thought might show she was responsive and could indeed hear us. My sister held the phone to my mother's ear and I told her how much I loved her and how sorry I was for what I had done. I explained how much I wanted to be there with her. I promised that if I ever got married I would wear a kilt in her family colours. I asked her to please stay with us as she would miss seeing our children. Neither Sarah nor I had any children yet. I told her to fight with everything she could muster, as we still had so much to do and live for. I finished and asked my sister if there had been any increase in her heart rate at any points. She said yes, there had, when I had mentioned having children and also wearing a kilt if I got married. I feel sure by her reaction that she heard those words.

That weekend was the longest ever. I sat and willed her to get better. I sent her energy and prayed for her to pull through. She was a strong woman, but her will to live had diminished over recent years and she had sunk further into depression. Life just seemed to be too much for her to deal with.

It was on Monday that the phone rang and it was my father. I knew what he was going to say and broke down in tears.

'Pete, it's over. She's gone. It's finished.'

I wept for hours, maybe days. I didn't want to see anyone or talk to anyone. I just wanted to be left to myself. I have never felt as lonely in the world as I did then. Thousands of miles from home and my mother had just died; no family here, no really close friends, just me in my cell on my own.

I stayed that way for nearly a week. My whole world stopped. I didn't want to know about anything. The only calls I took were from family and friends back in Britain. My father thought they might push through my parole application and release me on compassionate grounds so I could be back home in time for the funeral. I explained that life and death meant nothing in this country. Death, and violent death at that, was so commonplace that it didn't really mean a great deal. He said he was going to contact the Foreign Office and see if they might be able to do something. I told him to go ahead and that it would do no harm.

My sister and my mother's long-term partner were left to make arrangements for the funeral. They decided to have the service at the Quaker hall in the town she had lived in for the greater part of her life. She had helped in the restoration of the stained-glass windows with her partner – they had repaired nearly all the windows in the church over the years – and had always loved spending time around churches. Her remains were to be cremated, which I wasn't happy about as I don't like the idea of it. Sarah promised to keep some of my mother's belongings for me, not that she had much, but I wanted her papers so I could look into our family background on her side, which wasn't very clear to us. Apart from that I wasn't bothered about having anything. Sarah offered to send me some photos but I told her they would be safer kept with her. She said she would send me a copy of the order of service for the funeral.

It was a while before the funeral could take place as there were some complications with the hospital. When the day came, nearly 150 people came to pay their respects. She was well liked. Such a shame she died young, not having even reached 60. I prepared a speech for the day, which my father was good enough to read out for me. We did talk about trying to set up a computer link on the day so I could speak myself, using my friend's laptop through Skype, but we didn't quite manage it, so my father did me the favour instead. The speech was generally well received apart from by her partner, who openly blamed me for her death in front of quite a few people and said I should have apologised in my speech. I had already apologised to my mother when my sister held the phone to her ear and that was between me and her. I felt he should have apologised for having split my parents' marriage up and consequently our family, which caused everyone a great deal of pain. Sarah and I had lived with our father, there not being enough room for us in her partner's flat.

My sister had collected a pair of urns with our mother's ashes in, one for each of us to spread where we wanted to. Some of her ashes were spread around the beautiful little church near to the River Severn where her funeral was held. She loved spending time there. She would sit in the warm sun with the fresh breeze blowing through her hair, gazing out across the waters of the river and on over to the Forest of Dean, eating her lunch.

A few days after the funeral I received the results of my parole application. When I finally clarified exactly how much remission they had actually given me, I was glad that I didn't have to tell my mother, as the shock probably would have killed her. It nearly did me. They told me I would be inside for a further five years.

This all happened while I was becoming very ill with TB but before it had been officially diagnosed. Very soon after my mother's death I heard that my aunt, my father's only sister, was terminally ill with lung cancer. I chatted to her on the phone while she was staying at my dad's.

During this period, I was at the lowest ebb of the entire time of my sentence. Coping with my mother's death and then finding out that I had so much longer to do after the failure of my parole application, led me to pretty much give up hope of ever getting out alive, particularly now I had chronic TB.

CHAPTER TWENTY-SEVEN
SIMON

'*Cuentate, cuentate,*' the guards and *caporal* were shouting. It was the count or roll call, at 8am as usual. I quickly put on some clothes and emerged from my cell, bleary-eyed and heavy-headed, having had a few drinks the night before. It was a couple of months after the TB vaccinations and I was starting to suffer from the effects, although I didn't know it at the time.

Monday morning, the beginning of yet another day in another week in another month in what I had hoped would be the last year. I was still reeling from having been told a week earlier that I was now faced with being locked in this never-ending nightmare for a further five years. As I passed Simon's door, three cells down from mine, I gave it a knock to make sure he came out for the count. I did this every morning as his cell was situated at the point in the wing where we would have to pass the guard in order to be counted. We would all then have to wait at that end of the wing while they checked that the numbers tallied and that no one was asleep in a cell, or missing. For this reason, Simon tended to wait until the very end of the count, drinking coffee in his room, watching the early-morning TV, rather than standing around waiting for everyone to be counted. On a few occasions he had missed the count and this really annoyed the guards, as it meant they had to start all over again and re-count everyone until they got the right number. Missing the count could result in them taking you to the punishment block for up to a week, but usually meant you had to bribe them with five or ten dollars to leave you alone. So I always knocked and he would return the favour and make sure I was up, as I was prone to oversleeping. I knocked and he emerged with his usual cheeky grin.

'Morning Pete, you all right?'

'Yeah, not bad. Bit hungover but all right.' Simon used to find it funny when I sometimes appeared at the count still drunk as hell and I would amuse everyone with my wit (I thought I was witty anyway) while we waited. We filed through together and on the surface he seemed to be fine, cracking jokes with people, saying hello, but I knew him well and I could tell he was subdued. He didn't have that spark this particular morning. His usual energy seemed depleted.

Simon had been in this same prison for nearly nine years by now. He was initially sentenced to 25 years for his part in a major case, involving some 400 kilos of cocaine, which had been seized in Britain in containers that had arrived at Avonmouth docks near Bristol and originated from Guayaquil. Simon had not been present in Britain or arrested there as he had lived in Spain for nearly 25 years. He was arrested when he arrived in Ecuador on the basis of an English arrest warrant. He was not found to have a single trace of cocaine and the evidence was tenuous at best. After pressure from the British authorities, Simon was sentenced to the maximum of 25 years in prison in Ecuador.

Simon had for years been trying to get his sentence reduced to 16 or even 12 years. For some reason, sentences were always in a multiple of four apart from the exceptional cases of 25 or 35 years. It always struck me as odd that there were no in-between lengths of sentence. When Simon was first arrested, someone had introduced him to a supposedly excellent lawyer who guaranteed he would secure his release or, in the worst-case scenario, a short sentence. This was similar to what had happened to me with the first lawyers I had in Quito. These kinds of promises were commonplace, particularly when foreigners were involved who usually couldn't speak the language and would assume that Ecuadorian lawyers were of the same calibre as European ones who had studied for years and had degrees. Not a bit of it – nearly everyone I met in Ecuador had been robbed by a 'lawyer'. Undoubtedly, the person who introduced Simon to this character purporting to be a lawyer had been in on the scam.

In total, Simon handed over $120,000 and still received the maximum sentence, as the lawyer kept stringing him along. The problem was that once they had you on their hook wriggling around for your freedom they could keep making demands. For example, a story would be concocted that the judge was asking $50,000 to give you a 12-year sentence, so you would perhaps try to make a deal that you would pay half up front and the other half once you had the result. You would pay the $25,000, the lawyer saying yes, that was fine, and then after a few weeks he would come back saying the judge had refused and now wanted all the money up front. What do you do? You're not going to get your $25,000 back if you say no and you will then run the risk of a high sentence, so you pay because that's the only thing you can do and they know it. The scam artist 'lawyer' would then come up with numerous reasons for needing more money, such as having to pay off the deputies, the secretary of the court, to get documents stamped ... There were a hundred and one different reasons that could be used to extort money from the victim.

By the time Simon realised that this lawyer was robbing him, it was too late. After the first one vanished with his $120,000 he managed to come up with further funds to pay another lawyer. Using this second lawyer he set about trying to fight the sentence. Part of his problem, like mine, was that the British police were keeping an eye on the case and making sure he wasn't going anywhere. However, after nearly nine years in prison, the lawyer finally managed to get his sentence reduced to 16 years. Simon had been hoping for 12, which would have meant he would go free immediately. Now he was in the same position as me and we were both applying for parole at exactly the same time. His papers were in the same batch as mine, which was dispatched to Quito under the new system.

This new system functioned on the basis of merits for work, good conduct, education, sports and various other areas. You would be graded for each and it all added up to the recommended percentage you would be given remission. The maximum was 50 per cent. This was a problem for people like me who had already been in prison for years, when the system didn't exist and nor did any courses or work opportunities to be graded on. It just didn't work and so I received only ten per cent remission, meaning I had to do another five years: a total of 11 years out of 12. Practically the whole sentence. They were barely giving me anything. This had really unnerved Simon when he heard my result as his was due back any day. To him the prospect of another five years in prison was just too much.

Added to this, Simon was in trouble. Big trouble. He had been doing business with various people, including Los Cubanos gang, trafficking cocaine to various parts of Europe. The problem was, he couldn't cover the losses if something went wrong. He was also juggling money; using money from one deal to finance another hoping they would both come off, but they didn't. He had lost money one way or another, through either the drugs or cash being robbed. It's very hard to control the situation when you are locked up in prison thousands of miles from the action. If someone decides to take your money, what are you going to do, unless you have people overseeing everything for you on the outside, which Simon didn't. He ended up in debt to the tune of some $120,000 to the gang and another $80,000 to someone else. That's $200,000! He couldn't get anyone to do any more business so he was stuck. He just couldn't get the money. The gang had been sending people up to him on a regular basis now to put pressure on.

He had become depressed and despondent. He had even told the embassy he was in grave danger and feeling suicidal and that they needed to move him. They didn't seem to believe him, or couldn't arrange it, I don't know which. I remember sitting with him in his cell one day. He pointed to an iron ring in the ceiling of the cell and said if he was going to kill himself, that's how he would do it. I told him to shut up and stop talking crap.

After the count that morning, I went back to my cell and fell asleep. At about 9.30am there was a banging on the door. I opened it, bleary eyed. 'Come quick, come quick! Something's wrong with Simon.' I ran to his cell where his cellmate and another Englishman, Jake, were busy removing the air conditioner from the gap above the door to gain access to the cell. His cellmate had managed to get the air conditioner nearly all the way out when he started shouting that Simon was hanging in the cell. My heart started racing. 'Come on! Get this fucking door open!' I screamed. We took the air conditioner out and the cellmate went through the gap into the cell, dropped down and opened the door.

We charged in and grabbed Simon's legs to take the weight off the noose. Jake got a chair, climbed up and managed to loosen the noose and remove it from his neck. We dropped him down on to his bed, where one of the other inmates trained in first aid tried to revive him with mouth-to-mouth resuscitation and heart massages. But he was gone.

By now there was a huge crowd gathering at the door, all pushing to get a view. We cleared them back and someone called the guards. We decided it was best not to disturb the scene too much. Jake and I were discussing what had happened – things weren't right. The first thing we noticed was that all the chairs were neatly lined up against the walls, so what had he stood on? There was nothing. The noose was not a proper noose, merely a knot tied twice, and his head was touching the ceiling. So how had the noose tightened? There was no rope for it to have slid down. We reckoned that someone had knocked him out and then held him up while someone else tied the knot around his neck and attached him to the iron ring. Something else really puzzled me – I couldn't understand why he wouldn't have waited a week or two more to see if there was the possibility of his getting released and out of the potentially deadly fix he was in. Having wanted nine years surely a few more weeks wouldn't have bothered him?

When the guards arrived, one of them, who was friendly with Simon, went ballistic saying there was no way he had killed himself and that someone had done this. He was furious. The police were called and the forensics arrived a couple of hours later. They suspected murder; they took the names of a few people and later conducted interviews and more or less accused one person outright. Nothing came of the investigation, which they eventually gave up on. I believe Simon was killed by the gang because he hadn't paid off his debt. I had learned that the gang had given him up until the day in question – that Monday – to pay or they were going to kill him.

Isabel from the embassy was shaken when she found out, as she had known Simon for the entire nine years and liked him a lot. She had to inform Simon's ex-wife and his two daughters back in Britain. It was another rock in my heart, another heavy link added to the chain. I had spent a lot of time with Simon and he had become one of my closest friends there. I felt very lonely for a while after. At this point the British embassy really started trying to push for all of us to be repatriated as quickly as possible.

I had refused, because it meant my family having to pay $8,000 in fines imposed by the judge. I wasn't about to ask them to cover this, after having caused them so much trouble. I was still adamant that some change would occur in the law, or a presidential pardon might be issued. There were constant rumours circulating the prison, half of which I think were made up just to give the inmates some sense of hope; some light at the end of a very dark tunnel.

Repatriation was a long, complicated, drawn-out process that at its very quickest would take a year and a half to be arranged. You first had to send a letter to the minister of justice for Ecuador asking his permission to even be able to apply for repatriation. Once you got the green light, a dossier about you was prepared by the prison services and sent to

Quito where formal approval had to be granted, which could take over a year to happen. When you got approval to be repatriated to your home country the minister of justice for Ecuador would send the dossier to the equivalent department in your country, such as the Foreign Office in the UK or the State Department in America. They would then review your case and decide whether or not they were willing to accept you back in order to serve the remainder of your sentence.

The calculation of how much you needed to serve in prison once home varied significantly from country to country. For example, in Spain most people who were repatriated went free after a month or so in prison there. The English system was kind of unfair as they calculated how long you were to serve by working out how long you had left of the total sentence, so, for example, say I had served six years out of 12, six would be left. They then took the six and said you had to serve half of that, so another three. This meant I would serve a total of nine years out of the 12. This I thought a very unfair system because had I been sentenced to 12 years in England under the current laws I would only serve half and be automatically released, which would mean six years instead of nine. Not only that, but it was very likely that you would have just come from a prison with a far harsher regime and suffered a great deal more.

I know a lot of people would say tough shit, you shouldn't have done it in the first place, and that's fair enough. But just spare a thought for people in prison abroad – it could one day be you or your child or a family member. People are quite frequently wrongly imprisoned in foreign countries for all manner of reasons.

We were still being told that everyone in the prisons in Ecuador would be released after having served half their sentence in something known as a 'two-for-one' deal. So, seeing as I had served at this point six years – half my sentence – I couldn't see any reason to go back to Britain and have to do another three; that would make a total of nine when I could possibly be out very soon here.

There were various conditions you had to meet in order to be repatriated. You had to be sentenced and the sentence needed to be enforced and finalised with no ongoing appeals or further charges pending. You had to have served at least ten per cent of your sentence. Your home government had the right to refuse you if they didn't particularly want you back in the country. If however they approved you and the prison service in your country did too, then your application was once again returned to the Ecuadorians for final approval. The Ecuadorians would then give their approval if they were happy with the amount of prison time you were going to serve once home. You also had to pay the fine imposed by the judge along with the sentence and this I did not want to do. I was stuck.

In my case, the embassy told me they could make an application direct to the president, asking that the fine be waived so that I could be repatriated. They warned me that it might take a year or two for a reply to come back. I told them to go ahead and make the application for the fine of $8,000 to be waived. I would wait and see if I got lucky.

If I applied to be repatriated then I couldn't apply for the two-for-one as well and see which happened quicker. It was a case of either/or. I didn't like the idea of missing out on the chance of being released after six years and instead having to serve another three or so years in prison in England. It was a very difficult decision to make. Added to all this there was the distinct possibility that if I was repatriated I could face the prospect of being re-sentenced in Britain to 20-plus years in prison. That really put me off and was a key factor in me deciding to try to wait it out, as painful as it was in deepest darkest Ecuador.

CHAPTER TWENTY-EIGHT
TRASLADO –
TRANSFER

It was 1 December 2013. I was still really ill with TB having now been sick for well over two years.

'*Onze, onze, onze!*' came the shout just after the count. Fuck! A couple of people came running into the cell to tell me hundreds of police were descending on the prison. We could hear a helicopter overhead and see high-ranking police officers appearing on the rooftops surrounded by heavily armed police. Something major was happening and it wasn't good. Quickly word came that this looked like the beginning of the end. The dreaded transfers to the new regional prison. During his presidential campaign, Correa had vowed to completely reform the prison system. Now he was carrying through this promise and we were about to experience first-hand his vision for our futures. But many inmates were not too happy about it.

Everyone was running around like headless chickens trying to hide weapons and drugs, both of which the wing was awash with. Our wing, having become independent from Los Cubanos, was now one of the major entry points for drugs and firearms because it was outside of the gangs' control and therefore every Tom, Dick and Pablo could bring in exactly what he wanted. This was largely due to our recently installed prison director, who was the most corrupt I had seen in my entire time in Ecuador. He had made it very clear that if we wished to operate in 'his' prison there was absolutely no problem. The one condition was that he receive his piece of pie – and a big piece it was.

Intent on milking an over-fatted calf that was due to be slaughtered any moment, shortly after his arrival, he sent out an emissary in the form of his personal security guards. They travelled from wing to wing carrying a list of the key players in the drug trade from each wing. They invited all those named on the list to come and meet the director in his office in order to discuss how he wanted things to run. Basically, this was to sort out the fee he was going to demand.

Upon their return from this summit meeting the main dealers from the wing spoke to me to offer me the sole right to sell crack cocaine and cocaine to the entire wing with two or three people working under me, promising me security and backup from them if needed. The director had demanded $2,000 a week as a kind of licence fee to trade drugs, firearms, alcohol and whatever else. We debated how we could raise this kind of sum weekly, based on the average amounts we sold daily. It was possible but it was going to be hard work and take a huge chunk of the profits. This, however, was the only way in which we were going to be able to continue trading. If we refused to cooperate and ceased doing business altogether, he had threatened us with sanctions such as being transferred. So we were really between a hard place and la Roca!

The government had been threatening to carry this out for months now and we knew that the transfers to the new prison were imminent. However, we had discovered that a certain number of wings in better structural condition were to be left standing and occupied after some basic improvement, mainly to the security. The director decided he would offer guaranteed places in these wings, for a large fee, which was to be negotiated. He was trying to squeeze people for as much as he thought he could on an individual basis.

The authorities, all the way to the very top, were absolutely determined to wrest back control of the prisons and break the power of the gangs through divide and conquer. President Correa was pushing through the reforms as fast as he could as the prisons of Ecuador were becoming renowned worldwide as dangerous, violent, out-of-control, gang-run, drug-infested hellholes you would be lucky to survive if imprisoned in them. The murder rate in the prisons was spiralling out of control as the system broke down. At least while the gangs had controlled the prison they had maintained a strict level of discipline and order. Numerous foreigners had been murdered and this was becoming more frequent, which the various embassies were becoming alarmed about; this was really beginning to cause the president problems, as the embassies were complaining and threatening sanctions if their citizens were not properly looked after.

More and more police poured into the place. Various dealers arrived at my cell in a panic, asking me to stash drugs for them in one of my large, purpose-built hiding places. Most of these were by now compromised so I was reluctant to place myself – and their goods – in jeopardy. For those with whom I was more friendly, I accepted the items and placed them in some new spots that absolutely no one knew about, just to be sure. By now the entire wing was in turmoil.

Several thousand police, military, naval and air force personnel had descended en masse, marking the beginning of a huge operation to put an end to the mayhem. The *jefe de guia* called everyone to gather round as he was about to start reading out the list of people to be transferred. He explained that we were not permitted to take anything with us, absolutely nothing – no documents, photos, letters, clothes, money, *NADA*! This announcement was a body blow as we had received no prior warning. This would have allowed us time for friends and family to come into the prison and remove any valuable items for safe keeping. I wasn't particularly worried about losing material possessions such as my TV, fridge or DVD player, as they are easily replaced. I called Margarita to let her know what was happening and she said she would inform Isabel, the honorary vice consul, and try to salvage some of my belongings.

By now quite a few friends had gathered in my cell waiting to hear the *jefe de guia* call out the list of names. We sat around chatting and reminiscing. I gathered together a bag of medicines I needed with me, in the hope that they couldn't deny me my medication. My friends and I decided to consume what we had left of the various drugs in stock, coke and weed. I gave my Spanish room-mate Marco a quantity of bags of heroin in order to help him withdraw gradually once he reached the new regional prison.

I had rapidly packed a bag just in case I could chance it and get it through. As I had expected, it didn't take long for my name to come up. There were enough people wanting to take over my end of the business and I knew they had been plotting against me. I wasn't allowed to take anything and I went through a series of searches before being sent out into the exercise yard to await transfer. This was going to be quite an experience.

I sat in the shade and watched as slowly but surely every last person filtered through the door. It took a while for over 350 people to be searched and accounted for, by which time the sun was at its zenith and beating down fiercely on us. We had no food or water and people were beginning to suffer. The police called some of the shopkeepers forward. Their stock was all going to be wasted now, so they agreed to all the drinks being distributed. The police, however, in their usual disorderly fashion, just piled them all into large plastic bins and threw the bins one at a time into the yard. This provoked a mad scramble ending with people piling on top of one another like a rugby scrum, desperate for a drink. A bin landed just to my left and as I was reaching to get a drink, twenty or so people piled on top of me, knocking me to the ground.

I was completely crushed and nearly passed out as I couldn't breathe. I was still ill from the TB, with no strength. Both my elbows were badly cut in the fall and my friends, seeing that I was really struggling to breathe, persuaded the police to let me back into the wing for an injection of dexamethasone, which my good friend Carlos offered to administer. When I re-entered my cell to find the medication and a needle, I discovered that the cell had been completely ransacked by people looking for the drugs and money stashed there. Diego, my other Spanish room-mate, later told us what had happened. As soon as both Marco and I had been taken out of the wing, a group of inmates, along with two guards, had charged into the cell, hit Diego a couple of times and held a knife to his throat to get him to tell them where everything was hidden. He had no idea, so it proved fruitless, but they had totally trashed the cell. Everything was in disarray. I immediately recovered the drugs from the secret hiding place and put them in my underwear, thinking

240

it unlikely that I would be searched again before we reached the new prison.

After Carlos administered the injection, my breathing normalised and I lay down on a mattress in the cool and fell asleep. At one point a kindly policeman woke me and offered me some food that they had been pilfering from the shops. It was appreciated as I hadn't eaten anything all day. I ate it, and went back to sleep again. The next I knew I was being awoken by Marco; it was dark and people were milling about in the wing. I was confused. He filled me in on what had happened.

The police had begun by transferring the wings further inside the prison. Our wing would have been the last, but they had run out of time and manpower so decided to put us all back in the wing until they had the resources to make the change. This was expected to take place in the early hours of the next morning. We were to have one final evening in Atenuado Alto and then it was to be a fresh beginning. Along with virtually all the rest of the inmates from the Peni, some 5,000 people, we would be the first inmates, all guinea pigs, to be initiated into Rafael Correa's new penal system as part of his socialist experiment.

There was now very little food on the wing as most of it had already been either consumed, stolen or destroyed in the chaos. Marco managed to get hold of some platefuls of food, which the authorities had brought in at 7pm, so we tidied the place up a little, enough at least to be able to sit down and eat. While I ate my friends filled me in. The guards, it seemed, were having a field day and taking full advantage of the situation to grab as much as possible. The hardest-hit financially were the shopkeepers. Having had no warning that this was about to occur, they had been unable to take countermeasures. The shopkeepers had nearly all just

241

restocked their stores with thousands of dollars' worth of provisions. This had only been possible after much negotiation with the new director and substantial bribes being handed over. The authorities had really clamped down on anything coming into the prison in the run-up to the transfer, and many of the shops and restaurants had been forced to close because they were unable to acquire the necessary stock. To us it seemed like more than a coincidence that all these goods had been allowed in by the director himself, just a day or two before the planned transfer. He had profited hugely from the bribes and now had all the goods as well.

The guards had come up with a scheme to make money. They offered to deliver goods or money to people with families on the outside, for a hefty fee. A couple of the main store owners had been seen handing over large rolls of dollar bills to certain guards who promised to take money to their families. One even handed over some twelve thousand dollars. I was very sceptical that the money would ever reach its destination. A few of the dealers had sent money, drugs and phones out with guards. These were more likely to reach the right people as the dealers were gang members and the guards knew all too well the consequences for them if things should go missing for no matter what reason. They were certainly being paid well, that's for sure. A few of the guards had made multiple trips in and out of the prison that day, transporting goods. It really was a gold rush for them. For some of the guards this was to be their last chance at making quick money; they had not been contracted to work at the new prison, because they were known to be corrupt and not to be trusted.

As I sat at the table, I was keeping a watchful eye on things happening outside my door on the wing. Order had completely broken down. I saw a few people pass my door carrying knives and machetes quite openly. I had heard that people were settling scores while they still had the chance and trying to collect debts. This had resulted in a few people being quite badly beaten but as yet no one had been killed, at least on our wing. A few people had been robbed and it was getting dangerous even to go outside the cell. I told one of my friends to close and lock the door and not open it unless we were absolutely sure who it was and what they wanted, as I would definitely be a target for an attempted robbery. We all made sure we had weapons within reach: knives, bats, bars, whatever was available.

First of all though, we decided to go out and have a look around and see what was happening, so four of us left together, with our weapons. One friend stayed behind to keep the cell locked from inside until we returned. We opened the door on to a scene of chaos, mayhem and debauchery. It was like something out of Dante's 'Inferno'. People were consuming anything and everything that was left over. One of the main cocaine dealers was sitting outside his cell, giving coke away by the handful from a bag that had contained two kilos. People were cutting up lines of coke and smoking crack all over the place. The sweet smell of potent skunk hung thickly in the air. Bottles that had held alcohol littered the floor. It was madness. I felt as though I was watching what might happen if all society's controls and normalities were suddenly removed.

A few people asked if I had anything left I wanted to sell or give away. I had been producing home-made wine from the local fruit, which sold quite well once it had been left to stand for a good month. My good Russian friend would distil some of it into a really vicious spirit, but I had the best part of a 25-litre canister left, so I decided to give it away as my contribution to the end-of-the-world party.

243

Diego particularly liked to have a drink and immediately got stuck into Chateau Tritton. It wasn't long before he was well gone and started becoming aggressive. He was dead set on tracking down some guys who had roughed him up and stabbing them. He was brandishing a three-inch pocket knife, reeling around the room saying how he was going to cut their throats. We couldn't help but laugh, considering most of the guys he wanted to attack were currently wandering round the wing with two-foot-long machetes and 12-inch kitchen knives, and possibly guns. We calmed Diego down and gave him some more home brew on the condition that he relax and not leave the cell.

At around four o'clock in the morning the police arrived to discover virtually everyone either drunk or high and in a jubilant mood. We were again called out one at a time, searched and each assigned a police officer who was to escort us all the way to the new prison. I was taken to the very front of the queue because I was ill and was on the first bus out of the prison, leaving behind all my belongings. I was not allowed to take the letters and photos my mother had sent me over the years. As well as these I lost all the other photos I had in the prison, case papers and letters. I will never be able to replace those letters from my mother who I never saw alive again. That broke my heart and still hurts to this day.

CHAPTER TWENTY-NINE
A NEW BEGINNING

The buses didn't even go outside the perimeter wall of the old prison. The new regional one had been constructed right next door, so we weren't going far. They had punched a hole through the perimeter wall and built a temporary road so that the buses didn't have to leave the prison compound. Each bus was escorted front and back by patrol vehicles with armed police inside. There was also a helicopter circling overhead just in case someone should try to mount an escape attempt; there had been many recently in the old prison — even one in the early hours of that very morning.

After a four-minute ride we were taken off the buses and led into what was to be the visitors' waiting room with its banks of chairs. The director, formerly of the old prison and now the director of the new regional prison, was there, overseeing the transfer and making sure things went smoothly. The police officer I was handcuffed to approached him and explained my situation: that I was sick with TB and possibly shouldn't have been transferred there at all but rather to the clinic in the old prison, where they had nearly all the cases of TB in one area together.

I was hoping and praying that the director would agree and that I would narrowly escape this transfer. At first he said 'No, no, this man can't come in here,' but then he reviewed my clinical history and decided that as I was no longer considered contagious I could come in but would be held on a super-high-security isolation wing. *Que genial!* Just what I needed. I had served over eight years now, but I felt as though I was working backwards through the system, with the level of security in which I was being held gradually increasing, from the relatively relaxed Garcia Moreno prison in Quito, to the extremely dangerous and to some extent more secure Penitentiary Litoral de Guayaquil, and now this. A supermax high-security wing in a high-security prison was like being a double A category prisoner in England.

I tried to reason with the director, who remembered me from previous meetings with the British embassy, which had been held in his office. He was a former detective who had been in the police force in New York and spoke perfect English. He was a straight down the line kind of guy. Reasonable, but wouldn't take any shit, as opposed to the last director there, who was completely the opposite.

Various civilian workers were issuing the 'uniforms' we had to wear from now on. Gone were the days of gang members wandering around the prison in designer clothes, sportswear and expensive trainers. The uniform consisted of one T-shirt in the colour of your security status – yellow for low, orange for medium, brown and red for high security, and white for supermax high security – a pair of black shorts, one pair of boxer shorts and a pair of flip-flops. We were also given a bed pack, which contained two sheets and one pillow-case, along with a wash kit with shampoo, soap, toothpaste and toothbrush, flannel, towel and deodorant, but no razors. We were told to place all our clothes and shoes in a black bin liner that was to be marked with our name and wing. I looked around the room and saw a great pile of these bin liners from inmates who had already passed through here and I just knew we would never see these items again.

I had brought with me a leather wash bag, which contained a load of my medication for TB, including dexamethasone and syringes with which to administer it in an emergency. The woman who was dealing with me explained that I couldn't take anything into the prison, medication included. I was petrified by this, because when I suffered an attack and couldn't breathe, the dexamethasone was the only thing that kept me alive and now I wouldn't have it. The woman said she would pass my medication to the healthcare centre so they could decide if I could keep it or not.

I proceeded to get changed into the new uniform but kept my own boxers on and also my own Adidas flip-flops. My legs and feet were still swollen so I claimed that the ones they had issued didn't fit and would mean I was unable to walk. Once I was dressed in my new outfit, the policeman escorted me uncuffed past the long queue of inmates waiting to go through the security procedures. These included strip-searches, a metal detector, scanner and a hot seat to make sure we didn't have anything hidden away internally. All of the security was under the control of the police as the guards were no longer trusted and were only in charge of the wings and locking people up. Everyone entering the prison, including the guards, visitors and embassy staff, would have to undergo these strict security checks before being allowed entry.

I passed through the checks without problem. The police officers in charge of the strip-searches looked thoroughly fed up with the job. From here we proceeded into the prison itself. It almost felt like I had been transported to another country, the difference was so great between here and the squalor of the Peni. The director had instructed my police guard to take me to the supermax high-security wing. To gain entry to the wing we had to pass through yet another security control, again manned by the police. This time it was a metal detector and pat-down. We also had to fill out a movements log with my name and that of the escorting officer.

There were cameras everywhere – one at each end of the landing, one on the main gate and a central one above the exercise yard. The wing was L-shaped, with four floors including the ground level. The cells on this wing were designed for two or three people but were all occupied by just one person at the moment.

The policeman left me with one of the guards and explained that I was sick with TB, at which I could see the guard baulked a little. I was instructed to take a mattress and pillow from the pile that was sitting in the middle of the exercise yard, covered in dust. I did and he showed me to the last cell on the ground floor, in one of the corners. The gates on the entrances to the cells were barred with just an iron mesh over the top, but were otherwise open, unlike the solid doors we had in the Peni.

The guard slid the gate back to let me enter and then shut and locked it behind me. That was an unfamiliar experience as I hadn't been actually locked in a cell by a guard since Quito, nearly six years previously. The cell was thick with cement dust from the building work, which was probably the worst place for me to be with a breathing complaint. There were two concrete bunks on the left of the cell and to the rear a metal toilet and sink, and also a shower, which was welcome. There were two thin, vertical slit windows, like archers' slots in a castle, overlooking a central area between wings that was destined to become grassy football pitches and volleyball courts.

Dawn was approaching now and it quickly became light. I started to hear a little bit of movement from other cells and wondered who else was going to be on the wing. Seeing as it was supermax they were going to be fairly serious players, whoever they were. At around 8am I saw the servery staff from the kitchens wheeling in the breakfast on a large trolley. Shortly afterwards they went from cell to cell handing it out: some bread, a hot drink of some description and a banana. They gave me a bag with extra bread in it for later in the day.

The cell remained locked and I wondered what the regime would be like here. How many hours would we get outside the cell each day? I guessed that as the prison was new and in a state of chaos, and with movement from all the transfers, we would probably be staying locked up most of the time. This didn't exactly fill me with enthusiasm for my new home.

After a short while I heard some guys in the next cell – they were talking in English with an American accent. I called out to them and we had a quick chat. They had been placed in here as they'd been involved with the gang in the old prison and had been in control of a couple of wings. I recognised their names and even knew one of them vaguely. They were very friendly with some American friends of mine and Carlos, my friend from the Dominican Republic. They in turn had heard of me, so we were off to a great start. I felt instantly better. It is always a little unsettling coming on to a new wing as you don't know what the politics are and the general status quo. It can be a delicate matter where gangs are involved as you may end up in hostile territory unknowingly.

At around ten o'clock a guard started walking around opening cell doors to allow people into the small exercise yard. When he reached my door, however, he left it shut and walked off. This puzzled me so I called after him, but he didn't return. There were about 15 people on the wing at the time and most were either walking around the yard or washing clothes and utensils in basins.

One of the first to come and greet me was the ex-captain of police who I knew from Atenuado Alto and had fallen out with. He was a serious player who had been caught trying to load nearly a ton of cocaine on to a light aircraft belonging to the infamous Sinaloa cartel, the head of which at the time was Chapo Guzman. I couldn't believe it. One of the guys with whom I had had the most problems of late and here he was.

Shortly afterward, to my amazement, across the exercise yard strolled none other than the very head of Los Cubanos, Cubano himself. What the fuck! This guy was always kept in the most secure of locations. My head was reeling. Why the hell had I ended up in here?

The next person to greet me was Pedro, who had been one of the gang members of the Three Blind Mice. It was because of him that I had ended up moving wings to Atenuado Alto.

Not long after my run-in with the gang, Pedro had ended up in trouble with them and had turned informant in exchange for protection, by way of a transfer to the prison in his home region further up the coast. Then one night the police raided the prison and conducted a search of virtually all the wings. They brought someone in who was disguised with a balaclava over his face. We were watching from upstairs through the open area in the middle of the wing and instantly recognised his voice when he started pointing out all the cells in which the gang had drugs and weapons hidden in secret stashes. We couldn't believe it and started shouting insults at him until the police downstairs threatened to come up and beat us all.

Here this same man was, standing at my door, greeting me, being nice as pie, though looking rather nervous, I thought. I had to hold back my rage. I couldn't believe that I was now locked on a wing with the three people who over the years directly or indirectly had caused me the most problems. It was a cosmic joke. If I hadn't known that some of the others who had also given me grief were definitely dead, I would have expected them to appear as well and we could all have had a jolly get-together. I was almost glad my cell door was still locked, as it would give me a moment to collect my thoughts and work out how I was going to deal with this situation.

The guard eventually opened my cell door so that I could come out for a while and get some air. I spent the next hour or so talking to George and Wilson, the two Americans. I was keen to find out if anyone had a mobile phone in the prison yet. The answer was yes, but the guards were asking around $2,000 to bring in a BlackBerry, which was astronomical compared to what it had cost in the previous prison. There you could pay a guard $20–$30 and have whatever phone you wanted brought in. Obviously, you had to buy the phone as well. George told me quietly that he was actually waiting for a phone to be delivered any day now. He had already organised the money to be sent to a guard outside from one of his family in the States. The guard was then going to smuggle the phone in somehow; not the easiest of things to do, as he would be subject to searches by the police, including metal detectors.

However, to charge the phones we would have to give them to the guards as there were no power points in our cells. There also was only one light, which was positioned above the windows at the rear of the cell, and would come on automatically at 6pm and turn off at 10pm. There were no

TVs, DVDs, nothing. We weren't allowed pens or paper in our cells and no newspapers or magazines were allowed into the prison. No letters or notes could be received or sent. There were no telephones to use to call our families. We weren't allowed razors or scissors so there was no way to shave or cut hair. Not even books were permitted. Basically we weren't allowed anything at all in our cells. There was no exception to this. I have never been in a prison with such tight security. We were being held in effect incommunicado, which no doubt broke all sorts of human rights laws.

And yet there were already drugs in this high-security area of the prison, as there had been inmates there for a month or so previous to my arrival. Contrary to what you might expect, the drugs tended to originate from the highest-security wings as that was where you would find the more powerful and influential prisoners with the capacity to organise everything. George told me that the drugs were costing up to ten times as much here as in the old prison. I immediately saw an opportunity and my brain began plotting. I realised that whoever started getting drugs into the prison in volume would control the place. No doubt several other people were thinking the same thing. The transfers had completely split up the gangs and thrown them into disarray – it was as if someone had cleared the board or pressed a reset button and everything would have to begin afresh.

That first morning I was introduced to Cubano. He no longer wished to be called Cubano but instead Brother William as he was now quite religious, or so he claimed. I was sceptical. I had witnessed this so many times before – inmates claiming to have found God and changed their ways. Most often it was all a pretence to try to get time off their sentences for good behaviour. They would claim to be completely changed and reformed by religion, and yet once released they'd revert right back to killing and robbing. It really annoyed me as it was so false.

William, or Cubano as I still thought of him, was quite small and it reminded me of the so-called Napoleon complex, where smaller people have a bigger attitude – like a Jack Russell. Standing before me was a man responsible for literally hundreds upon hundreds of deaths, directly or indirectly. He wouldn't hesitate to kill for the smallest of reasons. I was amazed that Pedro was on the same wing as us because it was he who had ultimately instigated the downfall and loss of control of Los Cubanos in the old prison. He had revealed all the hiding places for the weapons and named all the key gang members. I could only guess that he had been placed here to gather information on Cubano. He was by Cubano's side throughout much of the morning, whispering things in his ear, going back and forth to the guards, plotting things with a couple of the others from our group of 15.

Lunch arrived around midday and was served through a slot in the main gate. It consisted of a bowl of soup, a plate of rice with a little sauce, a tiny amount of chicken and a fruit juice to drink. We were locked in our cells at this point, while the three guards went for their lunch. The cells were reopened at around 2.30pm.

Throughout the afternoon, I watched the comings and goings as various guards came to speak with William/ Cubano and also to George. I was familiar with a couple of the guards from the Peni, having previously done business with them. I greeted them and had a quick chat, dropping hints that I might be interested in trying to organise the entry of a couple of items. They were all fairly hesitant and nervous about things now as they were very much in the spotlight, following all the scandals in the Peni. Everything was on camera here, which added to their paranoia. They couldn't be seen fraternising with us inmates too much, otherwise the police would become suspicious.

We received dinner at 6pm – a plate of rice and two tiny pieces of meat with a little bit of some insipid grey sauce and that was it. We were locked in our cells until the following morning. The first night was spent adjusting to my new surroundings: the noises, smells and being physically locked up again after spending the previous six years in the Peni where our cell doors were open 24 hours a day. For the first time in a very long time I actually felt completely safe as I was locked on my own in a cell that no one, other than the guards, could access. I moved my mattress between the two concrete bunks to see which one offered the best position. Lower down was better as I found the oppressive heat warmed the air higher up in the cell.

I stripped naked and took an indulgent long shower. The cool water flowing over my hot body felt good. In the Peni showers had been something of a luxury, with a diminished water supply meaning we had to shower from large buckets in which we stored the water. It was nice to be in a fresh building and away from all the huge and millions of small cockroaches that infested the Peni. Having showered I stood and let the warm night breeze dry me in a matter of minutes, then lay down to sleep on my bed knowing that absolutely no one was going to knock on my door or try to kill me during the night. I slept well.

I had found out during the next day that half the people from my previous wing were housed in the adjacent wing to ours on a temporary basis until more space became available, as the prison was already nearing its capacity of 4,500 inmates. Not only had people been transferred from the Peni, but also from prisons in the surrounding area that were due to close. I had managed to call out to a couple of my friends as they walked past our wing and they found it hilarious that I had ended up on the same supermax security wing as Cubano. I was less amused. My friends told me that the conditions were bad on their wing, with five people to a cell, running water only a couple of hours a day and no showers in their room, just in the exercise yard. There had also been fights over the poor quality and meagre quantity of food they were receiving. Everyone was pissed off and fed up about this new regime already.

On the morning of the second day a group of social workers and a doctor arrived to check me out because of the TB. They were working their way around the prison, taking everyone's details. Margarita managed to get in to visit and she brought me in a tub of powdered milk supplementary drink. This proved to be of great help and I actually put on a little bit of weight, even in that first week – the doctors had weighed everyone at least a couple of times in the new healthcare centre for their records.

I decided to start the process of applying for repatriation as soon as we had been transferred here. In the first message I sent out I asked Margarita to please inform Isabel from the embassy that yes, I now wished to be repatriated to Britain to finish the sentence there as the conditions in this new prison were just unbearable. There was no way I could face serving another two or three years without even a pen to write with or a book to read, virtually no visits, no letters or payphone and thus no communication, and being fed rice and soup every day. I was now ready to go home to Britain and face the consequences. Come what may, I had had enough of the prisons in Ecuador.

At this point I didn't have a lawyer. I had decided to find one from Guayaquil as it was proving difficult and costly for Eva to travel the 425 kilometres from Quito to see me. Anyway, there hadn't been much call for her services once my sentence was finalised and all options to appeal thus closed.

My original plan with Eva had been to appeal my 12-year sentence after a few years had gone by and get it quietly reduced to six years, for around $20,000. Eva had this deal arranged so that I didn't even need to pay the money up front. The judges had said that they were happy to reduce the sentence as long as they saw proof that the money was in the country and available, for example in a bank account. Once they had reduced the sentence and I was happy they would receive their money.

I had one half of the money but had been waiting for the funds from the sale of my cells in Quito post-transfer to Guayaquil. However, Ruben, the person with whom I had left the responsibility to sort this out, let me down and never paid me the $10,000 he was supposed to. Had he done so I might well have gone free sooner. I tried to borrow the money from my family but they had lost all faith in the Ecuadorian legal system and all the crooked people involved at that time.

CHAPTER THIRTY
ESCAPE, PART 2

On the third or fourth evening following my transfer to the regional prison, I had been sitting in my cell eating dinner. Once I had finished it I had fallen asleep with the cell gate open, something I would never have done in the Peni, nor in Quito, as it was so dangerous. You would have woken up with your throat slit!

I woke up after a couple of hours feeling sick and immediately vomited as I sat upright. Perhaps it was something in the food. I gathered up my bedding and noticed that the gate to my cell was still wide open. What the hell? This was strange. It should have been locked hours ago, after dinner. What was going on, I wondered as I sat there, the smell of the vomit becoming ever more intense. Was this some kind of trap? Had they just forgotten to lock me up?

There was a camera mounted on the wall directly outside my cell, facing along the row of cells towards the guards' office. There was another one at the other end facing back this way, as well as the large one suspended over the centre of the exercise yard. Surely as soon as I stepped outside the cell I would be seen and provoke a shitstorm. It would almost certainly be classed as an attempted escape. But at the end of the day it wasn't my fault. I carried my bedding out of the cell and walked the short distance to the wash sinks in the exercise yard. As I stood there washing my sheets I thought, any second now the police will come bursting into the wing. Nothing happened. There were only 15 or so people on the entire wing. My next door neighbour George had noticed me out of my cell.

'You're going to get us raided, man. They will think you're escaping,' he said.

I had been out of my cell now for some 15 minutes and no one had come to investigate. I was amazed. The cameras were definitely working. Perhaps they just couldn't be bothered to walk the distance from the central booth where the police monitored the cameras. I sat back in my cell and pondered the implications. I had found a weak point in the security. It must be incredibly boring watching dozens of feeds from security cameras in a prison where everyone is locked up and there is therefore no activity. I wondered if I could manage to escape. The temptation was almost overwhelming, but the more I thought about it the more I realised there was little point in talking such a huge risk with such small odds of succeeding. There was an electric fence around the perimeter and armed police with orders to shoot to kill anyone trying to escape. I was just surprised that my cell door had been left open on a supposedly maximum-security wing.

However, for the next few nights I couldn't resist testing the system. Having collected my dinner, I would go back to my cell and slide the gate shut but not quite locked so that anyone glancing down the row of cells would think all the gates were closed. Sure enough my cell stayed unlocked again. This was crazy. I started to wonder if they were doing it on purpose to see if I would attempt to escape.

It happened yet again for the third night in a row, so this time I decided to leave it open all the way through until the next morning. When the guard came round to check the numbers and make sure everyone was present he found me asleep in my bed with the cell gate wide open. He woke me up and asked me what the hell was going on. I told him quite calmly that the guard had forgotten to lock me up the previous night. He eyed me suspiciously then slammed the gate shut, having first checked the lock to see if I had put anything there to prevent it locking properly. He stormed off muttering to himself and that was that. I sat and laughed to myself.

The new arrivals on the wing were all troublemakers and it didn't take long for them to start getting up to mischief as a way to entertain and occupy themselves. At this early stage of the new prison's occupancy all the empty cells' gates on the landings above had been left open so we could access any of them. The newly arrived group started seeing what they could break, steal or utilise. We received a stern lecture on how we would be confined to our cells much more from now on as we couldn't behave.

The guys who had caused the trouble didn't seem that bothered that now we would be locked up for more hours in the day. I couldn't work out why until later that day. I was standing at the entrance of my locked cell looking out at a deserted exercise yard when a cell gate on the opposite side slid open a little and one of these new guys cautiously peered out to check the coast was clear, came out of his cell and scurried a couple of cells along. He collected something from the guy in that cell, beat a hasty retreat to his own and quietly slid the gate to, but not closed. He saw me watching, indicated to me to be quiet and gave me the thumbs-up, laughing.

The lock on the cell gate was a fairly basic mechanism and obviously some of these guys had very quickly worked out how to keep it open. Later I asked the guy I'd seen open his gate how he did it. He gave me a demonstration. It only took a few seconds. The gate would even appear locked if tested from the outside. He explained that the cell gates were nearly all the same throughout the entire prison. People in the other security areas were running around all over the place. Someone somewhere is going to use this in an escape attempt, I thought.

Over the next few weeks, as more inmates arrived from the Peni, I was reacquainted with some old faces. One I vaguely recognised was a skinny young-looking guy nick-named Diablo, or Devil, and he did have a certain look in his eye that was far from saintly. This unassuming kid who was no more than 20 years old had a reputation as an escape artist, having already succeeded in escaping twice from the Peni and once from another prison. Our wing faced on to the highway, which ran past the prison north up the coast and south into the city of Guayaquil. You had a clear view from the upper landing and people would spend hours sitting there daydreaming, watching the world go by. You could also see the position of the nearest watchtowers and the perimeter fences. I began to notice that Diablo and a couple of others would often wander around together, looking up at the fence, gesturing and generally plotting.

One day I passed Diablo in the exercise yard and asked him, 'What's the plan then? When are you going?'

He looked momentarily shocked but then laughed nervously and carried on walking. I told him afterwards not to worry, but warned him to be more careful as others were beginning to take notice of his behaviour as well. I also cautioned him about the electric fence in the middle of the two other perimeter fences. He hadn't even been aware of this and asked me if I thought it carried a lethal voltage. I told him it probably did as otherwise what was the point? He thanked me for the information and headed off to discuss this with the others who planned to go with him. That was the last time we spoke of it as I didn't want to get involved.

I watched them, over the following weeks, making their preparations in the way of exercises to strengthen themselves for climbing and running. I wished them all the luck in the world. I loved it when someone managed to escape and get away. A buzz of excitement would go round the prison and everyone's spirits would be lifted for a few days until the monotony set back in.

One evening, it was pouring with rain so heavy that visibility was reduced to a couple of metres. We could hardly see the cells on the opposite side of the exercise yard. It was soon after 10pm – the light in the cell had not long gone out – when we heard some noise and the sound of movement on the landings. I asked my cellmates if they had heard it too and they confirmed that yes, someone was definitely out there. We moved to the door to have a look but I couldn't see a thing. Some other people had come to their cell doors as well and I could hear them saying someone was escaping. They must have decided to go tonight, using the rain as cover.

Two or three minutes of silence passed, then bam! Several gunshots rang out and we heard bullets hit the metal roof that covered the exercise yard. There were voices shouting from somewhere on the road but we couldn't make out what was being said because of the rain. An alarm had gone off and further gunshots could be heard. A minute or so later dozens and dozens of heavily armed, very angry-looking police burst into the wing like swarming bees.

They were running up and down the landings checking all the doors were secured. We heard them say that they had found open doors and we could hear the occupants who had remained behind being dragged out and beaten.

The wing was absolutely heaving with police and guards now. They brought a list and began checking who was present and who not. We quickly discovered that the two guys from the cell three along from ours had been in on the plan and gone with Diablo and some others. It transpired that they had opened the cell doors by the method I had been shown and scaled the fence of the exercise yard. They covered the razor wire on the top with foam and material cut from their mattresses and dropped down on the other side, where they had been spotted on camera and the police alerted. They had managed to scale the first of the three perimeter fences, by which point a couple of police patrol vehicles had arrived. The officers then opened fire on them, killing one and injuring another. They all surrendered and lay on the ground until the police arrived. They were lucky to not have all been executed on the spot, but times had changed and now it was all on camera and not as easy for the police to get away with. They were all brought back into the prison, two of them to the hospital wing for injuries and the others to maximum security. Diablo was one of them.

There was one final escape though, this time from maximum security. On this occasion the escapee managed to walk right out of the main entrance to the prison, having opened his cell door in the same way. This man was a renowned killer from an infamous case in Ecuador. He was recaptured some two weeks later in the city and brought back to the prison. That was the first and last successful escape attempt from the regional. Not long afterwards they modified all the cell doors and fitted extra locks so there was no way to open them. It seemed that the prison authorities had finally brought to an end years and years of escapes. Never say never though. I'm sure someone will find a weakness in the security and manage it someday.

CHAPTER THIRTY-ONE
THE REGIONAL

I was soon moved to the adjacent wing, which they had decided to use just for TB sufferers. For the first week, there were only six of us on the entire wing, which was designed to hold 300-plus inmates. We each had our own cell with a shower, which was great because of the heat.

We had now been in this brand new prison for three weeks following our sudden mass transfer on the first day of the month. It was nearly Christmas and, apart from the one occasion when Margarita had managed to see me, by late December none of us had received a visit yet. I had heard nothing from the embassy and Isabel, which was really beginning to worry me. She would always make contact whenever something momentous such as this took place. There was obviously something going on that was preventing her from communicating with me. I assumed the authorities were putting a block on anyone visiting for whatever reason.

Every year at Christmas in the Peni, Isabel, in conjunction with the big agricultural company the ambassador owned, would bring each of the British prisoners a huge cooked turkey and a black plastic bin liner full of baked potatoes, 30 or 40 in each. This was almost an institution and the whole prison knew about it. I would usually make up 60 to 70 plates and give them out to all my friends on the wing. I would then cook up a massive pot of minestrone soup using the carcass, beans and potatoes. This used to feed dozens of us as well. I was hoping and praying that they would bring one in this year because the food here was so shit. I had promised everyone else, all five of them, that it would arrive and we would all have a feast. Expectation was growing by the day, along with our hunger.

When I moved to the TB wing we had done our best to wash away the dust that coated everything. Dust, and particularly cement dust, which contains lime, is probably one of the worst things for a TB sufferer. It was making us all cough a great deal more than before. However, washing it just caused it to turn to cement and set everywhere. We complained to the guards and healthcare staff when they appeared but it fell on deaf ears. They said there was nothing they could do and that we would just have to clean the place. I asked to speak to the director of the prison but they told me there was no chance as he was so busy.

I was now facing the wing where one half of the people from Atenuado Alto had been placed. Luckily for me there was a very good friend of mine directly in front, who was quite a big trafficker. He had already acquired a mobile phone, so I passed some messages to him and asked that he send them to family and friends in England, which he kindly did. This really helped me out. My family were relieved to get news of me as they had heard nothing since the move. I asked my friend if he could arrange a phone for me. He said he could but that they were expensive. His had cost him $1,500 and the guards who had brought it in were now constantly pestering him for extra money and threatening to betray him if he didn't pay them. He said it was becoming more hassle than it was worth and he was considering giving it back and demanding his money be returned.

The guards were really taking advantage of the situation and making as much money as they could as quickly as they could. *Cabrones!* Bastards! I asked my friend if he had managed to arrange to get any drugs in yet so that we could start business again. He was working on it but again the guards were demanding astronomical prices. He said there were people who had managed to get things in but it was hard and really dangerous. It was a minefield and one into which, for the moment, I wasn't prepared to step. There was no point in me getting involved anyway as there were only a few people on the wing. I would wait until more people arrived so there was an actual demand, then attempt to take over the wing. At least for the moment I could start preparing by acquiring the necessary contacts to facilitate entry of the drugs.

At the beginning of the second week on the TB wing we had a few new on one of the normal wings arrivals who were all placed in cells on the opposite side of the exercise yard to me. These new guys were typical troublemakers: street thieves and robbers constantly on the lookout for something to steal. They were a pain in the ass right from the very first day. In a bid to get their hands on drugs they would feign illness in order to make the guard take them to the clinic. Once there they would attempt to steal whatever pills they could grab. They were particularly looking for painkillers or sleeping pills, anything for a buzz. They had taken to crushing up the paracetamol and snorting them to try to get high. They would come out of their cells with loads of white powder falling from their noses. Things came to a head when large quantities of pills were stolen from the healthcare centre and the police were brought in to search the cells.

They didn't find them but after that they placed an officer on watch in the clinic all day every day.

They took to hanging around the entrance gate to the wing trying to get food from the guards, who would always have extra portions and generally food of better quality. This little group had noticed that the guards quite often disposed of the surplus food from the evening meal in the rubbish in front of the wing office. They were so intent on salvaging this food that they would cut their arms and wrists badly enough to make them bleed and thus warrant a trip to the clinic to get stitches put in. On the way back they would quickly grab the bags containing the leftover food or convince the guards to give them some.

Hunger really is a terrible thing and will make you go to almost any lengths to appease it. We were literally starved for the first three months of our time at the regional. The worst thing was that there was nothing we could do about it. We didn't have shops where we could buy snacks or food to supplement what we were given. I have never been so hungry in all my life and will never forget the dreadful gnawing feeling that would keep you awake, constantly thinking about food. I would dream about eating and being in a sweet shop. I would sometimes wake up chewing and dribbling all over my pillow, thinking it was a delicious bar of chocolate. People would eat everything they were given. The bones from chickens, banana peels, orange peel, everything.

In the previous prison, where my friends and I used to cook for ourselves a lot, I was aware that there was always someone hungry who would gratefully accept whatever we offered them. Hardly anything was ever thrown away or wasted. Whatever I had left I would always offer to someone in case they were hungry. It was rarely turned down.

This little group of foragers would invent something new nearly every night, taking it in turns to be the sick man or casualty requiring treatment at the clinic. They realised it was better if they could feign an illness or injury that required the assistance of two or three others in order to carry the victim in a bed sheet. After a while the guards and healthcare team really began to tire of their antics and so the guards would pre-empt them by handing out any spare food to those they felt deserved it or needed it the most. This calmed the situation a little but they continued with the charades just for something to do and to get out of their cells for a bit. This really annoyed the guards as it wasted their and the health-care staff's time. It resulted in the guards ignoring cries for help as 95 per cent of the time it was a false alarm, 'crying wolf'. And you know the moral of that story. This was a worry for the rest of us who were genuinely ill, as the guards wouldn't come when called. There were a couple of occasions when people had become really quite sick and it took a long time before the guards realised it was a genuine emergency and came to assist. The cells had no call buttons or alarms, so the only way to get attention was to create a lot of noise by shouting and banging on the door until someone came.

During the day, I did exercises to try to build my strength up again but it was almost impossible with the small amount of food we were being given. The social workers told us that there were plans to start educational courses very soon. They also planned to have workshops where we would be able to earn a small wage. They wanted to have prisons func-tioning like those in developed countries where you are able to make productive use of your time and hopefully move some way towards rehabilitation. For far too many years Ecuador's prisons had become large holding facilities where people were merely warehoused until they were eventually released back into the community even more damaged and antisocial than when they went in. The new prison system aimed to change all of this and address the severe problems that had arisen with the old one.

For the time being, until they had settled and housed everyone in the appropriate security zones, nothing much would be starting so we would have to just occupy our time as best we could. One thing that was causing a great deal of discontent was the lack of visits. Hardly anyone had received one. From the prisoner's point of view, the most important things are visits, food and water, exercise and gym, communications, be it by phone or letters, and healthcare and safety. If you didn't get this right you were in for trouble and unrest.

There had already been protests by prisoners' families along the road that ran in front of the prison. Family and friends of inmates would come to the road and shout at the tops of their voices in order to speak to loved ones with whom they had been denied contact completely, in some cases for months. Tempers had flared and people burned rubber tyres and pelted the police with rocks and stones. The way in which we were being held incommunicado was causing a great deal of outrage and uproar in the country. It had been such a drastic change in circumstances and conditions that it had been a massive shock to most people. So severe had the shock been for some that they had taken their own lives. Added to that there had been over 20 murders in the first couple of weeks, a total of 35 deaths overall. It had been an unmitigated disaster all in all and the president was receiving a lot of criticism over the handling of the whole affair.

An estimated 80 per cent of inmates were going through drug withdrawal symptoms. Those who were suffering the most were the people heavily addicted to heroin. Those who had been sniffing loads of coke or smoking crack 24/7 merely fell into a deep sleep for a week as the stimulants came out of their systems and the whole world slowed down to a standstill for them. It was the reverse for the heroin addicts. They went from having been somnolent zombies to wide-awake owls unable to sleep. There were people screaming, crying, shouting and pounding the gates day and night for assistance, but help came only after a long delay, and only then if the person in question was seriously ill or having a fit or seizure. The clinics were under siege. They had to set up camp beds outside. Each security zone had its own clinic but they just weren't stocked and staffed yet and were completely unprepared for the vast problem of drug withdrawal they now faced. They didn't have any medication they could administer to relieve the symptoms, so they had to rush orders through and wait a couple of days until they were delivered.

No one had quite realised what a huge problem heroin had quietly become in the Peni. Both the main gangs were strictly opposed to selling the drug because they knew it would create all manner of problems and thus unwanted attention, bringing heat to them. It was only when the authorities began transferring the bosses and key gang members from all the wings that heroin began coming into the prison. Once the strict control of the gangs was removed there was no one to stand in the way of heroin's relentless march.

The authorities didn't seem all that concerned at this point. Heroin was a relatively new drug to Ecuador and only became a problem once it was made widely available after its production and purification began in Colombia and Mexico. I had witnessed the heroin epidemic in Britain in the 1980s and even more so in the 1990s. Several of my friends had died from overdoses and related problems.

I predicted that once heroin started moving south from Colombia and Mexico, Ecuador would suffer heavily with a high rate of addiction. Sure enough, the atmosphere changed in the prison with the increased use of heroin. It was ironic that after the gangs had been removed and broken up there was a sudden increase in the level of disorder, murders, robbery, assaults, shootings, stabbings, drug use and general criminality. The drug users in Ecuador thought heroin was like cocaine – you could have a heavy session and by the end of the next day you would be OK. They soon realised that wasn't the case and before anyone knew what was happening there were masses of heroin addicts, with no treatment available, no clinics, no methadone, just one option for not getting sick, which was to take more and more of the brown powder.

Now with a fresh start in the regional prison there weren't many people who wanted to see heroin seep into the wings again, with everyone having just kicked the addiction. The gang bosses were in a sensitive position and didn't need any problems or extra attention at this early stage, while they were re-establishing their business with so many eyes already watching for mistakes.

The huge number of murders that took place in the first couple of weeks occurred in part because the authorities paid little or no attention to the gang affiliations of inmates as they arrived at the regional. Consequently, people were placed in the next available cell with whoever was waiting in line with them. This resulted in enemies and opposing gang members being accidentally placed in the same cells. There were five people to each cell on most wings. Imagine what happened when there were four members of one gang and an enemy from another gang was accidentally placed in with them.

I wondered whether the prison authorities had mixed everyone up on purpose to get rid of a few gang members. It was very easy for them to claim it was an error, by which time of course it was too late. The director was relieved of his position after this fairly disastrous start to what was being heralded as the model of the newly modernised penal system. It wasn't really his fault as the whole mess was just thrust upon him.

It didn't take long for the gangs to start re-establishing control and installing bosses in each of the wings. Los Choneros really came to the forefront now as they had been some of the first inmates in the prison and were becoming ever more powerful. They were basically in control of the entire prison, from what I was hearing. This was great as JL, the boss of Los Choneros, and his brother Carlos were really good friends of mine, so I would be well looked after if I made contact with them. Every time I was taken from my wing to the clinic friends of mine from Atenuado Alto would start chanting my name out of the windows until there was a regular cacophony. No one else received this kind of reception, not even Cubano, who was the boss of an entire gang. The guards would look at me, wondering just who it was they were escorting.

There were a couple of really beautiful female guards who had previously worked in the Peni and were now working on my wing, both of whom I was very friendly with; but one in particular, Paula, now started to pay me quite a bit of extra attention. She was stunning with an amazing figure and a really kind personality. She would call me out to the wing office to chat and flirt and give me food, which I much appreciated. It was good fun and brightened my day. She would sometimes come to my cell door at night if she was on duty. I would be naked because of the heat and Paula would stand by the door for a while talking to me. It was great!

Everyone had been waiting for the day the canteen shop finally opened so that we could taste something sweet again and get some proper food to eat. The authorities kept promising us if we behaved ourselves then they would open the shop. When they did eventually do it you had to have money in your private account, which was held by the director of the prison. You were limited to spending $50 in minimum security, $40 in medium, $30 in maximum and only $15 in supermax, per month.

We soon worked out that if an inmate had no money coming into their account we could use some of their quota in the shop by paying money into their account. You could then purchase more goods once your quota was maxed out, which you'd split with the owner of the account. This worked for those of us with more to spend – because 30 or 40 dollars' worth of food did not last a month – and for the account owner who would get a share of the items in payment for the use of their account.

This also meant there was now currency again in the prison, which could be used for drug deals. It's difficult to earn a buck, if there's no bucks. The canteen shop also became a route for contraband to be smuggled in, and it didn't take long for the dealers to find people willing to earn extra money to bring in a parcel. Weed and coke were the two main drugs that started coming in and the gangs were back in action.

In the meantime, I was still stuck in the healthcare wing. On 23 December, over three weeks after our transfer, a couple of hundred people from the clinic at the Peni arrived. The turkey became a running joke among the small group of us who had arrived on the wing first. They kept asking me where the turkey was and I would reply it had flown off, to bitter laughter. I wasn't laughing though and as Christmas approached I became depressed and anxious. I had had no contact with anyone apart from two messages and the one visit from Margarita.

On 24 December I met up with my Estonian friend Enar. We agreed to see if we could arrange for Enar to be moved in with me so I had some company and someone to talk to. Changing cells here was not like it had been in the Peni where you just moved where you pleased when you pleased within the wing. Here we would have to get permission from the wing coordinator, which was complicated. Enar's name would have to be moved on the list, which meant reprogramming the details on the system. I went and enquired with the guards and they said they would see what they could do but that I really needed to talk to the coordinator personally to arrange this. Great! It looked like it would be a solitary Christmas. I told Enar and he said not to worry, we would do it as quick as possible.

As the afternoon of Christmas Eve drew on I became more and more despondent. I hadn't even been able to send a letter to my family wishing them happy Christmas, nothing. Dinner arrived early so that the guards could get us all locked away and go home to their families and friends to start celebrating. We on the other hand were given a 'special' Christmas Eve dinner consisting of a slice of turkey so thin I could see through it, a little bit of Russian salad – perhaps a teaspoonful – and, you guessed it, rice. Nothing sweet, not even on Christmas Eve, and it was back to my concrete box to be locked in for the night.

I ate my dinner and lay down on my bed lost in my thoughts of my family, my dead mother and my friends. This would be the first year of my life that I had not been able to speak to my family on Christmas Eve. I felt terrible. I hated myself for having committed the crimes that had put me here in the first place, separating me from everyone I loved. I lay on my bed in that cell, on my own 5,000 miles from home, and I wept. I just couldn't take it any more. I felt worthless, a complete and utter waste of DNA. I had failed everyone and become a disappointment and embarrassment to my family. My mother, aunt and cousin had all died in my time here, along with dozens of friends. If only I had not become involved with drugs perhaps my mother would still be alive. She would never see my or my sister's children as neither of us had had any by the time she died. For the very first time in my life I began to contemplate ending it all by committing suicide. But these thoughts only lasted a minute or two, during which I remembered when my stepbrother had killed himself, followed by his cousin four weeks later. I recalled the devastating effect that had had on the rest of my family. My sister, Sarah, had recently had a little boy and images of my newly born nephew who I'd never met flashed before my eyes and I knew I could never be so selfish as to kill myself.

I started to pull myself back together. I started cursing myself for being so weak and self-pitying. Around 8pm a kind, friendly woman who worked in the prison's healthcare team came around wishing everyone a happy Christmas. When she got to me she could see I was upset and she tried to reassure me, which made me cry once again. I told her I was OK, thanked her and wished her a happy Christmas and she left. At that point I broke down and wept until I could weep no more and fell asleep.

CHAPTER THIRTY-TWO
BACK INTO THE FRAY

In January, I was moved back to my wing. One day I was stood by the entrance gate on to the wing, which was made of cast iron or steel bars. I hadn't realised it was unlocked and another inmate suddenly pulled it open, catching and cutting my big toe in the process, as I was only wearing flip-flops. It was only a small cut, but within a couple of days of bathing in the open-air showers in the exercise yard it became infected. The infection rapidly spread to the skin surrounding the nail which became intensely painful and full of pus. It was agony. I left it at first, thinking it would clear up on its own, then a couple of people gave me various liquids and creams to apply to the area. None of these had any effect and it kept getting worse. I pleaded with the guards to allow me out to go to the clinic, which was only 100 metres away, but they were being bastards and wouldn't let me go.

The infection kept spreading, until the whole foot became swollen and inflamed. My body was losing the fight; I was no longer able to walk up and down the stairs. I finally snapped and got myself down to the main gate again, now on a Saturday. By chance I found it to be open so walked straight out of the wing. At this point a guard challenged me. Luckily on this particular day I knew both the *jefes de guia* and was on good terms with them. I point blank refused to return to the wing and told the guard to call his boss. I was in so much pain it had to be seen to. He eventually gave in and accompanied me to the clinic.

The doctor took one look at it and said had I left it another two or three days he would have had to amputate it. In order to save the toe, he had to pull the nail out then and there. Now, I don't know about you, but the idea of having my toenail torn away from the nerves by lifting it and then yanking it out was my idea of fucking torture. This is what I had expected to happen if I ever ended up on the bad side of a deal and was kidnapped.

Added to this, I had been sniffing coke for the last 24 hours and this was going to require an anaesthetic. I asked the doctor casually what the anaesthetic was. He told me it was lidocaine. Oh dear! Lidocaine is derived from cocaine and the fact that my body was full of it probably meant my tolerance was going to be through the roof, meaning the anaesthetic would have little effect. The doc came back with his small black case of tools.

'I am going to have to inject underneath the toenail, which will hurt quite a bit, and then also two further injections, one being directly into the main nerve which runs up the side of the toe.'

'OK, doc, fire away.'

Why the fuck does this only happen to me? I wondered as I lay back and gritted my teeth. At this point my good Russian buddy Ruslan appeared. Being a field-trained military doctor from the Russian infantry and a qualified chiropractor, he had quickly been taken on as an orderly in the already overwhelmed healthcare centre.

'Hi Ruslan. *Dobroe utro.*'

We chatted and joked, which was a welcome distraction from the pain that was about to be inflicted on me. I clenched my jaw as I saw the doc preparing a bloody great long syringe right in front of me. He pushed the needle into the vial of clear liquid that was lidocaine, then held the needle up and squirted a little into the air, clearing any bubbles. The thought of this foreign body being driven under my toenail was almost enough to make me faint. In went the first injection and it wasn't too bad as I was in such great pain already. It was the second injection directly into the main nerve that hurt like a bastard. My cold sweat spread from my forehead down across my chest and stomach. I lay back and the pain slowly receded from my foot. The doc started probing. Sure enough, I could still feel it when he poked around because of my high tolerance to cocaine and therefore to lidocaine. He gave me a couple more injections, up to the maximum level permitted, glancing at me occasionally to make sure I wasn't dying.

'If this fails to completely numb the toe, then you will have to come back another day and try again.'

Luckily it worked. By now my toe felt as if a giant was squeezing it with the pressure caused by all the extra fluid under the skin.

'Right, here we go,' said the doctor, putting almost his entire bodyweight on my leg and another inmate holding me down at the shoulders. There was a bit of a tug and a cold feeling where the nail had been. It was out. I heard the doc open the metallic bin and then a 'ting' as my toenail landed in the bottom. I could hear the pat-pat-pat of my own blood hitting the floor. Ruslan looked like he was about to faint.

They poured iodine directly over the exposed nail bed and bandaged it. I was warned to take great care that no one stand on it or that I accidentally bump it. As I was about to leave, the doctor enquired, with a glint in his eye, 'Do you have any other problems with your nails?'

'Why? Do you want to pull them all out?'

'No, just checking.'

'I thought you might have been starting a collection.'

During the next couple of months, I was called to the offices out of which all the functionaries for the medium-security zone worked. I had to undergo a series of psychological examinations in order to fulfil the criteria for repatriation. I also had to go through a long medical examination to ensure I was no longer contagious with TB. If I had been, that would have stopped the entire process dead in its tracks, probably along with me shortly afterwards. I also had to have interviews with various social workers and administration staff.

On one particular day, my room-mates had convinced me to smoke some potent skunk with them. I generally don't touch marijuana as I don't like the effect, but on this day I thought it might change my perspective a little bit and pass the day more quickly. A few lines of coke followed and then suddenly I could hear my name being called. Shit. Was it me being paranoid? Had I finally lost the plot? Another inmate appeared at the doorway and said I was being summoned to the offices and that there was a social worker waiting at the main gate. Just what I needed while I was stoned!

I limped down the stairs, my foot still being bandaged, and left the wing with the social worker who seemed to be looking at me more than normal – or was this just my paranoia? I tried to stay cool and collected. Once we arrived at the office, it transpired that she was one of the psychologists and had a barrage of questions awaiting me, which were going to take a couple of hours to wade through, including me having to draw pictures such as a house, a tree, a face – all the usual psychobabble. I laughed internally as I knew my answers were going to come out somewhat skewed and would probably have the shrink scratching her head. As we proceeded, the effects of the drugs gradually began to wear off, thankfully, and I relaxed and got into the questions. I never did see the results of that or any of the examinations, much as I would have loved to.

Upon my return to the wing, everybody started saying, 'Oh, you're going soon. Good luck! Stay in touch.' I wasn't so sure and managed to put in a call to Isabel to ask for an update on what was happening with the process overall. I received the usual response.

'A couple more months. You know we can't give you the date.'

'But is it going to be soon?'

'I can't say,' she replied, as my hopes and dreams of freedom slowly headed west along with the setting Ecuadorian sun.

A couple of weeks after having moved back to the wing, there was a commotion at the gate, so I went to see what was happening. Someone told me that they had just overheard one of the officer's radios reporting that one of the wings in the low-security zone, which was situated next to ours, had started to riot and there was a mass breakout taking place with dozens of people scaling the chain-link fence out of their exercise yard and over into the medium-security zone. I stood by the entrance to the wing. All of the wing entrances were double-gated. The idea was that the guard could let you through the first gate into a holding area, close that gate behind you and then open the outer one, or vice versa. Thus no one could suddenly rush out of the wing. Some of the other inmates on my wing had slammed shut the outer gate and unravelled the fire hose located in this holding area. They had then pulled the hose into our exercise yard, slammed shut the inner gate and stood waiting to blast anyone that attempted to gain entry to our wing.

The next thing we see are a couple of guards and police running across the open area in front of the wings where the football pitches were meant to be. As one of the policemen is running from the mob that we can hear approaching from our left, he turns with handgun drawn aimed towards the pursuing inmates. He must have thought better of it, as how many people can he hit with one clip before they are on him tearing him apart? In his panic, he fumbles the gun and drops it. Having no time to retrieve it he high-tails it following the rest of the guards to where they had locked themselves in an area on a wing to our right.

Within seconds, dozens of people went racing by, all carrying weapons from knives and machetes to iron bars. Jesus Christ! The guys manning the fire hose opened up at anyone who attempted to even get near our gate. By now the mob had managed to rip the gate off its hinges behind which the guards were cowering. They started to beat the hell out of the guards and police officers with whatever they had to hand as they ran back across the open ground in the direction of the office buildings, seeking shelter. The mob were smashing and breaking anything they could. They managed to break into the shop and looted everything. They also tried to break into the clinic to steal drugs but the security there held. A police helicopter was now circling overhead and a cordon of police had encircled the entire prison in readiness to prevent an escape.

The guys at our gate maintained a defence against the marauders who tried to break into our wing and pelted the guys manning the hose with rocks, clods, mud and sticks. After a while, hundreds of police in riot gear came charging in, releasing tear gas. The police managed to chase everyone back to their wings and brought the situation under control. Miraculously, no one was killed but quite a few were injured. All the ringleaders were transferred to other prisons, having been identified on the cameras. That was the only actual riot I witnessed in all the years I was imprisoned in Ecuador. There had been the protests or *paros*, but never a riot like this – up until then.

CHAPTER THIRTY-THREE
ADIOS

Six months had passed. It was November 2014. Payano was trying to get my attention. Payano was a Dominican who saw himself as a bit of a politician or revolutionary and liked to get involved in the daily running of the wing however he could.

'They're calling you into the offices,' he told me with a knowing look in his eye and a wry smile.

Isabel the vice consul from the embassy had been in touch and told me that I was going to be transferred any day now but she couldn't give a specific date because of security. They were concerned I might attempt an escape mid transit. I was on tenterhooks, barely able to sleep with the anticipation.

I had kept news of my ongoing repatriation bid reasonably quiet as people were extremely envious here and just loved to cause you problems if they thought you were doing better than them. I had seen other people, over my many years in prison, keeping their release date a closely guarded secret, so that one day they would be there and the next gone; disappeared as if dead. I used to think it strange when people kept their release date secret, but I learned over the years that it was in fact the best thing to do, just in case someone wanted to get you into trouble at the very last moment.

I was now seen as one of the bosses on the wing. Even most of the guards treated me with a degree of respect. The gang knew I was someone dependable, with whom they could do business. I was involved in the sale of cocaine on the wing and helped to oversee the running of everything else as a whole. But that could also make me a target for someone who was jealous of my status. I had seen on numerous occasions that when someone started doing well for themselves other people on the wing would become envious, and it often ended in trouble for the one doing well. Quite often someone would cause a problem just out of pure spite. I was worried that someone would try to get me busted with 50 or 100 grams of coke. That would quite easily get me another 12 years.

However, what was worrying me even more was the prospect of being arrested upon arrival in Britain and charged with conspiracy to import some 85 kilograms of cocaine. The memory of the threat the British police had made when I was first arrested, of a 20-year minimum sentence in the UK, still hung over my head. Fuck that! There was no way I would accept that without a serious fight. I had been mentally preparing myself for this coming battle for several months now, ever since it was confirmed that I would be getting repatriated to Britain where I would complete the remainder of my sentence.

My friends in Britain were divided on the issue, half saying I was going to get stuffed if I came back and the other half of the opinion that, seeing as I had served nearly ten years and gone through all the traumatic events I had, the British authorities would consider it sufficient punishment and call it a day. My stepmother had managed to speak to one of the police officers who had been involved in my case. He had more or less said to her that they considered the case closed and I had been sufficiently punished, so they wouldn't be pursuing me any further. I wasn't sure whether to trust that or not.

I had no idea what was going to be the actual outcome, but whatever happened at least I would be home in my own country, in my own culture and near my family and friends, who I hadn't seen for nearly a decade. God, it was going to be strange.

The thought of seeing my family was actually making me feel quite nervous. I knew my own face had changed drastically. When I looked in the mirror the face that stared out at me was one that bore signs of extreme mental trauma. My eyes appeared anguished and constantly on the verge of tears. They were eyes that had witnessed horrific scenes of death and torture. Where once I had longish hair I now had a shaved head. I was also looking gaunt and ravaged from the effects of the TB, which had nearly killed me, and the minimal prison diet.

Nearly ten years had gone by since that day I had left my father standing on the French train station platform. My sister had told me he had aged quite a lot and now had a full head of grey hair and had lost a tooth or two. I tried to envisage a gap-toothed, decrepit, bent old man, but found that impossible to imagine, as he had always been such a big, strong person.

In the time I had been away, my sister had got married and had a child, so I was now an uncle. I had only seen photos of my new nephew and couldn't wait to meet him in person. She had named him after the character in a story I created when we were children. I would ad-lib it to her in the evenings or if she was feeling upset, so it had stuck with her. When I found this out it touched me deeply to know these stories had left such an impression on her. She was now a woman and mother, not the little sister I had left behind.

I went over to the offices with the inmate dispatched to find me, wondering what they needed to know now. Over the previous weeks, I had been called to the offices on a number of occasions so that they could gather all the information necessary for my repatriation. I had to undergo psychological examinations, talk to social workers, have medical check-ups, compile a dossier of what I had been doing with myself for the last nine years and have a security check in order to make sure I wasn't preparing to escape during transit. This check was basically once again a series of psychological tests for risk assessment and a couple of interviews. No doubt they had their informants on the wings letting them know exactly what was going on. They took my fingerprints and photo-graph several times, and I don't know how often I had given my details and those of nearly all my family members.

The whole process of repatriation was expected to take about a year; however, it quite often took a lot longer, with some people having waited up to three years. It wasn't guar-anteed that you would be accepted, either. First of all, the Ecuadorian government had to agree in principle to my repa-triation, then the British government had to do the same. All my prison history would then be sent from Ecuador to Britain for them to take a better look at me and my case. This was then returned to Ecuador with anything the British had to add, such as my criminal record and British prison history. The Ecuadorians then had to make a final decision and approve the transfer. At this stage I had to pay the fine I received as part of my sentence, which in my case was $8,000; I couldn't be transferred until this was paid. I then had to cover the cost of the airfare back to the UK, which would be quite high as they informed me they were not able to purchase the ticket until the last moment because of the way they operated. The prison service uses normal airlines but has to get special clearance from the company due to the possible risks involved in transporting convicts. After all this was done they would go ahead and make the arrangement for British prison officers to come from Wandsworth Prison in London to escort me home. This could take a good few months to sort out as there is only a small group of prison officers who travel around the world bringing prisoners home.

I would not be informed of my transfer date until the day before it happened. This had been driving me mad. It seemed to me that every time I called the British embassy to enquire when I might be going home, they would say, 'Oh, in a couple of months.' It felt as if my transfer date was getting further and further away. Christ, I had nearly served my entire sentence already and they had awarded me an extremely generous ten per cent off my sentence for not behaving well! This meant I had to serve just under 11 years in total.

I'd been told that the presidential pardon I had applied for in respect of the $8,000 fine could take years to be granted. I didn't want to spend $8,000 plus another $2,000 in airfare just to go back to prison in Britain for God knows how long.

The tragic and brutal death of Simon, and the death of another British prisoner under very similar circumstances, had quite rightly caused a scandal. British prisoners being targeted and killed was not acceptable when the Ecuadorian government had a duty of care. The embassy was also aware of the poor conditions and lack of food.

The Ministry of Justice had promised to speed up the process of repatriation but refused to back down on the issue of the fines, which was one of the main reasons a lot of people couldn't go through with it. In Simon's case the fine had been over $80,000. An incredible amount. That was the highest I'd heard of. The average was a couple of thousand dollars, with the Spaniards receiving the lowest, often just a couple of hundred. The money raised from the fines was supposedly used to fight and prevent drug trafficking in Ecuador.

I had kept refusing to let my family pay the fine as it was a lot of money and I felt terrible that they would have to pay it. I thought something would come up and I would get released, but I kept waiting and waiting all in vain. I missed out on a couple of things that might have seen me released years earlier because of technicalities and poor work on the part of lawyers. This to some extent was lucky, as had I not served very long the British police would have attempted to extradite me to Britain to be re-sentenced there. Either that, or I wouldn't have been able to return to Britain for a very long time. In the end my stepmother paid the fine that would allow me to be released.

I arrived at the office block for my area of the prison. There stood a well-dressed Ecuadorian woman, looking rather nervous, with a walkie-talkie in her hand.

'Are you Pieter Tritton?' she enquired in Spanish.

'Yes,' I replied, wondering what the hell was going on now.

'Right, then you are leaving to go home to Britain right now.'

'What?' I stammered, while my heart rose up into my throat and a ridiculous, uncontrollable grin spread across my face. 'But I don't have any of my things.' I had actually sent out most of the things I wanted over the preceding weeks with Margarita to ensure they reached Britain safely. I also didn't want to carry any phone numbers with me on the return journey because I was worried about being questioned on arrival. I was worried that if the police found these numbers it might cause problems for the people concerned. It could also have possibly caused me problems, as some of the numbers on the list belonged to very serious traffickers.

'You are very welcome to go back and get your things if you want,' the woman said sarcastically. She had been talking rapidly into the walkie-talkie, confirming she had me next to her and was due to deliver me any second now. I decided I would rather leave the few things I had in my cell. Probably best to leave the couple of grams of coke I had just got that morning ... I felt momentarily bad for not having been able to say goodbye to all my friends, some of whom I had known since my very first days of captivity in the Interpol cells in Quito. Whenever anyone left it really felt as if they had died, as quite often that would be the last you ever heard of them. It was sometimes very emotional if a very close friend left. Part of you didn't want them to go, however happy you were for them that they were getting out. I felt both sad and ecstatic at the same time. I was sure my friends wouldn't begrudge me not saying goodbye.

The woman asked me to follow her to the main reception block where the offices of the director and senior prison staff were. I was ushered into a holding cell, one of three large cages. There were some twenty-five people in the holding cell, including a couple whom I knew from my years in the Peni. They greeted me warmly and made space for me on one of the plastic-covered mattresses on the floor. The woman told me I was going to have to wait a couple of hours before we left for the airport with an armed guard. She explained that I should have been taken from the wing I was housed on and brought here the night before to keep me in isolation so that I couldn't inform anyone, in case I was preparing to escape. It also meant they would have me ready and waiting to be escorted by Interpol and the other policemen to the airport. Apparently there had been some sort of mistake and they had forgotten to collect me. I was due to leave the country at 5pm, but it was now 1pm and they hadn't even started the process of filling out all the relevant paperwork.

The first stage was for members of the prison service to sign the permission needed to transfer me to Britain. Next, the police had to run a few checks on me, such as finger-prints, to confirm my identity. I was then thoroughly searched for weapons of any description. As we were going through this process, a group of four heavily armed police officers more akin to military personnel arrived. They were carrying M16 assault rifles and Glock handguns, and were wearing camouflage fatigues and maroon berets. These four plus another four waiting outside were to be my escort all the way to the plane.

The last people to arrive were four Ecuadorian Interpol officers in whose car I would be travelling. They searched me again and then handed me some normal civilian clothes into which I could change. Margarita had bought some navy blue trousers and a polo top, fresh new underwear, new shoes and a jumper for the flight and sent them in via the embassy. She was due to meet me at the airport along with her son Gustavo, Isabel and a few other people who had organised the transfer. It sounded as if it was going to be quite a send-off.

I was in utter shock that after the best part of a decade of constantly trying to survive I was actually going home and this nightmare would finally be over. I kept thinking any minute now I would wake up and still have another ten years to go. It was really happening – it really was!

I had been told previously by the embassy and by lawyers in both Britain and Ecuador that if I was to face further charges in Britain the police would have to, by law, notify me 24 hours before travel. It therefore appeared that I wasn't going to face further charges upon arrival in London. I was still nervous but the pressure was starting to lift.

The plane was due to leave at 5pm and we needed to arrive at the airport with lots of time to check in. You may think you have it hard at the airport with security, but imagine the security checks I had to go through. I had to be patted down countless times and then go through a scanner to make sure I hadn't swallowed capsules, and of course my bag was thoroughly searched.

I was so happy as we pulled away from the prison that I couldn't stop smiling. Our small convoy headed towards the airport in Guayaquil. I was in the middle car, accompanied by the four Interpol officers, all armed, and in front of and behind us were jeeps, each carrying four armed police. As we travelled along, one of the Interpol officers turned to me and asked, 'So don't you like it here then?'

'Why do you ask?' I replied, a little confused. Although the answer was obvious it sounded like a loaded question.

'Well you tried to escape, didn't you?' the Interpol officer responded knowingly, all his colleagues laughing.

'Ah!' I thought that this information had been long forgotten – it hadn't. The tunnel project had come back to haunt me one last time. I had never had it confirmed that this was the reason behind my transfer seven years previously, but finally I knew the answer. They all found this very amusing. The fact that this had come up now helped to explain a few things, for example why I had been transferred from Quito to Guayaquil in the first place. I had paid someone a fair amount of money to supposedly have this erased while I was in the process of applying for parole. No wonder they had only awarded me ten per cent remission off my sentence.

'So you won't be coming back any time soon then?'

'I can't, as you well know. But I will in the future as I have business I want to conduct between here and Britain.'

They all looked at one another and laughed again. They didn't realise I was serious. Just not drugs next time.

At the airport they cordoned off an area of the car park and surrounded me with armed police to prevent me from doing a runner. I wasn't allowed to get out of the car. It was only when Margarita, Gustavo, Isabel, Tanner and a few others turned up that they finally gave in and let me have various photos taken alongside my friends. Members of the public wandering by were peering over at us to see what all the fuss was about. I was dressed in reasonably smart, brand-new clothes and they had removed the handcuffs as we were surrounded by heavily armed police. It probably looked as if we were some important dignitaries.

We were travelling economy class on a commercial passenger airline. I hadn't yet been told the route we were taking. There are no direct flights to England so I knew we would likely be travelling through North America, Spain or Holland, these being the most commonly used routes. I had for a while planned in my mind the possibility of escape if I had thought there was any chance of my being re-sentenced upon arrival in London. I couldn't face another long sentence. I knew that we would have to get off the plane for a stopover at some point, so I'd thought I might be able to slip some crushed-up sleeping tablets into the drinks of the guards accompanying me. They were bound to have some coffee or tea when we stopped. The plan was to then take my pass- port, which one of them would be carrying, and disappear off out of the airport somehow. I had gone so far as to acquire the necessary tablets and had them crushed up ready. It was lucky I was taken without warning, as they would almost certainly have discovered them when I was searched.

An hour or so had passed when the three British prison officers from Wandsworth arrived in the airport car park and introduced themselves. They had the typical look of prison guards about them – short hair, strong but rather fat, smartly dressed. They seemed quite surprised by the level of security around me and the amount of serious hardware the police had on display. They looked rather underdressed for the occasion, with just a pair of handcuffs, compared to the others' M16 assault rifles and Glock handguns.

I had a brief chat with them about my sentence, what I had done and how the prisons compared with the ones in Britain. They had been in Ecuador since the Monday of that week and it was now Thursday. True to form and Ecuadorian efficiency, some of the paperwork hadn't been completed when they arrived, so I couldn't be released into their custody. This had meant we missed the first airline booking, which was due to go through the USA. They had to buy new tickets, passing through Madrid on Avianca and then swapping to BA.

I said my goodbyes to Margarita and Isabel, who had become very dear to me. I view Margarita as a second mother and Isabel as a third! Without the pair of them and all their help I would almost certainly have ended up dead. They looked after me as if I was their child, with such love and care. They are two of the most incredible women I have ever met and it broke my heart bidding them farewell after all those years. We were all quite tearful.

I had jokingly written out a list of things I wanted them to buy me for the journey: fruit, chocolate and all manner of other food and drink. Of course it was all denied. Rocío did manage to bring me a chocolate brownie and a hot chocolate, which tasted divine after so long in the last prison without anything decent to eat. The craving for something sweet is incredibly strong when you can't satisfy it.

Members of the press and a human rights group were at the airport in order to make sure I left the country in one piece. I was handcuffed before walking through the airport, at gunpoint and surrounded by the police. It was quite a spectacle, with women pulling young children out of the way and people pausing to take photos. I was experiencing culture shock. Everything appeared shiny and glowing with colour. Everyone either seemed to have a phone glued to their ear or was staring at one. Everyone looked smart and well-presented and it all felt really fast. I thought, if I'm feeling in shock here, I can't imagine what London will be like.

We proceeded further on into the depths of the airport, being ushered past worried-looking officials and members of the airport security. A couple of Human Rights Watch workers were busy snapping photos at every stage in order to show the world how well Ecuador treats its prisoners and so that, should I arrive in bits, they would have proof they weren't responsible. Also in tow was a journalist documenting my journey. Prior to the security checks and searches the British prison officers officially took charge of me. All three of them then posed beside me for a photo, with one of the policemen dressed in military fatigues complete with beret and M16 assault rifle. One for the scrapbook and to show the grandchildren!

Next we had all our bags searched, at which point I was ushered into a room with a high-tech scanner and X-ray. One of the customs officers asked me if I had swallowed any capsules of cocaine and assured me that if I had I would be going directly back to the prison to begin a fresh 12-year sentence. A few people in the prison had tried to talk me into swallowing capsules prior to leaving, insisting that I wouldn't be searched as I had just come from prison. There was no way in hell I was doing that. I never had and never would ask anyone to do so for me, as it is inherently dangerous and just not worth the risk. After nine years I just wanted to go home. I didn't want to spend a single minute more in a South American prison.

They took their time examining the scanner and X-ray results, scrutinising every last centimetre of my intestines and colon. Good luck to them! It reminded me of some of the men I had seen in Quito with fresh red scars running the entire length of their abdomens where they had had the capsule extracted on the operating table in order to 'save them'. Their scars resembled the sewing I had seen on the mailbags in the prison workshops in Britain. Frankenstein's monster looked better.

We then passed through into the departure lounge and found some seats next to the gate. The armed police had left now and the only ones who remained were the Ecuadorian Interpol officers who were tasked with seeing me all the way on to the plane to make absolutely sure I was no longer a problem for their government. They reminded me that I was banned from returning to Ecuador for the next five years.

I was now left with just the three British prison officers and a couple of Ecuadorian Interpol officers. I sat quietly for a while, collecting my thoughts. Then I noticed, directly in front of us, a chocolate shop. The brownie and hot chocolate Margarita had given me earlies had reminded me of my love for chocolate and Ecuadorian chocolate is some of the best in the world, so I persuaded one of the guards to accompany me into the shop. I walked out the proud owner of my first bar of chocolate since I'd gone to prison, and God it tasted good.

We had to wait until everyone else had boarded and then we took our places in the last two rows of the middle section, reserved for us. I had a prison officer each side of me and the third was seated behind. It still felt unreal. As we taxied along the runway I was smiling from ear to ear, and when we finally took off I couldn't help but laugh out loud. I was away! I had done it! I had survived nine years in one of the most dangerous prisons on the planet. People had tried to kill me, I had seen people killed every which way, torture carried out, gunfights, grenade attacks, machete fights, riots. Some of my close family had died while I was away, and lots of friends. I was changed, but alive.

We rose up into the stratosphere and sped across the Atlantic towards Spain and Britain. That chapter of my life had closed. I drifted into one of those all-encompassing deep sleeps you only experience after severe trauma and prolonged periods of intense stress. I was safe, perhaps for the first time in a decade.

CHAPTER THIRTY-FOUR
HMP WANDSWORTH

Fyodor Dostoyevsky said: 'The degree of civilisation in a society can be judged by entering its prisons.' He should know. He did four years' hard labour in Siberia.

I awoke somewhere over Portugal, rather disorientated and achy from being squashed between the two large prison officers. One of them was asleep and the other reading a magazine. I asked him how much longer to go and he told me it would be about an hour until we touched down in Madrid. We had to wait a couple of hours in the Spanish capital before our flight left for London. If there was going to be any chance of escape then that would be the most likely time I could attempt it.

During the flight I had been quizzing the guard who seemed to be in charge of our little group as to whether or not there was any mention of an active arrest warrant with my name on it. He told me that he had not seen or heard anything about further charges or pending cases back in Britain, which came as a huge relief. Although I had been told that they would have had to notify me before we even got on the plane in Ecuador if I was going to be arrested upon arrival in England, I wouldn't fully relax until at least a couple of weeks had passed back home. For nine years I had wondered almost daily whether or not I was going to be charged on my return to Britain with the alleged offences in connection to the case in England and Scotland. It seemed that I would very soon be able to put that out of my mind and start planning the rest of my life.

We landed in a sunny Madrid late in the afternoon of 14 November 2014. The plane emptied and we were the last to disembark. It felt fantastic to finally step on to European ground. I couldn't stop grinning. I was led, handcuffed to one of the guards, to a waiting area located in what appeared to be the airport police or customs offices. There were a couple of holding cells and various interview rooms. A few people were brought in, handcuffed and accompanied by the police officers who had just detained them. I wondered whether any of them had just been arrested for drug trafficking. There was I on the way home, having nearly finished my sentence for drug trafficking, and here were these people possibly about to start a period of detention for the same reason. This business will never cease. There will always be people willing to risk their liberty smuggling drugs unless they are legalised.

It was finally time to board our flight to London Heathrow. As we were mid-air heading towards England the sun was setting in the west and to me it felt symbolic, as if that was the end of one journey and another was beginning. I felt good. We descended through the clouds and the lights of the city of London came into view, spreading out below us. One of the guards turned to me and said, 'There's your new home down there.' Somewhere below us was HMP Wandsworth, soon to be my home for the remaining ten months of my sentence.

We landed at Heathrow at around 6pm. When we presented our papers at immigration, the border force officer looked at me with a grin and said, 'Been a naughty boy have we?' I couldn't help but laugh. The English sense of humour – how I'd missed it! From here I was led to a waiting prison van and we began the journey from Heathrow down the M4 motorway towards London. I was feeling tired and overwhelmed by this point. The sense of freedom I'd experienced during the flight began to evaporate as we got nearer to Wandsworth prison.

HMP Wandsworth is an old Victorian establishment with a capacity for just under 1,900 inmates, making it one of England's largest prisons. All repatriated prisoners come here first in order to be assessed to determine their security status, calculate how long they are to serve and a host of other things. Prisoners arrive on an almost daily basis from all over the world. As well as repatriated prisoners Wandsworth holds those on remand waiting for trial, people awaiting deportation and a large number of foreign nationals. Once you have been assessed you will probably be allocated to the prison where you are going to serve out the remainder of your sentence. This is unless, like me, you only had a short period left to complete. In that case, you are more likely to remain in Wandsworth.

We arrived at the gates around 9pm. They led me to the reception area, where the handcuffs were removed and my details taken. As it was so late and the guards all wanted to leave for home, they decided to leave the full admission process until the following day. I was shown to a temporary cell, complete with television. Watching British TV was something of a treat after nine years of Spanish-language *telenovelas*. I sat down in the cell grinning quite contentedly as I drank my cup of English tea and ate some biscuits (not cookies, English biscuits!), chocolate, cereal and other junk foods they had supplied in the induction pack. I felt so very, very happy to be in prison ... in England. I was probably the happiest prisoner in the entire place that night. As the relief and exhaustion washed over me I fell back into a deep sleep without the sounds of gunshots or screams in the night. I was in my home country and at long, long last safe.

I awoke in the morning to the sounds of Wandsworth prison; keys jangling up and down the landings, metal cell doors banging shut, people shouting and talking, bells going off and the multitude of other noises from within the walls. The guards came round a short time later and opened up the cell for exercise, so I went downstairs out into the chilly November air and had a wander round the yard. Luckily I was still wearing the clothes in which I had been transferred, including a black jacket. It was my own jacket from when I went over to Eaodar and had been in the safe keeping of the embassy and later Margarita in Guayaquil. As I walked round the exercise yard I overheard snippets of conversation from some of the other inmates bemoaning their situation and how hard it was in this prison, how bad the conditions were.

I know prison wherever you are in the world is hard; it's meant to be. That's the whole idea – so that by suffering you don't repeat whatever put you there in the first place. You do have to remember that there are always people worse off than yourself and in far harsher conditions elsewhere. I completely agree that you should stand up for your rights and always fight for better conditions. But prison in Britain is relatively easy. You get fed well and on time, you have clean water to drink, TV, regular visits, clean clothing, bedding, mattresses to sleep on, education, workshops, good gyms in most places and many other benefits.

Later I had a hot shower, my first one in years as we only had cold water in Guayaquil. I also called my family, who were so relieved to hear that I was safe and sound and back on British soil. They said they would put some money into my prison account so that I could buy some phone credit and snacks from the canteen, which you could access once a week. They also said they would set up an order at the local newsagents for the *Sunday Times* to be delivered every week. What luxury. This was like heaven to me after what I had been through.

My family assured me they would be down to visit me as soon as they could. This would be the first time that I had seen their faces in nearly a decade. One of the first things I wanted to do was get checked out by the medical team here to make sure I was clear of TB, as I still had a cough. I also wanted to make sure I hadn't brought any other tropical diseases back with me before seeing my family and my new nephew, who was only a year old.

In the morning of the second day I was taken over to see the doctor for the standard check-up everyone receives upon arrival in the prison. I explained that I had just recovered from TB but still had some symptoms including a cough that I was concerned about. I also had a painful infection under my right big toenail – which had only just about managed to grow back after being pulled out in Guayaquil – which needed looking at. Swabs were duly taken and sent for analysis. The doctor took my weight, blood pressure, height and some other vitals and sent me on my way saying they would be in touch.

Upon my return to the cell I found someone else had been placed in there with me. His name was Justin. He had been repatriated from Spain earlier that day and had just come on to the wing. He'd been living around Marbella and Málaga for several years but had been convicted of fairly minor cocaine dealing and given a four-year prison term, of which he had already served 18 months in Spain. We chatted, watched TV and recounted tales of prison and drug trafficking from our pasts. It didn't take long for us to make an incredible connection, the chances of which must have been extremely small. It transpired that he had known Simon, my friend who had supposedly hanged himself in the Peni in Guayaquil. They had been acquaintances in Spain many years before and Justin had known virtually everything about the case and Simon's arrest. This completely broke the ice and we spent the rest of the evening talking about Simon and the circumstances surrounding his death, his case and the prisons in Ecuador. Justin and I were together for three or four days and tried our best to get allocated to a wing and cell together, but didn't quite manage it. Having completed our induction period, he was transferred to D wing and I to B wing.

I was placed in a cell with a Polish man called Rafau. He was a tall, big guy with fair hair and a light complexion. He, along with four others, had been arrested for importing various drugs from Holland including heroin, cocaine and cannabis. To transport the drugs they had been using lorries, one of which Rafau had been driving when captured at a service station on the outskirts of London. He was still on remand awaiting trial and I could tell he was finding it all very stressful. It was his first time in prison and he didn't view himself as a criminal – and I suppose to some extent he wasn't. He was yet another victim who had been caught up in the drugs trade. I settled into the cell and the general routine of the prison and made a few friends on the wing. I found a couple of Chileans and Colombians to talk to, which was good, as it allowed me to practise my Spanish and meant

I could help them out when they needed some translating. I also met a guy from Oxford called Darren who had spent several years in prison in Peru. It was really good having someone to chat with about the whole experience who fully understood what I was talking about. I generally didn't bother telling people as most would look at you as if you were crazy.

Then I heard from my family that they were coming to visit. I suddenly became very anxious and apprehensive. I was worried about my appearance and I also didn't want to show surprise at how anyone had changed in the time I had been away for. I had seen very few photos while I'd been in Ecuador. With each passing day the tension ratcheted up another level to the point where I could barely sleep.

However, on the day everyone's nerves (which were of course mutual) soon settled down after the initial shock of seeing each other for the first time had worn off. My father's hair had greyed a lot more and his face had aged but then so had mine! My sister looked pretty much the same, just more like an adult woman and mother now compared to the younger sister I had left behind ten years ago.

The visits were over all too quickly, being only an hour and a half in duration, and soon it was time to say goodbye once again. My father promised they would try to visit once a month if they could. They said that once I was released I could stay at the family home in Gloucestershire for a while until I got myself back on my feet and organised with a place to live and work. I was grateful for this as I knew it was going to take me a while to readjust after such a long time in prison and in a different country.

I wanted to go to our house in France, but I wouldn't be able to as my passport was being withheld until I repaid the cost of the airfare from Ecuador for my repatriation. This came to over £2,000, which I would have to pay to the prison governor of HMP Wandsworth.

I had finally succeeded in getting the medical staff to pay attention to the cough that I just couldn't shake, and was transferred to the isolation ward of the hospital wing. Once the results of the tests had come back showing that I was non-contagious and didn't have TB, I was transferred back into the main prison. This time I was sent to D wing, which was generally the drug rehabilitation wing but also for those who were sick and needed regular medication. I was placed initially in a double-doored single cell for high-security prisoners. The prison officers seemed to take that sort of approach to me. It didn't bother me that much, but I was kept in that cell for over two weeks and not allowed out for anything. They wouldn't even allow me to go down for exercise; I had my food brought to the door of the cell and on a couple of occasions they actually forgot to feed me. I went absolutely ballistic and reminded them I was sick and not being punished and they soon sorted out something to eat.

I hadn't anticipated that I would experience such a degree of culture shock as I did. I had arrived on 14 November just as the Christmas advertising campaigns were getting into full swing on the TV. I found this all very overwhelming and quite upsetting, having just come from a country where there was such poverty and suffering. The greed and consumerism of our society was very hard to stomach, and to some extent still is. It took a few months for me to become accustomed to everything again, which I had really not anticipated. One very marked change was the massive influence of technology. From what I could see the whole of society had changed, with everyone now seeming to have smartphones and iPads. The drinking culture of Britain had changed a lot, with a vast number of pubs and clubs having closed down, and people drinking at home more these days and communicating instead via social media, which barely existed when I had left for Ecuador.

As the months went by I changed cells several times within D wing and got a job as a wing cleaner, which kept me out of my room nearly all the time. I was able to use the gym and started getting fit again. With only a couple of months remaining, I was suddenly transferred to the category C unit at Wandsworth, where there had been quite a lot of trouble in the last few months. This meant I lost my job and was back to spending almost 22 hours a day locked up.

There were two major disturbances on the unit while I was there when the guards completely lost control of the wings and a specialist riot squad had to be brought in. They came in with dogs, wearing body armour, and let off flash-bangs and tear gas. Just what I needed right at the end of my sentence! This reminded me of the *paros* in Quito, when the police would storm the place to regain control, while firing live ammunition.

During the last few months at Wandsworth, a very beautiful, dear friend of mine started writing to me. We had been at school together and I had always had a really big crush on her, so I was thrilled when I started to receive her letters. We corresponded frequently and I began to hope there was something more to the letters than just being friends. I hoped and prayed I was right as I had loved this girl from the very first day I saw her when I was 14 years old. I arranged to make contact with her upon my release, which she had thought would not be for several years yet. I now had something else to look forward to once I was out. Things were really looking up.

The last few months raced by and it was soon my day to be released, having completed ten years and ten days of a 12-year sentence. I was ready and packed at 8am, just waiting to go. But the authorities kept stalling. I started to get really nervous and wondered if I was about to be arrested by the police and charged with something else.

I went down to the wing office to find out what was happening. I saw that the senior officer on the wing was there. I approached him and asked, 'Sir, I'm due to be released today but no one has come to get me yet and I'm starting to worry I might be gate-arrested. Could you please do me a favour and check on the system to make sure that isn't the case?'

'What's your name and number and I'll have a look,' he replied.

'Tritton DF67855, Sir.'

He tapped it into the computer and I held my breath, half-expecting it to explode.

'There's nothing on there that I can see so I would say you are OK,' he said finally.

'Why haven't I been released then?' I enquired.

The SO looked me in the eye and said, 'Your guess is as good as mine. This place is so disorganised, underfunded and short-staffed it's a wonder there hasn't been a serious riot here.'

Great, I thought, just what I bloody need. He went on, 'You can be held up until 6pm, by which point if you haven't been released we have to start paying you for the privilege of your company as you will be illegally detained.' And with that he walked off. There's a saying in British prison: we, the convicts, are a bit like mushrooms insofar as we are kept in the dark and fed shit!

I called my family and they started ringing round to find out what was going on. I suggested they call my probation officer as well in order to advise them I wouldn't make it back to my home town in time to report to them, as you are duty-bound to do upon initial release. But to my relief, the guards finally came for me at about 4pm and took me to reception to collect my belongings and sign my release papers. I couldn't stop smiling, but I was still so on edge.

CHAPTER THIRTY-FIVE
HOME

26 August 2015. I was free. I stood outside HMP Wandsworth just absorbing that fact. As I walked across Wandsworth Common, in my imagination I had a large luminous yellow tattoo on my forehead saying 'EX-CON'. I thought everyone I passed must surely know I had just been released and was wary of me. I felt really self-conscious. It was a horrible feeling and one that didn't subside for quite a while. All the traffic seemed to be travelling fast and all the people appeared to be rushing around at breakneck speed. I was enjoying being able to walk on grass and touch the leaves of trees, and hear and see birds as I strolled along. Every little thing was as if new to me. I saw with the eyes and heard with the ears of a baby, as if learning everything afresh. The colours and smells of London swept over me like a tidal wave of sensation, an LSD trip without drugs.

My friend Jen had offered to help me get to Paddington. When she arrived, I explained to her that I was feeling quite strange and very self-conscious. She told me not to worry and we headed towards the tube station, where Jen had to explain what an Oyster card was. She gave me a spare one of hers to use with credit on and we headed underground. On the tube journey, I again felt very self-aware and as if people would be able to tell I had just come out of prison. Jen reassured me this wasn't the case. At Paddington she made sure I was certain of which platform the train was leaving from and that I had exchanged my prison-issued travel warrant for rail tickets. With all this in hand she wished me well and headed off into the evening, leaving me with my thoughts.

I was finally on my way home. I phoned my father to let him know what time I would be arriving in my home town. He said he would be there waiting for me with the car. Ten years ago my father had seen me off from the train station in France. He was now going to meet me at the other end of this train ride. In a way it seemed to have been one long journey, which was finally coming to a conclusion. I was lucky to have survived that ride and certainly couldn't have done so without the help of my loving family and my many friends who supported me by sending money and letters.

The journey back was uneventful. I watched the beautiful lush fields, trees and hedgerows of the English landscape race by. I hadn't seen this in a decade. New housing developments and tower blocks had gone up here and there but apart from that it was much the same. We descended through the beautiful West Country valleys that led to my home town and then suddenly we were pulling into the train station. My father was waiting on the platform, the relief written all over his face. My journey was finally over and my new life was about to begin.

ACKNOWLEDGEMENTS

I would like to thank the many people who helped me through the last eleven and a half years of my life, which were extremely hard at times, not only on me but more so on those around me.

Firstly, I would like to thank Sara Cywinski from Ebury Publishing for having chosen to publish my book, and also Liz Marvin for the fantastic job you have done of editing and moulding my writing. All the rest of the people who have worked on the book who I am not even aware of are due a big thank you as well.

Of course, none of this would have happened without Shaun Barrington. Thanks Shaun.

I wish to say a huge thank you to Mary Moore for typing all the chapters of the book, and making untold corrections and amendments. Not only that but also all your support both financially and morally throughout my life. Thank you so much.

I want to thank my father for supporting me both mentally and financially through the years and fighting to get me repatriated: I can never tell you just how sorry I am and how very much I care for you. Thanks also to my sister who also stayed in contact, giving me much-needed support.

A very big thank you to the staff of the British embassy in Ecuador for all your help and support throughout my time in prison. I particularly want to thank Sofie Deeks, Veronica Ruiz and Annika Dann. An especially big thank you to Rocío Torre CBE in Guayaquil. You undoubtedly saved my life and made it much easier to survive the harsh conditions we faced. You helped so many people.

Mercedes Quezada Lopez, you truly are an angel. A most amazing woman who has helped so many people. If anyone has a place in heaven it is you. I can never thank you enough for all you did for me. It is only possible for me to write this today because you saved my life.

I want to say a big thank you to all those friends who most generously helped financially by sending money to keep me going, and also letters and photos. Without your help life would have been unbearable and I would probably have perished. Laurie Howard, Alix Chalk, Lizzie Chadwick, Mark Short, Melissa Moore, Guy Robson, Lachlan McDonald, Kate Gilday, Nick and Sarah Dalgliesh, Waheed Beeg, Imran Bashir, Jo Broughton, Jamie Fletcher, Tabby and Chiggels, Ben Hogg, Marty McClenaghan, Gustavo Orozco, Shaun Knight, Istvan Pataki, Massimo Del Marino, Vladimir Gabidulin, Rebecca Rosenberg, Samir Narvaez, Mark Franklin, Laura Copley, Haim Yam, Massimo Gallo, Alexander Zellweger, Sallyanne Cole, Larissa Chambers, Mayli Harrison, Ryan Harford, Jennifer Fleetwood, Carlos Hierrero, Tony Slatter and so many more. Sorry if I haven't named you, but you know who you are.

The charity Prisoners Abroad should be thanked for all the help they provide to British prisoners and their families. If you wish to help a prisoner, please donate. Thank you.

In Remembrance of Those Who Didn't Make it Home to Tell their Story

Freddy Murphy

Ronny Walker

Stephen John Tull

Peter Hoffman

Alejandro Giraldo

Norman Kirkland

Tropico

Pescado

Payano

Clive Harding

El Gato – David Cecilio
  Álvarez Andrade

Pangora – Óscar Caranqui

And all the others who fell along the way. Rest in peace.

The memories of you will always live on.